Encyclopedia of
HORSES

Tony Newbury (Great Britain) on Warwick.

Controlling the horse at the walk.

Trotting poles.

Encyclopedia of
HORSES

Edited by Robert Owen

 CHARTWELL BOOKS INC.

Published by Chartwell Books Inc.
A Division of Book Sales Inc.
110 Enterprise Avenue
Secaucus, New Jersey 07094

First printed in 1979

A Grisewood & Dempsey Book
produced for the publisher

© Grisewood & Dempsey Ltd 1979
Grosvenor House 141/143 Drury Lane London WC2

ISBN 0 89009 295 8
LOC 79 53361

Printed and bound in Hong Kong
By South China Printing Co, Ltd.

Contents

Designed by John Strange

Artists:
Elizabeth Turner
Fred'k St. Ward

Contributors:
Jennifer Baker
Michael Clayton
Judith Draper
Elwyn Hartley Edwards
Georgie Henschel
Jane Holderness-Roddam
Gareth L. M. Hunter
Jane Kidd
Jill Ogden, MRCVS
Robert Owen
Julie Richardson
Robin Serfass
Sylvia Stanier
Sallie Walrond
E. A. Weiss
Dorian Williams, OBE, MFH

Horses of the Camargue.

Introduction

In recent years there has been an increasing interest in the horse by many who have not owned or ridden. Millions now watch televised sport, hundreds of thousands attend each year the major horse shows staged throughout the world, and tens of thousands of young and not so young have specific interest and involvement in one or other of the active equestrian disciplines. For these, participants or not, this book has been prepared to discuss and explain some of the questions arising from what is a wide and diverse subject.

No one book could hope to be *complete*; volumes would be required to deal in depth with any of the chapters included here. But the *Encyclopedia of Horses* will, it is intended, add to the many useful and informative works now available. The contributions in this book are from writers who have had years of experience and practical knowledge, and who are accepted as authorities in their respective fields. Their text is supported by carefully selected illustrations.

Throughout the *Encyclopedia of Horses* the aim has been to consider first the welfare of the horse, a priority of the organising bodies and equestrian associations throughout the world, and the preoccupation of owners and riders alike. The importance of the horse's welfare can never be over-stressed and it demands from all a better understanding, not only in the manner in which they should be kept and cared for, but an awareness that "welfare" begins even before the breeding process. And this becomes the theme of two of the five parts comprising this book.

As an essential introductory chapter we open this book with a study of understanding the horse, leading as this must to a contribution on breeding and stud management. A history of some of the better known breeds also includes specially commissioned contributions about American and Australian horses.

Part Two covers saddlery and equipment, probably one of the most talked about aspects of riding among novices and the experienced alike. Although basic equipment is traditional and, apart from slight variations and modifications has altered little for centuries, equestrian sport is of such recent origin that the variety of saddlery has enabled man to ask his horse to carry out activities which fifty or so years ago would have been unheard of.

The breaking-in and schooling of a young horse is the area covered in Part Three. This section has two important chapters; one, dealing with the young horse, and the other dealing with the horse's health. But, as mentioned earlier, perhaps the most important section for many of the younger riders and those whose experience is somewhat limited are the chapters which now follow on the care of both the stable-kept and grass-kept horse, including detailed information on feeding, watering, grooming and travelling.

The concluding Part deals with competitive sports, from Showing through to Driving, with contributions from many of the most experienced and practising authorities.

This 18th-century engraving is one of a series of scenes showing the disciplines of haute école. *Here the horse demonstrates the vaulting trot. The sandbag on his back is to simulate the rider.*

Part One:
The Horse

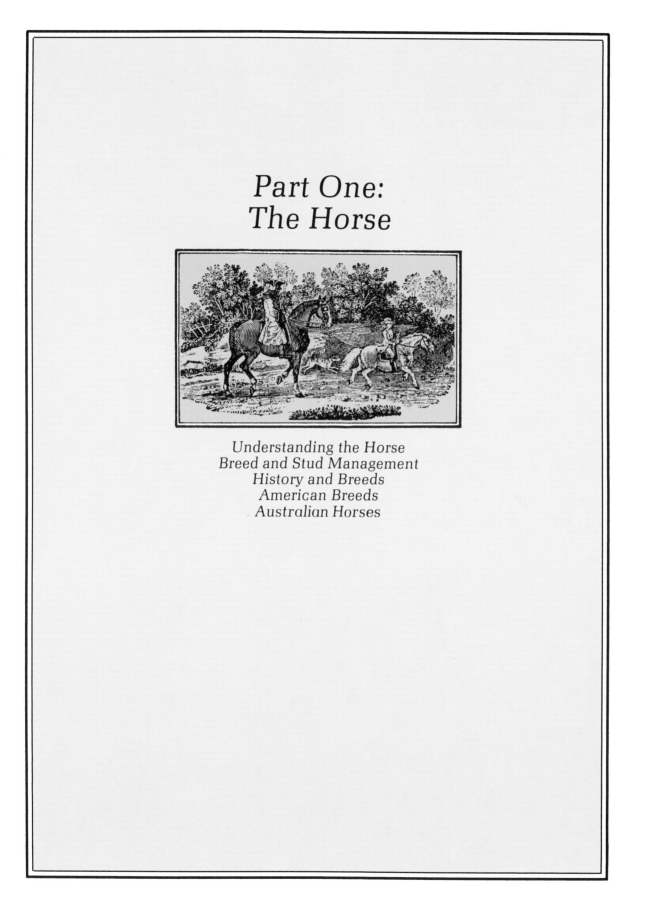

Understanding the Horse
Breed and Stud Management
History and Breeds
American Breeds
Australian Horses

Understanding the Horse

by Elwyn Hartley Edwards

In a society that is conditioned by the mechanical and the electronic it is hardly surprising if the horse, despite much lip-service being paid to the contrary view, is regarded almost subconsciously in terms of the machine. Present-day standards of instruction may unwittingly give support to this erroneous view by concentrating too much on the technicalities of riding and by failing to emphasise that a satisfactory and successful relationship with horses, particularly if the concern is with training, or even with owning one, has to be based on an understanding of the physical and mental make-up of the animal.

Understanding horses involves an appreciation of three factors: *physical structure; the digestive system and the utilisation of food* and, finally, the *horse mentality*.

It is not perhaps essential to be an expert on the anatomy of the horse, but an overall understanding of the physical structure is essential in planning a training progression and in appreciating the amount of work which can be given safely to a young and immature horse. Indeed, without some knowledge of the structure the trainer is working in the dark, not knowing what it is that he is trying to achieve, nor being aware of the faults in carriage and outline that are bound to occur.

A knowledge of the digestive system is, of course, an essential for any horse-owner if the horse is to be kept fit for the work required of him.

Just as important is the understanding of the horse mentality, which will provide rational explanations for what may at first sight appear to be irrational actions on the part of the horse. The training of horses is, in fact, concerned as much with the conditioning of the mind as with the development of the physique. The former is obviously impossible unless the mental processes and the seemingly paradoxical motivations of the horse are first understood.

Physical structure

The body of all animals, including the human one, is composed of cells, one cell in relation to the complete organism being like a grain of sand upon a beach. Each cell is in itself a living entity, which has to be fed and then cleansed by the removal of waste matter and which has its own specialist function within the complete organism. The liver cells, for instance, make bile; the muscle cells develop the power of contraction, a most important ability.

The function of the multitudinous cells forming the organism is to feed in order to reproduce. This is achieved by the division of individual cells, a process which is rapid in youth while declining with advancing years. Similarly, cell multiplication is encouraged when the organism is in good health and decreases under opposite conditions. For instance, in the young, healthy horse, muscle development, as well as the efficiency of the muscular system, will be at a high level, while in the older horse the system will have begun to degenerate and will in consequence be less efficient, more prone to strain and slower to be repaired by natural agencies.

The framework of the body is made up of the variously shaped bones comprising the *skeleton*. Bones act as supports to the body mass and move to effect locomotion when *joints* are activated. A *joint* is, in simple terms, the junction between two bones and while its con-

The anatomy of the horse.

1. *Phalanges of pelvic appendages*
2. *Metatarsal bones*
3. *Tarsal bones or hock joint*
4. *Tuber calcis*
5. *Tibia*
6. *Fibula*
7. *Patella*
8. *Ribs*
9. *Ulna*
10. *Pisiform*
11. *Os pedis*
12. *Os coronae*
13. *Os suffraginis*
14. *Metacarpal bones*
15. *Carpal bones*
16. *Radius*
17. *Sternum*
18. *Humerus*
19. *Scapula*
20. *Mandible*
21. *Maxilla*
22. *Atlas*
23. *Axis*
24. *5th cervical vertebra*
25. *Scapula cartilage*
26. *Tubis coxae*
27. *Sacrum*
28. *Ilium*
29. *Femur*
30. *Sesamoid bone*

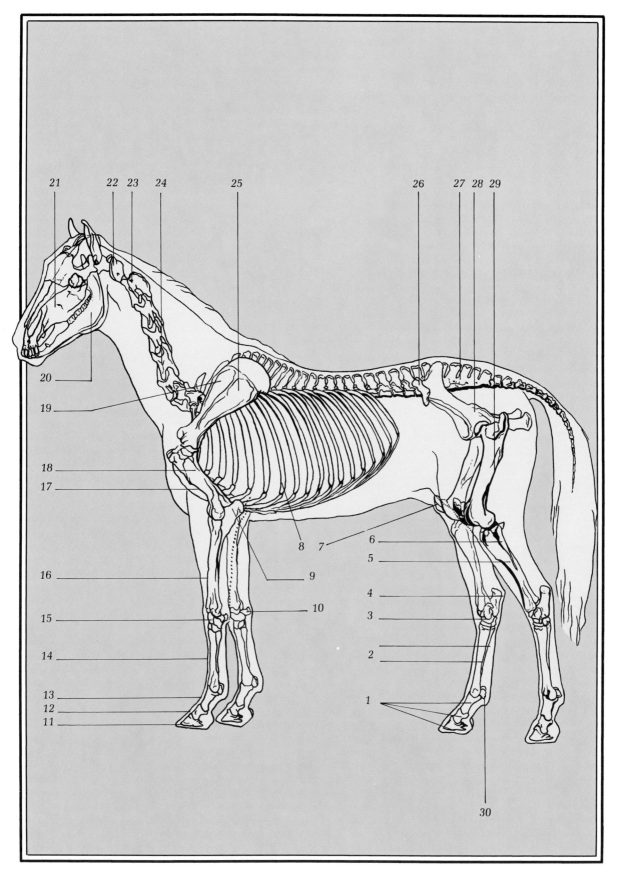

21 22 23 24   25   26   27 28 29

20

19

18
17

8 7   6
          5

16   4
          3

15   2

14

13   1

12
11

10

9

30

Body muscles of the horse.

1. Sternocephalicus
2. Brachiocephalus
3. Deltoid
4. Triceps
5. Posterior deep pectoral
6. External oblique abdominal
7. Biceps femoris
8. Tensor fasciae latae
9. Intercostal
10. Latissimus dorsi
11. Trapezius
12. Cervical rhomboid

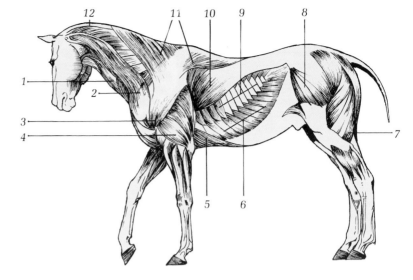

The early training of the horse, beginning at three years of age, concentrates on building, developing and suppling the muscles correctly. It is important that the training should encourage the rounded top-line and that muscles should not be allowed to develop so that the opposite (a hollow back) becomes inevitable.

struction is remarkable and very strong it remains, nonetheless, the weakest point in the structure.

Where a joint occurs in the skeleton the articular surface of the two bones is of a greater density than is found elsewhere as a preventative against undue wear caused by friction. As an additional precaution the bone surfaces are separated by layers of gristle called *cartilage*. The two bones are held together by *ligaments*, which not only serve to join the two together but also limit the extension of the joint, permitting its movement only so far as it is capable. The whole joint is encased in a two-layered capsule, the outer layer of which gives further support to the joint while the inner layer secretes an oily fluid (joint oil or synovia) which allows the joint to operate in a state of perfect lubrication.

Should the ligament suffer damage, it follows that the movement of the joint will be affected and the horse will become incapable of work.

Young horses, whose co-ordination will be insufficiently developed, can pull or strain ligaments very easily, and the same applies to horses brought up in soft condition and put too quickly into work.

Muscle movement
The substance covering the skeletal frame is called *muscle*. It is attached to joints and its function is to cause movement in the latter and therefore in the whole frame. The greater the muscle development the greater will be the efficiency of the movement in the body mass.

Movement is achieved by the contraction of the muscle which draws together the points of attachment to the bones. But although muscle has the property of *elasticity* to a high degree, it is soft and easily torn. To prevent damage to the muscle substance muscles are equipped with strong, *inelastic* ropes running throughout their length. These are called *tendons*. One end of a tendon is fastened securely to a bone and the other is virtually plaited into and through the muscle substance. Following the contraction or expansion of the muscle the joint is activated by the tendon acting in response to the muscle's movement.

The action of the joint is impaired by any damage caused to the tendon. The seriousness of the damage depends upon the extent of the tendon injury. Tendons, by being strained, sprained or even ruptured, are the cause of the majority of serious breakdowns in the structure.

Muscle, when not actually contracting or extending, is held in a state of slight tension, known as *tonus*, the purpose of which is to prevent violent movements causing joints to be flexed or extended and so to suffer damage. *Lack of tone in the muscles, as occurs in tired horses, in unfit ones, or those which are either very old or very young means they are likely to be unco-ordinated.* The risk of the joint components suffering undue strain is then very great.

The elasticity of the muscles and their ability to contract produces movement in the limbs. Contraction, however, has a peculiar property which is of particular relevance in the training of the horse. It is that the power of contraction is proportional to the extent to which the muscle can be extended. It must follow that the greater the power of contraction in one muscle, or in a group of muscles, the greater will be the flexion possible in the joints they activate and the greater will be the mechanical efficiency of the structure. Given that the degree of muscle contraction is dependent upon the muscle's power to extend then it is clear that the early training of the horse should be directed to this end.

In schooling horses, particularly in the early stages when we are concerned with the stretching of muscles, an important group of muscles to be considered is that running from the neck along the "top-line" of the horse on either side of the spine. These muscles are arranged in pairs on each side of the powerful, elastic ligament which extends from the poll to behind the withers and then continues in a less elastic form along the top of the spine to the sacrum at the croup of the horse. Up to the wither the ligament goes under the name *ligamentum nuchae*, after which it becomes *ligamentum nucho-dorsale*. In English it is referred to as the cervical ligament.

This ligament is important to the schooling of the horse, since it is involved in creating the rounded outline already mentioned. By inducing the horse to extend and lower the head and neck the ligament is stretched over the fulcrum then formed by the withers. As a result a degree of tension is obtained in the spine and the back is rounded slightly. This action, combined with that of muscles acting in opposition i.e. one extending while another contracts, results in the hind legs being brought under the belly and thus contributes to the propulsive effort of the quarters.

Any sort of pronounced propulsive effort is impossible while the back remains slack, and efforts to impose a carriage by forceful means while the cervical ligament and its accompanying muscles are undeveloped and unstretched is likely to result in a U-shaped, upside down horse incapable of engaging the hindlegs under the body.

The *voluntary* muscles, which have so far been mentioned, are of two kinds: the *flexors*, contracting to flex joints, and the *extensors*, which stretch, or extend, to fulfil the opposite purpose. Muscles frequently act in pairs, but they also act in opposition as in the case when the back is rounded. In this instance the large back muscles act as extensors, while three muscles on the side of the abdomen and three running from the fifth and ninth ribs to the pubis act in opposition, as flexors to complete the rounding, raise the abdomen and bring forward the hindlegs. Similarly, the muscles on the underside of the neck are matched by the opposing dorsal muscles on the top of the neck in order for the head and neck to be supported and to be carried without effort.

An example of muscles acting in pairs, each compensating for the movement of its opposing partner, are the dorsal muscles on either side of the spine and those covering the abdominal wall. The compensatory effect occurs when the horse's body bends in making a correct turn. The muscles on the inside of the body then contract while those on the outside must compensate and allow the bend by extending to the same degree.

Unequal development of these muscles, caused by incorrect or negligent schooling, will result in the horse becoming "one-sided" and unable to bend with equal facility to either hand.

The remaining types of muscles are the *involuntary* muscles, like those giving movement to the bowels, and the *cardiac* or heart muscles, both of which act independently of any stimulus.

From this brief survey certain lessons emerge with clarity, particularly, perhaps, those concerned with the adequate preparation of the structure.

The structure of the horse cannot be said to be mature until about the sixth year of the animal's life and up to the age of three or four the

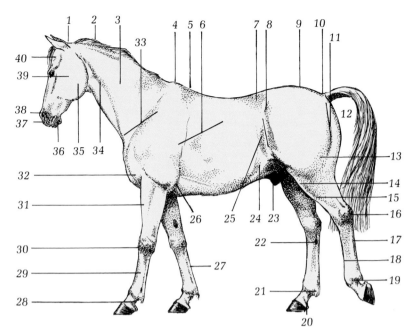

The points of the horse
1. Poll 2. Crest 3. Neck 4. Withers
5. Back 6. Ribs 7. Loins 8. Point of
the hip 9. Croup 10. Dock 11. Hind
quarters 12. Buttock 13. Thigh
14. Stifle joint 15. Gaskin 16. Point of
hock 17. Flexor tendons 18. Hind
tendons 19. Fetlock joint 20. Hollow
of heel 21. Ergots 22. Chestnuts
23. Sheath or prepuce 24. Belly
25. Flank 26. Elbow 27. Back tendons
28. Coronet 29. Fore cannon 30. Knee
31. Forearm 32. Breast 33. Shoulder
34. Jugular furrow 35. Jowl 36. Chin
37. Muzzle 38. Nostril 39. Cheek
40. Forehead.

component parts are still in a state of development. Bones in young horses up to this age are still "green" and the imposition of weight, in terms of a rider, combined with injudicious work will put too much strain on them and may even cause malformations.

The digestive system

The digestive apparatus of the horse and an appreciation of the size and positioning of the relatively small stomach is a subject vital to the animal's management and is the reason for the two golden rules of feeding: *Never work after feeding* and *feed little and often*. There was once a third golden rule which said that horses should be watered before feeding. Today water is made constantly available, which is more sensible, more satisfactory and in no way damaging to the animal's well-being.

The explanation of the two rules is simple enough. A horse should not work immediately after a feed because of the position of his stomach in relation to the lungs. The stomach is separated from the chest cavity proper by the diaphragm, a section of muscle which is in contact with the lungs. After feeding the small stomach becomes distended, as do the bowels, which may still be digesting a previous feed. As a result the stomach presses on the diaphragm, a matter which is of no concern while the horse is at rest, but which can cause a chain of complications if the horse is saddled up and ridden. The exertion will naturally cause the horse to breathe more deeply and consequently to expand the lungs. Such an expansion exerts pressure on the elastic structure of the diaphragm which in turn will press on the distended stomach. The breathing will obviously be impaired and the digestive processes will be interrupted. The result will be a fairly sharp attack of indigestion which could develop into a severe colic. Were the horseman to be so stupid as to attempt to gallop the horse the result could be even more serious. The lungs could in those circumstances become choked with blood and a rupture of the stomach could occur. To avoid such dire ills, horses should be given at least an hour after feeding before being exercised.

To appreciate the second rule of feeding, feed little and often, it has to be understood that the stomach and the whole of the digestive apparatus is designed for the slow and almost continuous ingestion of food. The horse's stomach is small in relation to his size but the bowel structure is capacious; there are, in fact, two bowels, the small and the large, the length of intestine being 70 feet (20 metres) and 30 feet (10 metres) respectively.

In the natural state feeding is a near continuous process, and once the stomach is about two-thirds full the food passes into the bowel at the same speed at which more food enters the stomach.

Ideally the feeding of the domestic horse kept in a stable should follow the pattern set by nature, but since this would involve feeding a few mouthfuls every five minutes it is obviously not possible. None the less feeding must resemble the natural way as closely as possible, even though the stabled horse is eating what for him is unnatural foods which are far less digestible than grass.

Feeds of corn, bran and other concentrates have to be given in small quantities at frequent intervals. The capacity of the stomach and the ability of the digestive system to cope with the food intake does not exceed between 4–5lb (2kg) of concentrates, and so with a hunter in hard work it may be necessary to feed four times a day.

Horses are not very sensible about eating and most are greedy. If an animal was given one very large feed, he would make every effort to eat the greater part of it and to do so with great rapidity. His small stomach would then become distended to a point where the *involuntary* muscles involved in digestion would become incapable of doing their work. The digestive process would then be brought to a halt, the food would ferment, giving off gases, and in all likelihood the stomach would rupture.

Hay, which actively aids digestion in the stabled horse by assisting

A well-made horse, i.e. one of good conformation, is an animal whose component parts – head, limbs, trunk, quarters etc – are in proportion one to another. The horse should then give an impression of strength (substance) combined with refinement (quality).

In the HEAD, *which should be lean and finely chiselled, the eye is an important feature. A big, bold eye is looked for since this denotes a generous temperament. The nostrils should be wide to allow the maximum air intake to the lungs.*

The head needs to be well "set on" to a fairly long, graceful NECK, *that blends into the shoulders. In stallions a "crest" to the neck is usual and permissible.*

The slope of the SHOULDER *is of particular importance in the riding horse. It should be well-sloped from fairly prominent withers to its point to allow for a full extension of the forelegs.*

The FORELEGS *should be strong and muscular in the forearms, with big flat knees and short cannon bones running into well-formed fetlocks and hard, open feet.*

The GIRTH *needs to be deep to allow room for the internal organs, and the ribs well sprung.*

The BACK *has to be strong and neither too long nor too short. The former is weak while the latter inhibits the action.*

The QUARTERS, *the power-house of the horse, must be of great strength with powerful second thighs and good well-formed hocks.*

in the breakdown of the rich concentrates, can be given in much larger quantities because it is eaten so much more slowly.

Semi-wild horses from the Camargue. In the feral state the horse lives in herds following the lead of the dominant stallion.

Digestive process

The process of digestion begins in the mouth where the food is rolled by the tongue and chewed by the molar teeth. The chewing action stimulates the release of saliva from glands under the tongue and in the jaw. The saliva reduces the food to a rough paste-like consistency.

The teeth are clearly a vital element in the process, and yet at a recent conference a distinguished veterinarian stated that in his view and experience eight horses out of ten would benefit by attention being given to their teeth.

It is very possible for the teeth to wear unevenly and in some instances to become so sharp as to lacerate the mouth. When this occurs, the process of mastication is affected and so, therefore, is the process of digestion. Diseased teeth may cause "quidding" when half chewed food is dropped from the mouth and so has no chance of getting further in the system of digestion.

From the mouth the food mixture is forced into the stomach by the muscles of the gullet. In the stomach the large involuntary muscles knead the food paste still further, assisted by the *gastric juices* which the stomach releases.

The food, now a smooth creamy paste, passes into the small bowel, into which empty the ducts from the pancreas and liver to add their own secretions to the digestive process. Bile, from the liver, helps to prepare the food for use by muscles and is also a disinfectant for the bowel. During its course through the bowel the food, now reduced to a liquid, is absorbed into the body. The large bowel receives the unabsorbed matter from which all possible nutriment has been extracted by constant movements of the gut. What is left is passed out as excrement.

Various fluids assist the digestive process and perform specific functions as follows:

Saliva helps to convert starch to sugar and assists in preparing food for swallowing.

Gastric Juice, an acid, changes proteid (flesh-forming elements) into peptones, which are more easily absorbed. It dissolves fibrous matter and assists the starch to sugar conversion.

Intestine secretions continue the process of splitting peptones and sugars into easily absorbed substances which pass through the bowel wall into the lymphatics and blood vessels.

Bile converts fats into an emulsion as well as disinfecting the bowel.

Pancreatic Juice continues the process of converting starch to sugar, protein to peptones and emulsifying fats.

The digestive system is remarkably complex and efficient but in the stabled horse, dependent upon rich concentrate foods, it can easily be put out of gear by careless or incorrect feeding, poor quality foods and so on.

In the fit, healthy horse the system works to maximum efficiency. In the horse that is off-colour its efficiency is reduced and this is also the case with old horses.

By far the greatest cause of disruption is the incidence of parasitic worms in unacceptable numbers. Their control is basic to good horse management.

As a general summary the body can be compared to an engine into which fuel is added. The product of the fuel is energy; what is not used for this purpose is expelled as waste.

Food enters the horse, is converted and made absorbable and the resultant nourishment enters the blood and is circulated through every organ, entering the muscles and being converted into energy. Food conversion into nutrient and its use for work produces heat. This heat is regulated so that the horse has an almost constant temperature largely by the actions of the skin (sweating) and the lungs (breathing) helped by bowels and kidneys.

Waste products are excreted by the bowels, the kidneys and through the lungs and the skin surface.

The mentality of the horse

A common failing in animal-lovers is to regard the objects of their affection in human terms. This anthropomorphic approach is entirely non-productive in so far as the training of the horse is concerned, as indeed it is in attempting to build a satisfactory relationship between human and equine.

Most horse-lovers also make the mistake of endowing the horse with an intelligence which the animal cannot possibly possess. Much may depend on the interpretation of the word "intelligence", but what is certain is that animal "intelligence" cannot be equated with that of the human.

The brain of the horse is very small, far smaller than that of a turtle, for instance. Since we do not ride turtles that point is not entirely relevant.

In the broadest terms it may be said that the horse is a creature of instinct and not of reason. The instincts motivating his behaviour are those which he developed in the wild state as a means to survive the natural hazards of the environment in which he lived, and as a defence against predatory carnivores, including man.

Horses are herbivorous, non-aggressive, herd animals whose defence mechanisms are based on the ability to move swiftly away from danger or from suspected danger. The instincts of the horse and his highly developed senses are all in the main directed towards flight as a means of preservation. To the horse it matters not one jot that in his domestic state the original stimuli have long been absent. He remains a creature still governed very largely by his instincts and any study of the horse personality in relation to training must take account of these factors. Additionally, it has to be remembered that the greater part of

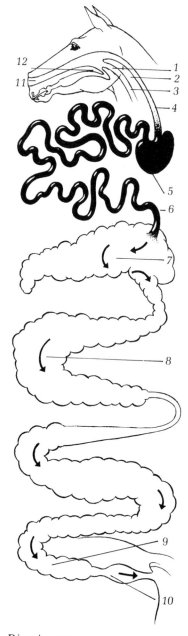

Digestive system.
1. Larynx 2. Pharynx 3. Windpipe 4. Gullet 5. Stomach 6. Small intestine 7. Large caecum 8. Large colon 9. Small colon 10. Rectum 11. Nasal passages 12. Soft palate

the horse's feral life was devoted to the search for food, a commodity which still plays a very large part in the life of the modern horse.

The mentality of the horse is perhaps most easily understood by considering the following characteristics and then by studying, briefly, the senses and the remarkable memory which go to complete the personality.

Some of the following characteristics present difficulties in training while others can be used to the trainer's advantage. (All, of course, are to some degree inter-related):

1. The herd instinct. 2. Security. 3. Following instinct. 4. Excitability. 5. Nervousness 6. Sensitivity.

The *Herd Instinct* is possibly the strongest of all and exerts great influence on the behavioural pattern. Like other aspects of instinctive behaviour it can never be subjugated entirely, but its worst effects can be overcome by training and it is possible to use it to our own advantage in schooling.

An example of the instinct being overcome by training is when a show jumper leaves the collecting ring, and his herd of the moment, to jump his round in the arena. Wise course-builders will usually place the more difficult fences so that they are jumped towards the collecting ring and the "herd".

Racing exploits the herd instinct by creating a simulation of the herd flight. To a lesser degree exploitation occurs when a young horse is taken hunting and because of the presence of companions jumps fences he would not consider in cold blood, thus gaining confidence in his own ability.

Horses naturally seek the company of their own kind and it is noticeable that horses kept in a group rarely develop the problems that can occur with horses kept singly. These latter can develop what amounts to neurotic traits.

Security is closely connected with the herd instinct for the horse finds security in being a member of a group. In the domestic horse security is probably centred on the stable and its immediate environs. Stables, of course, are also associated with food, a major pre-occupation with the horse.

Appreciating the importance of the stable in the horse's life it would be unwise to place a schooling area alongside. The horse would hang continually towards the stable and also be distracted from the work in hand.

On the other hand, the stable and food, like the herd, can be useful. Every horseman knows how a horse quickens his stride when turned for home; this characteristic can be exploited when introducing young horses to traffic, for instance. The horse is taken out down quiet roads and brought back by a route on which he is likely to encounter traffic. In most cases the thought of home and food will result in the horse ignoring the cars and lorries.

The importance of the stable and the security it offers is very well demonstrated when horses are sold on. Quite frequently a formerly quiet and well-mannered horse will become difficult, shying on the roads, napping and so on, when first put into new surroundings, often after a long and uncomfortable journey. Given a few days and quiet kindly treatment the horse will settle down. On the other hand, tough treatment will probably only increase his sense of lost security and make him far worse.

The Following Instinct. Most horses are followers by nature. In the wild the herd is controlled and led by the dominant stallion, who makes himself responsible for the herd's safety and well-being and, when necessary, disciplines those who step out of line. In the domestic horse the need for leadership still remains and fortunately horses appear to accept the dominance of man in substitution for the herd stallion. They can come to repose a great deal of trust in their human leader who, like the herd stallion, cares for them.

Respect, however, in any sphere is not given unconditionally – it has to be earned. Young horses in training or newly purchased older

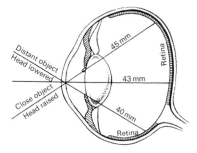

Above: Unlike the lens in a human eye, the horse's has no elasticity. It cannot bring distant or nearby objects into focus by contracting or relaxing its ciliary muscles. To compensate for this, the retina is not a true arc, and the horse, by raising or lowering its head, can manoeuvre the eye so that incoming light hits a point on the retina at the correct focal length, so that the object appears in focus.

The diagram shows that the horse needs to lower its head to see distant objects and raise it to see close ones.

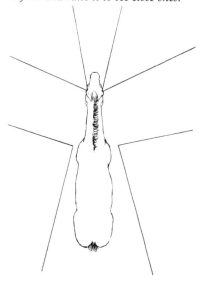

This diagram shows the limits of a horse's forward and lateral vision. If the horse is concentrating on objects on either side of its body, it cannot simultaneously see efficiently straight in front.

horses will, almost without exception, test the authority of the leader (as they would do with a herd stallion) by making resistances. Treated firmly such resistances are easily enough overcome, but should the horse be allowed to succeed in his insubordination he will very quickly attempt to reverse the roles of leader and follower. If that happens, he is best sold on to a more knowledgeable horseman.

Excitability and *nervousness* are closely allied and present to a greater or lesser degree in all horses. The highly strung nature of the horse derives from the flight instinct which is his first line of defence and is commonly manifested in shying, often at seemingly insignificant objects. Firmness on the part of the rider and the exercise of common sense will reduce shying, so long as it is not caused by defective eyesight. Horses will draw confidence from the rider's voice and hand and if they can be persuaded either to touch or smell the offending object, will normally make no more fuss. To punish a horse for shying is only to confirm his fear and to make him even more nervous and apprehensive.

Excitability is often more of a problem in the highly bred horse than in the one of more common ancestry, but in all cases feeding has an important influence. Too high a protein diet will encourage excitability, and insubordination too. It therefore behoves the trainer to balance the intake of energising food by a corresponding energy output in the way of work and exercise.

It is reasonable to assume that the horse, as a non-aggressive animal, is possessed of a greater sensitivity to pain and a lower pain tolerance than aggressive animals like dogs. It is the horse's instinct to flee from pain, or from the threat of it, and it is largely because of the innate sensitivity that the horse can be controlled and trained by humans possessed of so much less physical strength.

As an example, a tap from a whip delivered on the horse's flank will cause him to move his quarters away, and later when the action of the rider's leg is substituted for the tapping whip the quarters will be shifted in the same manner.

Occasionally there are reactions which appear to be out of character, although on examination they often prove to be quite logical. Horsemen, for instance, talk about horses "fighting" the bit. While it is true that excited horses in company will take a pretty strong hold, the use of the word "fighting", implying that the horse is deliberately opposing his rider, is wrong. It is far more likely that the horse is running away from the discomfort caused by the bit and the more the rider pulls the more urgent becomes the need to escape from the pain which is being experienced.

Stallions, of course, will fight to establish ascendency, but it is very rare for any horse, stallion, mare or gelding, to attack a man. Horses can, however, show signs of aggression in the stable, particularly at feed times. The ears will be laid back and the horse may even kick out. Such behaviour is probably a momentary reversion to the feral state. Not comprehending that the human has no interest in the food, the horse behaves as he might to his companions in a field, when he would threaten another horse to keep him away from his feed tin or haynet. More frequently the horse is expressing anxiety and impatience by kicking and so too much should not be read into his actions.

The Senses

The senses of the horse are, like those of all animals, highly developed and are integral to the personality.

Sight in the horse is peculiar to the species. It can vary between the heavy cold-blood horses and the hot-blooded types of riding horse based on the Arab and the Thoroughbred. In the former the eyes are set more to the side of the head and vision to the front is less effective.

In all horses the eyes do not, in general, focus together on objects directly to the front but they do afford very considerable lateral vision. Vision to the rear is also possible when the head is raised.

This all-round vision is part of the protective equipment, but its limitations have to be appreciated. It is not, for instance, ideal for jumping. At 15 yards (14 metres) both eyes see the fence. At 4 feet (1 metre) the lower part of the head makes the simultaneous use of both eyes impossible. The horse, if he is allowed, has to tilt the head in order to see the fence with one eye. Horses can, therefore, jump blind unless the rider allows sufficient freedom to the head.

Hearing in the horse is acute, since the head itself is rather like a sound-box. Horses respond to sound, particularly to the tone of the human voice. Their hearing is far more sensitive than ours both for the sound-box like property of the head and the exceptional mobility of the ears, which can be erected and directed at will towards the source of sound.

Just as acute is the sense of smell, and the old horseman's trick of rubbing an aromatic fluid on the hands is not as silly as it sounds. What is very certain is that horses can smell fear, both in their own kind and in the human. Human beings *do* give off a "fear smell" which is easily perceived by animals, who will react either by becoming upset and frightened themselves or by taking advantage in whatever way is presented to them.

The smell of blood and death is also quickly picked up by horses and very few remain unaffected by the smells coming from the older type of abattoir.

The sense of smell is used as a way of gaining reassurance as well. Once a horse has got close enough to smell some object of which he has been apprehensive he will usually accept it without further ado.

The sense of touch also appears to have a significance. Horses will sometimes touch a pole laid on the ground with a hoof and, having done so, will cross the object in the course of training without bother. Taste, it would seem, plays no more or less a part than in other sentient beings.

A sixth sense

There is evidence to show the presence of some sixth, animal sense. Horses certainly sense atmosphere and they are susceptible to the moods of their riders. Furthermore they are able to perceive timidity and hesitation in the human, as well as courage and confidence.

Finally, there is the horse's remarkably retentive memory, which is both an advantage and a disadvantage in training, for the horse remembers both the good things and the bad. Someone once wrote that in schooling horses we write on stone and what we have written can never be erased.

The horse cannot relate connected happenings separated by a period of time. It would be ridiculous to take a horse who has misbehaved in the ring back to his box and then to punish him for the offence, because he would not understand the reason for the punishment. The only result such an action would have would be to confuse the horse and make him resentful.

The horse can, however, associate immediate cause and effect. If he performs a movement well and is rewarded by the voice and a pat from the hand he will remember the experience with pleasure and be anxious to perform the movement when next asked. Conversely, a horse who kicks and is reprimanded immediately associates the act of kicking with something unpleasant and possibly painful and will not wish to repeat the experience. Were the horse to be hit five minutes after kicking he could not relate the punishment to the crime.

Horses are trained, right up to the very highest levels, by a system of repetition and reward. Some, like their human counterparts, learn quickly, while others are dull and slow. Intelligence, in human terms, is not in evidence, nor is the horse able to express affection very well – his long face is not designed for it. None the less most horses have delightful and very individual personalities, if they are allowed to develop them along with their minds and bodies.

The association between man and horse should be a partnership, in which each knows, respects and relies upon the other.

This younger rider, with her well turned out horse, shows quite clearly how any association between the human and the horse must be based on trust and respect.

Breed and Stud Management

by Georgie Henschel

If you own a nice mare, perhaps your daughter's pony which she has outgrown, or your own favourite hunter or competition horse, it is only natural that one day, you may want to breed a foal from her. Before you decide to do so, you should realise that breeding a foal involves certain responsibilities, and consider carefully whether you are willing, and can afford the time and the money, to accept them. Particularly nowadays, when too many horses and ponies are being bred indiscriminately, many of them to end their days in the meat market. You also need certain amenities, even if you only want to breed one foal from one mare.

Although you may want, and may be prepared to look after, a foal, and the mare during her pregnancy, are you equally prepared to look after the foal when it becomes a young horse or pony? To give it the care, attention and handling it will need if it is to mature into a sensible, useful and co-operative adult? If, for example, you intend ultimately that the foal will be used by your children, remember that it will be three years before it can begin its lessons, and four years, before it can be ridden seriously. The same, of course, applies if you are hoping to breed a horse for yourself. Or, if your idea is to sell the foal as a youngster, to recoup the stallion's fee and a bit over, are you prepared to be choosy about the home it goes to, and not sell to the first dealer who offers a good price?

Before putting a mare into foal, it is only right to try to answer these questions honestly. Because, in a sense, we play "God" to our equines; in deciding to breed from our mares, it is we who are causing new equine lives to come into existence; it is up to us, therefore, to do the best we can for those lives.

The necessary amenities are: a good field, and a loose box, or a field shelter which can be turned into a box by putting up slip-rails.

If you are a horse owner, you probably have a field. But to be suitable for a foal, it should be fairly level, be well fenced, have no odd bits of old wire lying about in it, a securely fastened gate, and – some shelter: trees or hedges. If it has running water, so much the better, but it should not have deep ditches into which a tiny foal can easily slip, and be unable to get out. A box or shelter is necessary, even if the mare is to foal outside. You may need it for emergencies: you will certainly need it when you want to handle the foal, and for feeding in winter.

Choosing a stallion

In all breeding, there is an element of chance. A good mare and a good stallion will not automatically breed a super foal, although they are more likely to do so than would the mating of two mediocre animals. The root of the matter is that the stallion should suit your mare; in breed, and in conformation; its good points compensating as far as possible for the weaker ones of the mare. Do not simply put your mare to the "stallion next door", unless that stallion is in every way suitable for her.

If your mare is a pony under 14.2 hands you will have to breed a pony from her. If you want one smaller than she is, choose a small stallion; if bigger, then the stallion should be bigger. If she is a registered Mountain and Moorland, the most sensible thing is to put her to a registered stallion of her own breed. Every breed has its own

Don mare and colt foal, bred at the Lugovskoi Stud, at summer pasture high in the Tien Shan mountains, in the USSR. Nothing is better for the young horse than to spend the first summer of its life on good grass, at freedom with its dam, visited regularly by sympathetic human handlers.

Society which willingly gives information about available breed stallions. If she is a pony of no particular breed, and you want a little more "quality", put her to a small Thoroughbred, or an Arab, or a Riding Pony Stallion. If she is one of the larger Mountain and Moorlands, Fell, Dale or Highland, you can breed a horse from her by putting her to a Thoroughbred. Welsh Cobs also cross well with Thoroughbreds, but are now so valuable in themselves that you would be best to put your Cob mare to a Welsh Cob stallion. Small pony mares – Welsh Mountains, Dartmoors or Exmoors – can breed slightly bigger foals by using, for the Welsh, Section B or C stallions, and for the Dartmoor and Exmoor, Riding Ponies.

If the mare is a horse and it is intended to breed a good all-rounder, you can do no better than put her to one of the Hunter Improvement Society's stallions. These are Thoroughbreds which have not only proved themselves on the racecourse, but have been assessed and awarded their premiums by first class judges. The Society will give you particulars of the stallions serving in your area. If your mare is rather light and you want more bone and substance, the Cleveland Bay cross is excellent. A Thoroughbred crossed with an Arab will give you an Anglo-Arab, which can be registered as such with the Arab Horse Society: good Anglo-Arabs are excellent riding horses. A pure bred Arab should go to an Arab stallion. If your mare is of that grand type that used to be known as "Irish Hunter", she should go to a Thoroughbred every time.

If your mare is a "maiden", that is, if this is to be her first foal, do not put her to a stallion very much bigger than herself, because the initial service may be both difficult and painful for her.

Before choosing your stallion, take a good look at your mare's conformation. If she has rather a plain head, and maybe a short neck, choose one with a good head, well set on to a good neck. If she is a bit short striding, particularly behind, the stallion must have a really free, swinging action, good quarters and well let down hocks. But above all, and whatever type of foal is to be bred, choose a stallion with a good temperament. This is vital; and particularly so when it is a question of children's ponies.

Always visit the studs where the stallions are standing; see how they are run, how the animals there look, and how they are handled. Your mare will have to spend some time there; you want to know she will be well looked after. See the stallions, both in their boxes, and led out; and if you see some of their progeny, so much the better.

Before taking your mare to the stallion, you should get your veterinary surgeon to examine her, to make sure that her reproductive organs are in order, and that she is not suffering from any form of equine venereal disease. Many studs nowadays insist on visiting mares being certified free from Contagious Metritis.

Sending the mare to stud

From early spring onwards, mares come into season more or less regularly every three weeks, individual mares showing slight variations in the number of days between their periods. It is at the culminating point of these periods that they can be successfully covered by the stallion. Watch for the rhythm of your mare's periods as this will help you determine when to take her to stud.

Mares carry their foals for an average of 333 days or about 11 months. When she goes to stud must therefore be eleven months before you want her to foal. When this is, must depend upon where you live. In a mild, southern climate, she can foal in April or early May; where it is colder, and the grass comes later, any time from mid-May until the end of June. If she is a maiden, she may not hold to her first service, so it may be as well to send her to stud three weeks earlier than the date you had worked out for the correct foaling time.

If the stallion lives close at hand, you can take the mare to him for service, but it is not easy for the inexperienced to know what is precisely the right time for this. It is better to take her to the stud when she comes into season about eleven months before you want her to foal, and to leave her there for at least three weeks: that is, until her next oestral period is due. If she does not come into season then, she is said to have held to the service; the stud will notify you that she can be collected. If she does come into season, she has not held; the stud will have her covered again, and will contact you to ask if you wish her to remain for a further three weeks.

Care of the in foal mare

For the first three months, a pregnant mare can be ridden normally, although she should not be asked for extreme exertion, and can be fed her normal working diet. Take particular care that all her food is of good quality: hay, grass, and oats, or cubes. She will benefit from extra minerals and vitamins: various seaweed additives are good, as is cod-liver oil. If she is kept stabled, she should be turned out for part of each day on good grass.

Between the third and fifth months, the foetus increases considerably in weight – from 4oz (115g) to about 4lb (1.8kg). Continue riding her, but do not do her girths up too tightly, and again, do not ask for extreme exertion. Her behaviour may change; placid mares may become restive; those usually hard to catch, come up to you freely, eager for company. She may show unwillingness to work, and will certainly show increased appetite, so you should increase her concentrate ration. If she lives out, or is turned out for part of the time, her companions should be friendly and known to her; she should not risk being bullied or kicked. She is better out with mares and fillies than geldings.

At five months, it is advisable to stop work, at least for a month, because between the fifth and sixth months, great changes take place in the unborn foal. It not only trebles in weight in this time, it quickens, and the mare must accustom herself to its movement inside her. At times, you will be able to see this movement.

After the sixth month, she can be ridden again very lightly for a couple of months. During this second half of pregnancy the greatest development of the foal takes place so it is really best for the mare to be turned out on good pasture and allowed to exercise herself at liberty – for the whole day, if she is stabled at night. As this part of her pregnancy, when the foal is making the greatest demands on her, will be during winter, she must have plenty of nutritious food. The best is good bruised oats, with a little bran added; if you prefer to feed cubes, use Stud Cubes, which are specially balanced for breeding stock. As there will not be much grass in her field, she should have a net of good

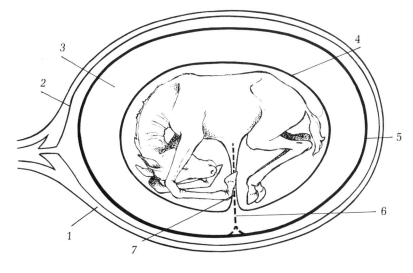

The normal position of a foal in the womb. Just before birth, the forelegs will extend forwards, with the head lying between them.
1. Cervix
2. Wall of the uterus
3. Allantoic fluid
4. Amnion
5. Placenta
6. Blood vessels running between the foetus and the placenta
7. Umbilical cord

hay in the morning, if she lives out, another, larger one, at night. She should have at least two feeds a day, but remember that the foal is taking up more and more room inside her, therefore cramping her stomach; no single feed should weigh more than 4lb (1.8kg). If after Christmas she seems to be going back in condition (as she may do if the winter is very severe), give her more hay, and an extra, third feed, rather than add to the weight of her normal ones. She should have a mineral or salt lick, or block, in her field or stable and always plenty of fresh clean water. About three weeks before foaling, cut down the oats and add to the bran. A good evening feed for her at this time is a bran mash with linseed, with a handful of oats added.

If you are in doubt as to whether your mare is in foal, there are three ways she can be tested. By rectal examination, by a veterinary surgeon. By a blood test, which can be taken between 50 and 100 days after her mating; and by urine, which can only be done after 110 days.

Pregnant mares should be wormed; but it is best to consult your vet as to the correct dose for her age, size and state of pregnancy. Feet should be trimmed regularly; as the mares become heavier, un-trimmed, over-long feet can split and cause discomfort. The mare should also be groomed; not as one would groom a stabled horse for a show, but brushed over regularly to keep the skin in good condition, and, if wintering out, to check for lice, which can appear on even the best fed animals. It is a good thing when grooming maiden mares to handle their udders gently from time to time; one of the reasons why it is sometimes difficult to get maidens to let their foals suck is that they are sensitive to any touch on their udders, and resent the "tickliness" of the foal searching for the nipples.

Shortly before foaling, the mare's belly will drop, and the muscles of her quarters slacken, so that the quarters will appear to droop. Her udder will swell; and when you see a waxy substance formed on her nipples, her time is not far off. Individual mares vary however; some develop an udder and "wax up" eight or ten days before foaling; some only the day before.

Foaling
Fortunately for breeders, the conformation of the mare is such that most foal both easily and quickly. Only about one per cent of mares have difficult foalings and most foals are "presented" correctly: that is, with the head lying between the forefeet. If your mare is expecting the first foal you have ever bred, for your peace of mind ask your vet to check that all is correct as soon as you notice she has waxed up. Vets are sympathetic to the novice breeders' qualms; if they suspect a mare may have an abnormal presentation, they will not mind being called upon for immediate help when foaling starts; and with any complications, help must be immediate, and never attempted by the inexperienced. If, however, all is going to be correct and normal, they will tell you not to worry.

If your mare is to foal outside, you should get her accustomed to you going into her field at night. However often you check, she will probably catch you out, and foal when you have gone to bed. All you need to do then, in the morning, is give the mare a bran mash and be sure that the foal is sucking, because it must get the mare's first milk, known as the colostral; and check that the mare has "cleansed" (got rid of the afterbirth). Go round the field till you find it, then bury it. If the mare has not cleansed, and does not do so within six hours of foaling, call your vet.

If your mare is to foal inside, she must have a deep bed of clean straw, well banked up at the sides and by the door, so that there is no draught at ground level. When foaling seems fairly imminent, her box should be cleaned out thoroughly every day and sprinkled with a disinfectant before a new bed of clean straw is put down. Rather than continually popping in and out of a mare's box to keep an eye on her, it is better to put a camp bed in the tack room, or a neighbouring box, where you can hear what is going on. Have a low-powered bulb left on in her box, so that the sudden putting on of a light does not startle her. The night you hear a lot of movement with the mare lying down, getting up again, and moving about restlessly, foaling is probably about to start. Go quietly to her box. Do not try to halter or hold her, but if she is used to you, she may appreciate your company. If all is normal, soon after the emergence of the "bag of waters", the mare will probably get up; then lie down, as her labour pains increase. Soon, you will see the emergence of a yellowish green membrane, the caul; this will normally burst with the pressure of the foal's forefeet, then comes its head, and finally, there on the straw is the newborn foal, wet and curly, alive, and as surprised to find itself in the world as you probably are to see it. The only complication with which you can deal is if the caul does not burst as the forefeet emerge. It is tightly stretched; a little pressure of the finger tips between the foal's feet will break it.

The mare, after a few moments, will get up, and in doing so, will normally break the umbilical cord. She will, or should start licking the foal; if she does, leave her to do this: it is the best thing for them both. It warms and dries the foal and stimulates its circulation, and encourages

The forelegs visible.

If help is given, the helper takes each foreleg and pulls gently each time the mare strains. The head is still enveloped in the caul. Pressure of the emerging forelegs normally breaks the caul, enabling the foal to breathe.

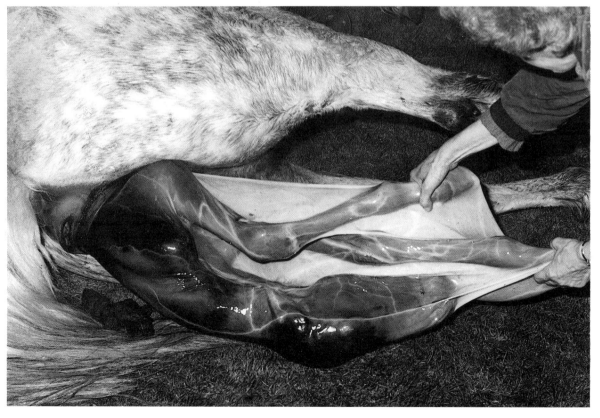

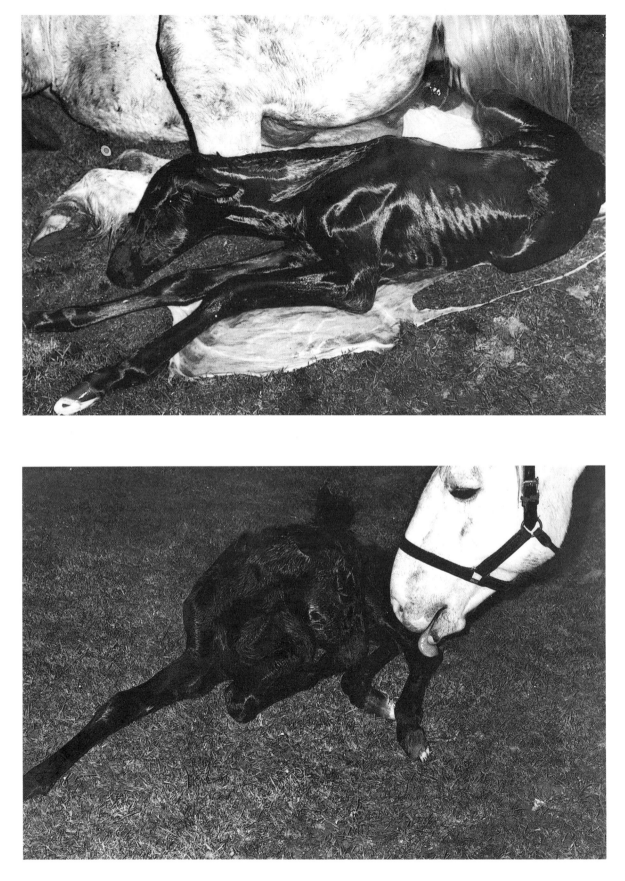

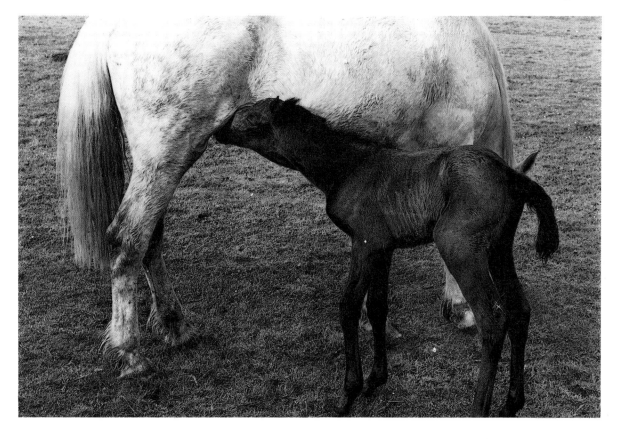

Above left: Just arrived, wet and cold.

Left below: The mother licks the foal to dry it, warm it and stimulate the circulation. If the mother does not do this, then human helpers must dry and warm the foal with soft towels.

Above: Warm, dry, on its legs, and happily feeding.

the mare's maternal instinct. If, however, she does not, you must dry and massage the foal yourself, using a soft warm towel. If the mare has sweated a lot, she should be rubbed down as well, but always see that the foal is warm and dry. It will soon start trying to get to its feet; if it finds this very difficult, you can help it. Having once succeeded, it will soon collapse on to the straw again, when you can give the mare a bran mash, and leave them quietly together, as the foal will not want to suck for an hour or so. Again, you may have to help it to find the right place!

As soon as the mare cleanses, remove the afterbirth; take out all soiled straw and replace with plenty of fresh. Dab some iodine on the foal's navel, and wipe down the mare's flanks. Provided the foal is sucking, tie up a hay net for the mare, see that she has water, and leave them in peace and quiet. If both mare and foal are well and strong, and the weather is fine, they can be turned out on the second day, as grazing is the best keep for mare and foal; oats should not be given for several days after foaling; give the mare a feed of bran mash on coming in at night.

Handling foals
The sooner you can handle a foal, the better. This is why, even if your mare lives, and has foaled, outside, you need a box or shelter of some kind into which you can bring them both, and while a helper holds the mare, you catch the foal. To do this you will probably need to get it in a corner behind the mare; then put one arm around its bottom, the other round its chest. The first time you do this, just gentle it until it will stand quietly, probably quite enjoying being rubbed and scratched. Next time, put on a foal slip which, if it fits correctly, can be left on in the field. The following day, attach a strong webbing lead to the foal slip, and try leading the foal in to the box beside its dam. It may refuse to walk at all, when you must encourage it with an arm round its bottom. It may fight; if it does, do not worry, even if it gets quite

violent and throws itself down. Above all, do not let it go. Once it realises it can not get away from you, it will give in, and in a few days will be leading happily beside, or even away from the mare. Be firm with the foal, but do not get angry with it. Remember it is a baby; and while it must learn to respect you, you must not teach it to fear you. Therefore, "make much" of it when it gives in to you.

Once it has learnt to lead, you can teach it to stand while you brush it over lightly with a soft brush and pick its feet up. You need not repeat these lessons every day; only often enough for it not to forget them. Do not leave the foal slip on in the field now; with patience, it will learn to come up to you and be caught when you catch the mare. When weaning time comes, a great deal of time and temper will be saved if the foal accepts being haltered and led.

Before weaning, the foal must also learn to eat from a manger or feeding bowl. Foals start nibbling grass, and hay, very early, but before they leave their dams they must be introduced to concentrates. In late summer, when the grass is beginning to go off, bring the mare and foal in during the afternoon and put a feed of bruised oats and bran into a low manger, or a large feeding bowl on the ground. Out of curiosity, the foal will want to sample what the mare is eating. Bring them in again next day, and this time, tie the mare while she eats, and put a small feed down in a separate bowl for the foal. Do this daily, sometimes putting a few sliced carrots, or cubes, into the foal's feed, so that it learns about different kinds of food. If the mare and foal are alone in their field, you can do this feeding outside; holding the mare while she eats so she does not push the foal off his feed. Once the foal has discovered the delights of oats, you can put the feed into one trough or bowl: the foal will see to it that it gets its share!

Quite young foals can be turned out in a small headcollar, called a "foal slip".

Mares and foals at pasture, behind the safest of all types of fences, post and rails.

Weaning

Foals should not be weaned until they are at least five months old. Weaning can be done gradually, by taking the mare away for lengthening periods of each day, which is a bother because of the problem of what to do with the foal. Or it can be done in one fell swoop, simply removing the mare from the field and putting her somewhere where the two are out of sight and hearing of one another. This is probably less traumatic than gradual weaning, which must produce a continual state of uncertainty in both mare and foal.

Whichever way the foal is weaned, it must have company to which it is already accustomed before the dam leaves it. If you have other youngstock, put them in with the mare and foal some time before weaning; if not, another mare or a gelding: geldings often make excellent "uncles" to weaned foals. The mare will probably make more fuss about the separation than the foal; but by five to six months her milk will be drying off a little anyway. If her udder is still pretty big, you can wipe it over daily with a cloth soaked in vinegar, and take off a little milk if it seems very full, but do not milk her dry, this will simply encourage the supply. Once she starts quiet work again, she will soon stop thinking about the foal, and for the first week or so, give her only hay and a little oats. She must, however, stay out of sight, and hearing, of the foal. You may have to keep her stabled for a few weeks, with, of course regular, gentle exercise to get her back into condition.

The foal must continue its concentrate feeds, which can be increased to two daily, to make up for the loss of milk; its oats and bran can be supplemented with some milk pellets, or milk powder. A guide for the feeding of foals through their first winter, after weaning, is that they should have 1lb (450g) of concentrates for every month of their age; up to a maximum of 8lb (3·5kg). The concentrate feeds should consist of 65 per cent oats, 20 per cent good bran, and 15 per cent cubes, or soaked sugar beet, or, for a change, cooked flaked maize. They should also have a mineral or salt lick. During the winter, cod-liver oil or a vitamin additive in the feeds will benefit them.

Highly bred foals should come in at night from mid-October onwards; all, even the hardiest, should be in at night from December

onwards. If you have two foals, they will happily share one box; hang up two hay nets, feed in separate mangers and provide two water buckets.

It is vital to feed the foal well during the first winter of its life; what is skimped then can never be made up later.

Foals should have their feet trimmed when necessary; should be wormed regularly (your vet will advise the correct dosage for their size); and should have anti-tetanus injections.

Youngstock

In the first spring of its life, your foal will become a yearling. As soon as the grass comes, and the weather turns kind, it should be turned out; grass is the best possible keep for it; a few weeks before completely turning out, concentrate feeds can be gradually cut down. From mid-May on, it will need only grass until early autumn. Keep on handling the youngster; bring it in now and then for brushing, checking for cuts or scratches, and for reminding it of its stable manners.

During their second winter, youngstock need less oats and more bulk. If they are out on a sufficient acreage, and are given plenty of hay, one feed a day of between 3 to 4lb (1.5 to 1.8kg) oats is plenty for them. If they are highly bred and therefore thin skinned, they should be brought in at night from November on, but the hardier types can winter out, so long as their field has good natural, or a field, shelter.

As the grass comes again in spring, reduce their hay ration; when you find them leaving the hay, they are getting enough grass; and again, from about mid-May onwards, they will need nothing else till autumn.

Colt foals should be gelded as yearlings: your vet will advise you about this. Some are very precocious and are capable of serving mares at not much over a year; if they are not gelded in time, and you also have mares, you may be landed with a few "little mistakes" the following spring.

No young horse should be broken before it is three. At two and a half, however, it can in the autumn be given short lunge lessons, concentrating simply on obtaining obedience to the voice at walk, trot and halt. It can learn to wear a roller, but should only be lunged from the cavesson. Once it is calm and obedient, turn it away for the winter; it will not forget, and you can start again in spring where you left off. At three, it can be "backed", preferably on the lunge; and taken subsequently for short rides in a field or a schooling arena. But do not ask for anything more than forward movement, and obedience and keep your lessons short, and interesting. Again, turn it away, lesson-free, for the winter, and at four, it can begin more serious work.

If a young horse is worked too soon, its working life is shortened, and all the good feeding and care you have given it will have been partly wasted. No horse or pony, however "grown up" it may look, is fully mature until it is five, not only physically, but mentally. Whether or not we consider horses to be intelligent, they do indisputably have minds of their own kind, which develop with age and experience as do our own. Roughly, one year of a horse's life is equal to four of a human's. You would not expect a 12-year-old child to be of Olympic athletic, or University academic, standard; neither, therefore, should you expect your three-year-old horse to be capable of understanding, or performing, advanced and difficult schooling or jumping exercises. If more people understood this, there would be far fewer young animals spoilt and soured by being asked to do more than their bodies are ready for both physically and mentally.

While some horses, dependent on their heredity, have easier temperaments to deal with than others, it is safe to say that it is our handling which can make them or mar them. A young horse that has been firmly, sensibly and kindly handled from foalhood upwards will be a pleasant pupil when the time comes for its serious lessons to begin. Because it will have learnt to have confidence in, rather than to fear, human beings, it will do its best to co-operate.

Ideally there should be a natural supply of fresh water in every field or paddock. Where this does not occur, fresh water should be piped into a trough. The water level should be controlled by a ball-cock. Any container should be regularly scrubbed and cleaned.

A typical attitude of protection and maternal affection.

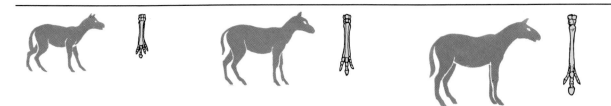

The earliest ancestor of the horse was Hyracotherium (above), or Eohippus. It lived in the forests of North America 55 million years ago in the Eocene period. It had four toes on its forefeet and was the size of a fox.

Mesohippus (above) was larger than Eohippus and lived between 40 and 25 million years ago in the Oligocene period. Its legs were now three-toed and had pads similar to a dog's foot. Its teeth, too, had changed and were now efficient for browsing on soft plants.

Merychippus (above) was the earliest form of the horse as we know it today; it lived in the Miocene period between 25 and 5 million years ago. The feet had lost their pads and the horse's weight was carried almost entirely on the enlarged central toe, enabling it to move much faster. Its teeth had now adapted sufficiently for it to thrive on the stunted vegetation.

History and Breeds

by Jennifer Baker

For the first ancestor of our modern horse we must go back some 60 million years or so to Eohippus, the little "Dawn Horse" which roamed across the swamp lands of Europe, South America and Asia when these land masses were still connected. A skeleton of this animal, found in North America, shows Eohippus to have been about the size of a fox and to have had pads similar to a dog's foot with four toes on his forefeet and three on his hind. Unlike hooves, the pads spread to allow him to wander over the wet marsh lands, and the scarcity of herbage ensured that he grew little beyond a foot in height.

As the land masses dried and the environment changed, the Dawn Horse's successors, first Mesohippus and then, about 25 million years ago, Miohippus, grazing on the by then stunted vegetation, grew to about the size of a sheep and lost one of his four front toes. Merychippus, slightly larger, with better-formed teeth and using only the middle one of his three toes, followed, and then in the Pliocene period came Pliohippus. About the size of a donkey this was the first of the horse ancestors to have properly formed hooves.

With the coming of the Ice Age and the final disappearance of the land bridges many animal species disappeared and others, including the horse ancestors, were reduced. They became extinct in America and until Christopher Columbus landed in Hispaniola in 1492, taking with him 30 horses, no equines were seen in the American continent. They did not get established in that continent until the *Conquistadores* landed in Mexico with a complement of mares and stallions in 1519.

From the horses that survived the Ice Ages, and the environmental and climatic changes that this entailed, four basic types emerged to which all today's various breeds and types can be traced. These were the Forest horse, the Steppe horse, the Plateau horse and the Tundra. The last mentioned has had virtually no part to play in influencing

The Przewalski wild horse – ancestor of the "warm bloods". A small herd was discovered in the Gobi desert in 1881 by the Russian explorer, Colonel N. M. Przewalski. A number are preserved in zoos throughout the world.

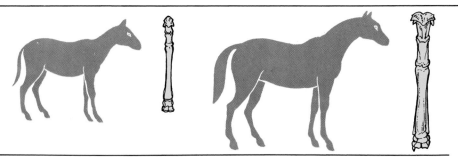

Between five and two million years ago (in the Pliocene period) the descendant of Merychippus, Hipparion, crossed into Asia, where it spread into Europe and Africa. Meanwhile Pliohippus (above) remained in the New World and provided the model from which Equus was to develop.

Several million years later, the horse as we know it today, arrived. Called Equus, it had by this time entirely lost its three toes and had properly formed hooves. Its better formed teeth had also been adapted for grazing. Equus spread into Europe and Africa, via Asia; and as it arrived the last of the three-toed horses became extinct. Finally, about 8,000 years ago, Equus became extinct in the Americas, leaving the modern horse to flourish in Europe, Asia and Africa.

today's breeds with the possible exception of the massive Yakut horse which lives in the Polar regions. The Forest horse was a solid, heavy type of animal with a big heavy head and large feet, and can be regarded as the basic founder of the "cold-blooded" breeds, while the Steppe and Plateau horses are jointly responsible for the "warm-bloods". The Steppe horse can be considered the ancestor of the Oriental and light horse breeds, being finely built with long limbs, and the last survivor of this primitive type can be seen in the Tarpan (*Equus przewalskii gmelini Antonius*), a breed that lived on the Southern Russian steppes in Eastern Europe. The last wild Tarpan, a mare, is reported to have been killed in Russia in 1879 and the last one in captivity to have died in 1919, but a herd very similar in type derived from Polish Konik mares and Przewalski stallions now live in a Polish government reserve. The Plateau horse still exists in the Przewalski (*Equus przewalskii przewalskii Poliakoff*) the wild horse of Mongolia, a small herd of which was discovered as recently as 1881 on the Western edge of the Gobi desert by a Russian explorer, Colonel N. M. Przewalski. Whether any still exist in their wild state today is not known since, owing to their having been hunted extensively by the Mongolian tribesmen, who know the breed as Taki, they retreated into the impenetrable desert and mountainous regions as well as into China. They are, however, preserved in a number of zoos throughout the world.

These four types spread over the land masses; the thicker, heavier types, such as the Forest and Tundra tended to inhabit the colder, wetter climes; the little Steppe horse favoured the warmth and dryness of North Africa and Asia; and the Plateau horse settled for Europe and Northern Asia.

Although environment, and natural selection through survival of the fittest, are the principal factors governing the evolution of the horse in his wild state, once he had become domesticated the interference of man played an increasingly large part. The first records of horses being domesticated come from China over 4,000 years ago and refer to raids by nomad horsemen who had the "same customs as the latter day huns", from which it can be taken to mean that the horses were ridden. By the end of the 13th century following the Christian and Moslem clashes in the Crusades and the capture of Oriental stock, selective horse breeding started to be practised world

The Byerley Turk, one of the three founding sires of the English Thoroughbred.

(reproduced by kind permission of Fores Gallery Ltd)

wide. By breeding selectively for specific purposes such as racing, driving, ploughing and so on, and feeding artificially in consequence, bigger and faster horses resulted in the numerous breeds and types of horses and ponies that we know today.

The breed to have had the greatest influence on the development of horses and ponies in general is undoubtedly the Arabian, a horse known to have existed in that part of the world from where it takes its name for many thousands of years. One noted Arab historian, El Kelbi, claimed that the first Arab horse to be captured belonged to a great-great-grandson of Noah and certainly as far back as the 13th or 14th century BC Egyptian monuments and rock carvings depicted horses looking very similar to Arabs. Mohammed too, appreciating the importance of horses in the desert lands, gave strict orders to his followers concerning the development and care of these horses. Under these conditions the Arab horse flourished, the "dry" look was fixed, and he developed the speed, soundness and stamina for which he is noted today. After Mohammed's death his followers spread Islam throughout Egypt and North Africa and carried it into Europe as far as Spain and France on the backs of Arab horses. Thus the Arab horse influenced the existing stock in all the countries throughout Europe, and generally upgraded them.

The accepted height for a pure-bred Arab today can vary between about 14.1 hands to 15.2 hands and with his short head, dished profile, huge widely spaced eyes, flared nostrils and pint-pot muzzle he is probably the most beautiful of all our breeds. He makes an ideal riding horse with his unmistakable "floating" action and high tail carriage and can carry weight out of all proportion to his relatively small size. However, his metier probably still lies in long distance riding, where his powers of endurance are brought into play.

The Thoroughbred's Oriental Sires

Although the Arab's influence has spread to practically all Europe's breeds his most noteworthy contribution must surely be as the progenitor of the Thoroughbred since it is generally accepted that three Oriental sires, the Darley Arabian, the Godolphin Arabian and the Byerley Turk are responsible for the founding of the Thoroughbred and that all present day Thoroughbreds are descended from

The Hackney Pony's spectacular action makes it popular with driving enthusiasts.

Below left: The Exmoor – probably the oldest of the British native pony breeds. The height limit for a stallion is 12·3 hands and mares should be an inch smaller. The only acceptable colours for an Exmoor are brown, brown-dun, or bay with no white marks, and all must have a mealy muzzle and 'toad' eyes.

them in the male line. "Running horses", however, which were probably of Spanish descent were imported into England during the 12th century and were certainly racing in England by the 14th century, and it is probable that a crossing of these "running horses" with earlier imports of Oriental stock and later with the three Arabians resulted in what we know as the Thoroughbred.

Of these later imports the Byerley Turk was the first to appear. He was foaled in 1680 and captured from the Turks at the Battle of Buda by Captain Byerley who brought him back to England and subsequently used him as his charger at the Battle of the Boyne (1690). He was the founder of the Herod line which sired The Tetrarch. The Darley Arabian was foaled in 1700 and was of the Kehilan strain being brought back to England by Thomas Darley in 1704. He sired Flying Childers and in due course founded the Eclipse line. The Godolphin Arabian, originally named El Sham and foaled in 1724, had been given to Louis XV of France by the Sultan of Morocco, but was sold on and eventually bought by Edward Coke who found him pulling a cart in Paris. Coke brought him back to England in 1729 and gave him to his friend Lord Godolphin to use on his Derbyshire Stud as a "teaser". A chance mating by this "teaser" produced a colt foal, Cade, which founded the Matchem line.

Organised racing, as opposed to matches between two owners for a wager, started on Newmarket Heath under the aegis of Charles II who competed as well as organising races and establishing rules. Later, in 1711, Queen Anne opened up Ascot Park for the same purpose. But it was not until the General Stud Book appeared in 1793 that the Thoroughbred became a recognised breed, although the breed was not established, and the word Thoroughbred not used, until 1821. In spite of his speed, the Thoroughbred is not confined to racing, since he makes a superb riding horse, having quality and intelligence, and when crossed with half-bred mares makes an ideal horse for hunting and jumping.

Theoretically, the crossing of these two first-rate breeds should result in the top horse *par excellence*, combining the soundness and stamina of the Arabian with the quality and speed of the Thoroughbred but without displaying the characteristics of one breed to the exclusion of the other. The Anglo-Arab does, in fact, frequently

The Welsh Cob (above) is a larger edition of the Welsh Mountain Pony, and makes a splendid ride and drive animal. Welsh Ponies and Cobs are registered in one stud book with four sections. Section A is the Welsh Mountain Pony, Section B is the Welsh Pony of Riding type, Section C is the Welsh Pony of Cob type and Section D is the Welsh Cob.

The Welsh Pony, section B, is similar to, but slightly larger than the Welsh Mountain Pony but with more quality and less knee action.

display all these desirable qualities and is a useful all-round riding horse being used for hunting, jumping and eventing with equal success.

In France the formation of State studs, which first came into being in Louis XIV's time in the 17th century, have had a beneficial influence on the French Anglo-Arab. Based on native Meridian half-breds crossed with the Oriental horses that were the mounts of the Moors, four studs, founded in the early 1800s, are prominent in South West France, these being Pau, Tarbes, Pompadour and Gelos. New infusions of Arab blood were introduced following the Napoleonic wars, but it was not until 1830 that English Thoroughbreds were introduced. The mares now visit both Thoroughbred and Arabian stallions, but in order to be recognised by the stud the progeny have to possess at least 25 per cent of Arab blood. The stallions, too, have to pass a selection test based on conformation and performance on the racecourse.

The Andalusian – an equine elite

Long before the English Thoroughbred was regarded as the supreme horse, the Andalusian of Spain was considered the elite of the horse world. It is probable that the Andalusian evolved from the crossing of the native lightweight stock, possibly of Barb type, with the Barb horses from North Africa that were left behind in Spain and the surrounding countries following the Moorish invasions of Europe. The Carthusian monks bred the Andalusian at their monasteries in Seville and Jerez de la Frontera and they are still bred in this South Western area of Spain today, principally for use by the *rejoneadores* in the bull rings, since they are tractable and agile enough to be schooled to the very high level required, and as parade horses for the Spanish festivities. It was these same horses that the 16th century *Conquistadores* took with them to America, and their influence can still be

A horse or pony is measured in hands from the highest part of the withers to the ground. A hand is 4 inches (10 cm).

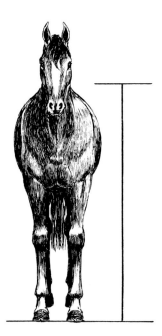

The Fjord pony from Norway flourishes throughout Scandinavia. It has a characteristic stiff mane and is always dun in colour. The fashion of hogging the mane dates back to Viking times.

The Fell inhabits the western side of the Pennine range. It is very similar to the Dales Pony which comes from the Eastern side of the Pennines.

The New Forest Pony is a mixture of breeds, including Arab. It can be any colour except piebald or skewbald. The least shy of any native British breed, it is quick to learn, quiet in traffic, and makes a very safe ride for children.

Far left: The Holstein, the ancestor of the German medieval warhorse. This fine all-round horse contains Andalusian and Thoroughbred blood.

Left: The massive but docile Percheron comes from the Perche region of France. This workhorse's somewhat overgrown Arab appearance can be traced back to oriental forebears in the Middle Ages.

Below left: The Hanoverian, formerly a carriage horse, is descended from the Great German Horse. By infusing it over the last 20 years with East Prussian and English Thoroughbred Blood, the Hanoverian has emerged as one of the best saddle horses for sporting events.

Below: The Lipizzaner, the mount of the Spanish Riding School in Vienna, is a direct descendant of the Andalusian.

seen in such horses as the Quarter Horse and Appaloosa. Their elevated, extravagant trot, and elegant carriage combined with a proud bearing made the Andalusian the mount of kings from the 14th century onwards and he became the supreme riding horse of the Renaissance period being ideal for work in the *manège*, the only type of riding which was practised in Europe at that time. A small horse, standing no more than about 15.2 hands and usually grey or bay in colour, he has immense presence and is strong and well-proportioned with a notably crested neck, short back and a wealth of mane and tail. His principal characteristic, however, is his hawk profile that is still, to a large degree, seen in the Lipizzaner, a direct descendant of the Andalusian. The Archduke Charles II imported nine stallions and 24 mares to found the stud at Lipica in 1580. It is from the Spanish Andalusian that the famous Spanish Riding School in Vienna gets its name, the Andalusian being the original horses used for *haute école*.

The Lipizzaner is not the only European breed to have developed from the Andalusian. Denmark's Frederiksborg and Knabstrup are both virtually direct descendants, the Royal Frederiksborg Stud formed in 1562, being based on Andalusian blood. The Alter-Real, who hails from Portugal, is also descended from the Andalusian but has had recent infusions of Arab blood added in an effort to upgrade the breed after French mares had been introduced and the breed declined in quality. Czechoslovakia's Kladruby can also claim Andalusian descent, the Emperor Maximilian II importing Andalusian horses to found his stud at Kladruby in Bohemia.

It is not only the foreign breeds, however, which have benefitted from the Andalusian influence. Britain's Cleveland Bay has also had infusions of Andalusian blood through the Kladruby, although the influence is less defined than in some other breeds. The British Isles, too, has a wealth of pony breeds, the nine native ponies being, Dartmoor, Dale, Fell, Highland, New Forest, Shetland, Connemara, (an Irish breed), Exmoor, the oldest and most "pure" of all the Mountain and Moorlands and the Welsh breeds of which there are four different types – the Welsh Mountain, the Welsh Pony, the Welsh Pony of Cob type and the Welsh Cob. Most of these natives have had infusions of outside blood at one time or another, mostly of Arabian blood, and the New Forest in particular has had Arab, Thoroughbred, Fell and Welsh all introduced at various times.

In common with Ireland, Britain has a reputation for hunter breeding which is the envy of the world. Although a hunter is not a breed, it has become a recognised type the best being half or three-quarter Thoroughbred crossed with a half-bred mare or possibly out of a native pony mare such as a Highland, Welsh Cob or Connemara. Some, of course, are heavier and contain Irish draught or Cleveland Bay blood, but Thoroughbred will be present in the best of them. The cob, too, the steady, solid and stuffy mount suitable for elderly gentlemen, is again a type rather than a breed, and is probably a Welsh Cob or Irish draught Thoroughbred cross. The hack, on the other hand, another type, is almost always Thoroughbred or at least with a high percentage of Thoroughbred blood in his veins, or possibly Anglo-Arab.

With the end of the Middle Ages and the Age of Chivalry, when the heavy carthorse type resulting in The Great Horse, was used to carry the knights and their heavy plate armour, both into battle and for tournaments, our "heavy", cold-blooded horses gradually became lighter. Our present day Shire is the last descendant of the English Great Horse. Standing up to 18 hands he is very docile for his massive bulk and his function today lies mainly in ploughing and draught work. Britain's other heavy horses are the Suffolk, always chestnut and hailing from East Anglia, and Scotland's Clydesdale.

Europe has its fair share of heavy "cold-blooded" horses too. Percheron, Breton, Boulonnais, and Ardennes from France, for instance, and the Jutland from Denmark; the Flanders Horse from Belgium and Germany's Schleswig Heavy Draught as well as Scandinavia's Swedish Ardennes.

While the light horse breeds have, with the general upsurge of riding and horse interests, an assured future, it is debatable whether the same can be said of the heavy horse breeds.

4

*Left: Head markings. Markings are
areas of white hair.*
1. *Star*
2. *Blaze*
3. *White face*
4. *Stripe*
5. *Wall eye*
6. *Snip*
*Wall eye is a white or blue-white
colouring in the eye, caused by lack of
pigment in the iris.*

5

6

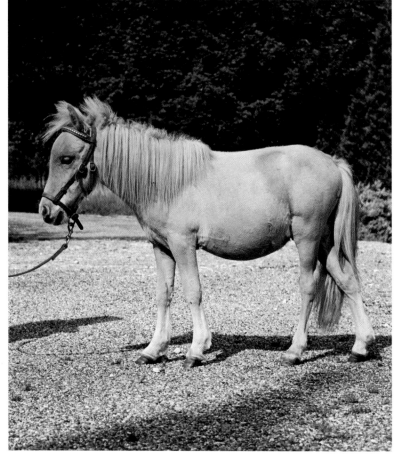

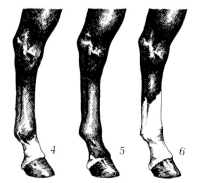

Left: Leg markings.
1. *Stocking*
2. *Fetlock*
3. *Coronet*
4. *Pasterns*
5. *Heels*
6. *Socks*

*The Falabella is the smallest horse in
the world. It was developed by the
Falabella family in Argentina from a
small Thoroughbred inbred with
Shetlands. Its height does not exceed
30 inches (76 cm).*

4 5 6

Colours. *If there is some doubt as to the colouring of the coat, then the points (mane and tail, muzzle and tips of ears) are the deciding factor.*

1. Liver chestnut
2. Palomino
3. Chestnut
4. Skewbald
5. Strawberry roan
6. Piebald
7. Black
8. Grey
9. Bay
10. Iron grey
11. Dun
12. Appaloosa

11 12

American Breeds

by Robin Serfass

Left: The American Quarter Horse was the first breed developed in the Americas. The breed is founded on Arabs, Barbs and Turks brought to America by Spanish traders and crossed with mares from England. Its early use as a mount in match races, usually run over a distance of a quarter of a mile, gave it the name "Quarter" horse.

Left: The Appaloosa gets its name from the Palouse river which drains the area in the north-west of the United States, where the breed was developed. Horses with the Appaloosa's distinctive colouring are seen in Ancient Chinese and Persian Art. In fact, the Appaloosa probably originated in Central Asia and then spread via Spain to America.

The United States is a vast country with a wide variety of geographical regions. Due to these enormous variations of physical areas, a large number of highly different breeds and riding styles developed over the years. Although many of these breeds are considered indigenous to North America, they are in fact descendants of horses brought from Europe by the Spanish *Conquistadores*. Breeds were then developed according to the demands of various regions in America through importations of bloodstock from England and Europe. Thus, unique breeds were created in America: among these being the Quarter Horse; the so-called "colour breeds" of the Appaloosa, Palomino, Pinto, and Paint; the American Saddlebred; the Tennessee Walking Horse; the Standardbred; the Morgan; and the American Thoroughbred.

Three riding styles

Three riding styles are popular in America – hunt seat, which originated in England for foxhunting; stock seat, used by the American cowboy for riding the range as well as herding and roping cattle; and saddle seat, developed in the Old South when cotton plantations and huge estates were the order of the day. Although all breeds can be ridden in any of the three seats, usually one seat is predominant. For example, American Saddlebreds and Tennessee Walking Horses are usually ridden saddle seat, while the Quarter Horse is most commonly seen in a stock seat saddle, and Thoroughbreds are primarily ridden hunt seat. All the various breeds in the United States have their own association; each determines the rules and regulations for that breed as well as for horse shows offering classes for the breed. But no person or authority has the legal right to recognise a breed in the United States; the development of breed registries came about with the Tariff Act of 1930, which allowed pure bred animals to enter the United States duty-free, provided the animal was registered in its country of origin. Breed associations have evolved in the United States due to the interest of people who wanted to see a particular breed refined and developed.

The Quarter Horse, the breed most often associated with the American Old West and the cowboy was, in fact, developed as the colonies were being settled – most notably in Virginia. Plantation owners would have match races down the main street of town, streets that were seldom more than a quarter-mile in length. Thus, the name Quarter Horse came into being, and even today, Quarter Horse races are popular events at local tracks.

This early emphasis on quick speed caused the Quarter Horse to develop very powerful hindquarters and well-developed muscles throughout his body. The breed is the most popular registered breed in the United States today, followed by the Thoroughbred and the Appaloosa. The Quarter Horse is popular not only as a speed horse over short distances, but as a working cowhorse, a show horse, and as a family pleasure horse. The compact, powerful body of the average Quarter Horse (14.1 to 15.2 hands) enables him to move quickly and with great agility. The Quarter Horse is also known for his even temperament as well as his intelligence, which makes the breed easy to train and exceedingly versatile. As show horses in the United States, Quarter Horses compete in a variety of events including stock, trail, pleasure, and reining, as well as gymkhana events that are judged on speed and agility, such as barrel racing and pole-bending. In all these

The Morgan, named after Justin Morgan, founder of the breed, has enormous pulling-power in draught and is capable of high speeds as a saddle horse. The breed can be traced back to a single sire, Figure, who was probably a Welsh Cob with a touch of either Thoroughbred or Arabian blood.

The Paint or Pinto (from the Spanish, pintado meaning painted) are colour variations of the same breed. The two associations registering the breed are the Pinto Horse Association founded in 1956, and the Paint Horse Association founded in 1965. The ideal pattern for a Pinto is half white and half some other colour, though standards are being set to ensure that the minimum area of a "spot" is 75 square inches (448 sq cm).

This Paint Horse is known as an overo, having a predominantly white marking on a coloured coat. A tobiano horse is one where again there is a basically white colouring, but the markings are a much darker colour than with the overo.

competitions, horses are shown with a Western or stock saddle, but Quarter Horses are also shown successfully in English tack in hunter, jumper, and hunter under saddle classes.

The breed was established in 1941; the first registered Quarter Horse being Wimpy, whose descendants are well known both on the race track and in the show ring. The American Quarter Horse Association has its own point system by which horses win points to earn the register of merit award, but Quarter Horses are strong contenders as well in open horse shows where all breeds compete in the same classes.

While the racing Quarter Horse is usually kept at a lighter weight than a performance (or show) Quarter Horse, both types feature the same basic physical characteristics. The short, compact body is dominated by the broad and heavy hindquarters, with a powerful stifle, gaskin and thigh. The head should be fairly small but with a pronounced and strong lower jaw and a small nose. The neck, too, is usually compact and strong and set on the shoulder at a good slant. The forelegs should appear short and very muscular, and the back and barrel should be short-coupled and broad with well-sprung ribs.

Several breeds popular in America are closely related to the Quarter Horse, but the animal's colour instead of its breeding became the criterion for its registration. The Paint Horse Association, formed in 1965, requires that any horse having been foaled after 31st December 1969, should have at least one registered parent, but it can be a registered Quarter Horse, Thoroughbred, or Paint. Paints must be at least 14 hands in order to be registered and most Paint horses are built similar to Quarter Horses due to the large amount of Quarter Horse bloodstock used in developing this breed. Paint horses are divided into two colour classifications: the overo, which is a solid-coloured horse with white extending upward from the belly, and usually with dark legs and a solid-coloured tail; and the tobiano, a white horse with large areas of dark hair all over his body. The colours other than white to be found on Paints are black, bay, brown, chestnut, dun, palomino, and roan, and the mane and tail are usually streaked with one or more colours. Often Paints have blue eyes, and the skin should be pink underneath the white hair.

The Pinto Horse Association was formed in 1956, and includes horses of all breeds which conform to the colour criteria outlined by the Pinto Horse Association. Pintos, like Paints, are divided into the two categories of Overo and Tobiano. In order to be registered as a Pinto, a horse must be at least 14 hands by the time he is five years old and meet the colour requirements of the association.

The Appaloosa, the colourful spotted horse, first became popular in the United States with the Nez Percé Indians in the states of Washington, Oregon and Idaho. The American Appaloosa Association has stringent rules regarding an animal's eligibility for its registration, and the original papers must be presented at the horse show office when competing at a recognised Appaloosa horse show. Again, Quarter Horse blood and characteristics predominate, and the Appaloosa Association was formed in 1938 as an effort to recognise a type of horse that, despite the physical similarity to the Quarter Horse, was ineligible for registry with that association. Appaloosa horses *must* fulfill three requirements in order to become registered animals: (1) the horse must have white extending around his eye; (2) the skin must be mottled black and white; and (3) the hooves must be vertically striped with alternating dark and light sections. A mature Appaloosa must exceed 14.1 hands and his colour can vary – usually the animal has a white area on his hips and loins that is covered with round or egg-shaped spots, and this area is referred to as the "blanket". However, Appaloosa horses may be white or light-coloured over the entire body with spots covering the whole body, as in the "leopard" Appaloosa. The colourings of the Appaloosa can encompass a range of hues from bay to roan to dun, as long as it meets the ever-important requirements of eye, skin and hoof.

continued

The Tennessee Walking Horse is well-known for its distinctive gait. Notice the extension of the right hind leg on this horse shown at the running walk.

American Saddlebreds

The American Saddlebred is a breed of large, high-headed horse with natural animation and elegant carriage. This breed was started in the bluegrass country of Kentucky when a Thoroughbred named Denmark and a pacing mare were bred in order to provide smooth gaits – thus, a horseman could ride for pleasure instead of necessity. The modern American Saddlebred has been selectively bred to enhance the extreme refinement and the highly animated leg action.

Saddlebreds are commonly 15.2 to 16.3 hands, with a naturally high head and tail carriage. The shoulder is long while the back is round and short-coupled; the hindquarters are rounded and powerful; and the legs are long and fine. This breed is used primarily in the show ring, ridden saddle seat, and as a pleasure mount.

In three-gaited, the American Saddlebred is shown with a shaven mane and tail, and he performs at a walk, trot and canter; in five-gaited, the horse wears a full, flowing mane and tail and performs, in addition to the three natural gaits, the two artificial or man-made gaits – the slow gait and the rack. These two gaits are true four-beat gaits and are very difficult for the horse to do properly, especially the rack, which is the very fast and animated version of the slow gait.

American Saddlebreds are also shown with a full mane and tail in fine harness events at an animated walk and a show trot. Most young Saddlebreds begin their show ring careers in harness classes before they are trimmed for three-gaited or are taught to slow gait and rack for five-gaited competition. Horses in Saddlebred events are judged on their brilliance, animation, quality, conformation, and style.

Tennessee Walking Horse

Another popular breed in America is the distinctive Tennessee Walking Horse. Shown in the saddle seat style of riding, the Tennessee Walker performs at three gaits: the flat-footed walk, the running walk, and the canter. The spectacular running walk is a gait unique to the Walking Horse, developed on the plantations of the Old South when an owner required a comfortable yet speedy gaited horse on which to oversee his property.

The Walking Horse breed, true to its name, was developed in Tennessee as a cross between the Thoroughbred, Standardbred,

Morgan and the Saddlebred. The Tennessee Walking Horse Breeders' Association was established in 1935, and the stallion Black Allan, a direct descendant of Hambletonian, is considered the foundation sire of the breed. The Walking Horse stands from 15.2 to 16.1 hands.

Tennessee Walking Horses are ridden both for pleasure and for show. Those of the breed that compete in the show ring are shown with a "set" tail and his gaits are more exaggerated than a pleasure Walker's. Even when his gaits are more defined, the Tennessee Walker gives an exceptionally smooth ride unlike any other breed. The slow, flat-footed walk is a four-beat gait and the horse nods his head slightly; the running walk is a much faster version of the flat-footed walk in which the nodding of the horse's head is extremely pronounced and the hind foot oversteps the front foot, in some cases by as much as four feet! The canter of the Walking Horse is often called the "rocking chair" canter because the horse's forelegs extend in an upward, rolling motion while the hind legs remain fairly still. The hindquarters of the Walking Horse remain relatively level at all three gaits, which accounts for his reputation for being the most comfortable horse to ride in the world.

The Standardbred breed, although developed in the United States, had its foundations in England with the Thoroughbred stallion Messenger, imported to America in the 1780s. The breed was established when Messenger's blood was infused with that of horses who had been used in harness races at country fairs. Messenger's great-grandson Hambletonian became the first famous Standardbred race horse, for which reason he is considered the founding father of the breed.

Standardbred racers can be either trotters or pacers – trotters move with the fore and hind legs in diagonal pairs while pacers move the fore and hind legs on the same side in pairs. The name Standardbred originated when the American Trotting Registry, founded in 1871, established that horses could be registered only if they could trot or pace a mile in standard time – approximately $2\frac{1}{2}$ minutes. Of course, since that time, both trotters and pacers have broken the two-minute mile, with the record at one minute, fifty-two seconds.

The conformation of the Standardbred resembles the Thoroughbred, although the former is usually heavier boned and has more slope in his hindquarters. The average height is somewhat smaller than that of the Thoroughbred, ranging between 15 and 16 hands.

Even though bred for racing, the Standardbred possesses a wide variety of talents. At horse shows, classes are held for "roadsters to bike" or "roadsters to wagon," in which the Standardbred is judged not only on his speed while pulling either a "bike" or an old-fashioned buggy-wagon, but also on his style, presence and manners. These horses show at extreme speed in one direction only – the right – and in most horse show arenas it is very thrilling to watch the drivers "turn their horses on" at full speed, as the small circumference of the arena requires skilled driving on tight corners!

Standardbred horses have done well for themselves in other areas as well, including endurance rides and jumping competitions.

The Morgan

Another extremely versatile breed found in the United States is the Morgan. The breed is named after a man, Justin Morgan, who owned the stallion Figure, the founding sire. The Morgan breed developed in only one generation, and all of Figure's progeny inherited his short-coupled, compact but extremely hearty conformation. Although Figure was a working farm horse, he was successful, too, as a trotter, in harness races, as well as in pulling contests and under saddle in match races. Figure came to be called Justin Morgan, and when he died at the age of 32, the Morgan breed was established and popular.

Morgans are usually of a solid colour and stand between 14 and 15.2 hands. His conformation is compact but strong, but not at all coarse. In fact, the Morgan's head is similar to that of the Arabian, with a

The Standardbred is mostly used for racing in harness, and consequently is bred for speed rather than beauty. One-mile time standards were set as an admission requirement to the race, hence its name.

small muzzle, refined ears and a large, expressive eye. Morgans are noted for their even temperament, willingness and amazing versatility. Although bred as a working horse, he is one of the few breeds that can compete in any one of the three styles of riding.

The Morgan Horse Registry began in 1894 and the Morgan Horse Association was founded in 1930. The Association recognises breed shows throughout the United States, and quite often the same horse will compete in English pleasure, Western pleasure, fine harness, roadsters and working hunters – all at the same show! In addition to his show-ring abilities, the Morgan is a popular family pleasure mount and is a favourite for demanding long-distance endurance rides.

Without a doubt, the Thoroughbred is the most widely known breed in the United States, due to the popularity of racing and parimutuel betting. The Thoroughbred breed in the United States is governed by the Jockey Club in New York City, and all Thoroughbreds are registered through this association.

However, Thoroughbreds are not bred exclusively for racing in the United States; this breed is also very popular in the show ring as a hunter or jumper, and, on occasion, is used as an eventing horse. The Thoroughbred's temperament is usually too high strung to be a suitable family pleasure horse, but in competition, he is unequalled.

Hunter classes in the United States are quite different from those in Britain, as all American show hunters perform over fences and are judged on their style of jumping the fences and their pace between the jumps. There is only one event, the hunter under saddle class, in which a hunter is judged exclusively on his walk, trot, canter, and gallop. The judge, or judges, *never* rides the hunter in American horse shows, as the emphasis is on the horse's performance over jumps and the judge's evaluation is strictly visual.

Many horse shows in different areas of the United States offer special classes for Thoroughbreds bred in that state in order to encourage local breeders to raise Thoroughbreds for show as well as for the race track. Horses do not have to be registered Thoroughbreds to compete in hunter classes, but they must be registered in order to race. The result of this rule is that many race horses which are not successful at the track end up being sold as hunter or jumper prospects – hence, the large number of Thoroughbreds found at horse shows.

Australian Horses

by E. A. Weiss

Above: This is the Three-Gaited variety of the Saddlebred, which is trained to walk, trot and canter. Note the rider's balanced position and the horse's animation. The characteristic high carriage of the tail is created by surgically severing the depressor muscles.

The Saddlebred is ideal both for family use and show use, where it is particularly successful. An apt observation from an American exhibitor was that: "You want a horse that looks as though he is going to explode, but doesn't".

There is no native Australian horse. The many fine representatives of the various breeds now found in Australia are descendants of imported stock. A continent that was to depend on animal draught for transport of its primary products, most of which were both bulky and heavy, had no suitable indigenous animals.

The first horses were imported by New South Wales Governor Arthur Phillip, Commander of the First Fleet, in 1787. They were a stallion and three mares from the Cape of Good Hope, South Africa. These horses were of mixed breeding, containing what is described as, much "Spanish Jennet" blood. There followed larger imports of good stock from the same source in 1795, from England in 1802, and by 1820 there were over 4,000 horses in the new colony.

English pure-bred stallions had arrived by this time, the first Thoroughbred in 1799, followed by Arab stallions from England, Persia, and India. By 1830 recognised studs for particular breeds had been established, not only for Thoroughbred and half-breeds, but also Cleveland Bays, Shires, Clydesdales, and French Percherons.

But there were still not enough draught horses to pull the huge transport wagons, and clear and plough the country's vast plains. So teams of oxen were used. A team might number up to 22 in pairs, driven by "bullockys" walking alongside, their long whips controlling the slow but sure progress of the laden wool or timber wagons.

Horse numbers grew rapidly. In 1870, Cobb and Co., the great coaching company, were harnessing 6,000 horses a day to haul their fleets of coaches 28,000 miles (45,000km) a week over the atrocious outback roads. By 1918 it was officially estimated that there were 2.5 million horses and a human population of 5 million, a dramatic example of their importance to the country.

Oxen may substitute for draught horses, but they are too slow to ride, and so by the turn of the present century, a type of riding horse was becoming common which was to achieve world-wide recognition. This was the famous Waler. It was named after New South Wales, the original name given to the whole Eastern Coast of Australia's then settled area, and not merely the present State of New South Wales.

A well-known English sporting writer visiting Australia in 1850 commented thus about these horses: "Mounted police and bush police, heavy men frequently, with heavy accoutrements, bestrode chargers such as no horse regiment in England could or can turn out".

The Waler was not a distinct breed, being a stamp of horse rather as a heavy hunter is understood in Britain. But it was well bred, usually from good quality local mares crossed with imported pure-bred sires, and having a good deal of Arab blood.

With the drastic reduction in the numbers of Army remounts required after the First World War, and the general rural depression, horse breeding declined dramatically. The general standard of outback and station horses suffered. Many horses were "let go" or neglected, and joined the wild brumby herds.

The revival in popularity of all breeds and types of riding horses in Australia in the last 20 years has resulted in what was known as a Waler being absorbed into the Australian Stock Horse Society, officially formed in 1970.

The Society's Stud Book requires a high standard of breeding, conformation, and performance for registration. Anyone with an eye for a horse will readily recognise that indefinable stamp of a Waler. Such horses can be seen at any camp drafting competition, rodeo, bushman's carnival, or outback gymkhana, and at the many shows specially organised by the Stock Horse Society.

The standards required of a working Stock Horse were extremely high, and most were by Thoroughbreds which were often ex-racehorses. A long springy stride and ability to walk fast were major assets. The nature of their work meant covering long distances with plenty of galloping over rough country. A strong constitution combined with extreme sure-footedness were essential qualities of a good Stock Horse. This type of horse is still the mainstay of the station jackeroo, the drover, overlander and rural rider, for it has been bred for the country and can survive in its often harsh climate.

A type of Stock Horse which was used specifically in the "camp" for cutting out, came to be known as the "camphorse". Once trained for such work, it was used for no other. Most camphorses were geldings. This type can be seen today competing in the cutting competitions, a feature of many shows. Sloping shoulders, length of rein, high withers and a flowing springy stride were considered most desirable. Similarly bred to Stock Horses, the essential qualities of a camp horse were extreme quickness on its feet and a fast take-off as well as an almost inherent ability to anticipate the movements of the cattle they were working.

Interest in showing Stock Horses led to the importation of a similar type of horse, the American Quarter Horse. Developed from the "cowpony", as the Australian Quarter Horse developed from the camphorse, the Australian type is now increasingly modelled on its American cousin.

Australia now has its own Quarter Horse Society and Stud Book, with several hundred registered breeders. Recognised Quarter Horse stallions are imported from the USA.

The Quarter Horse of the show ring and the quarter mile sprint, after which it is named, is a far cry from the ordinary working Stock Horse. Although it may work in the ring, cutting out beasts from a mob with no help from its rider, it is too valuable to be risked in the outback. Dressed in all his finery of silver mounted and highly ornamented cloths and saddlery, a competitor in the "Pleasure Class" at a Quarter Horse Show is a magnificent sight, and is one of the great attractions of these events.

There is in fact little difference in conformation or basic training between Stock, camp and Quarter horses, although the latter are now somewhat finer than the Waler, which was bred rather more for stamina than speed.

The Arab Horse

The Arab horse is one breed that has retained all its distinctive attributes and grace, and it remains popular for both riding and breeding – particularly in respect of the Australian Thoroughbred racehorse. An Arab stallion that had influence in his time was Hector, imported from Calcutta to Sydney in February 1903. His progeny were racing and winning at Sydney Racecourse in 1910. Since then there have been regular imports of first-class Arab blood lines from Europe and the Middle East. Excellent studs are established in Australia, and the breed remains a firm favourite on the show scene.

Among other breeds, Appaloosa, Andalusian, Palomino, and the American Saddle Horse all have their devotees, with societies to foster their interests. In Australia riding for pleasure is now as important as using horses as part of a job. More and more horses are being kept in a land that was once almost completely dependent on them.

Probably as characteristic of the present Australian horse scene as the Waler was in the past is the brumby or "wild" horse. Feral would be a more apt description, for all are descended from domestic animals gone wild. Brumbys are most common in the mountainous districts of Queensland, New South Wales and Victoria. There they roam the sparsely settled areas in small mobs dominated by a stallion. Because of inbreeding, these wild horses are frequently of poor conformation with little stamina. When their numbers build up, they become a serious pest. They are then "run" or trapped, both methods using long

The Waler or Australian Stock Horse is an all-purpose horse. It is used in rodeo competitions for Bulldogging, Campdrafting and Buckjumping; and domestically, as a draught horse and a saddle horse. But the Waler is probably most famous for its use as a mount for the police and the army.

wings of brush or ropes, leading to enclosed yards or stockades.

Ponies

There are no indigenous ponies in Australia. Many European breeds have been imported, together with breeds from India, Iran, Hungary and the island of Timor, off the north coast of Australia.

To which European breed belongs the honour of being first in Australia is difficult to determine. There is mention of Welsh "horses" being there in about 1828, Shetlands in 1864, Exmoors in the 1870s, a black Hackney in 1880 and a Hungarian in 1884. However, in the early 1800s Timor ponies were well established in Australia. They were noted for their hardiness and stamina, qualities which the early explorers demanded above all other.

Timor ponies are the descendants of mainly Portuguese and Dutch stock introduced to what is now Indonesia. They are not a recognised breed. It was the blending of many breeds, together with much Arab and Thoroughbred blood which has resulted in what is now accepted as the Australian pony. Like the Waler and Stock Horse, it is more a type than a breed, but there are recognised strains.

If there is a general comparison possible between the Australian Pony and the English Show Pony, it would be that the former is inclined to be more stocky, "Welshie" in appearance, less fine on the leg than many of the miniature Thoroughbreds seen at British shows.

The Australian Pony Society originally maintained a Stud Book (first issued in 1937) in three sections: Shetland, Hackney, and Australian, the last accepting all those not placed in the other two. In the last 20 years more pure breds have been imported and there are now separate societies for the better known breeds: Welsh, Shetland, New Forest and Highland, although some of these still operate in conjunction with the Australian Pony Society.

With a growing interest in keeping a pony for showing, together with the increasing number of important shows that included riding pony classes, a finer type emerged. Some of the ponies now appearing in riding classes at the Royal Sydney and Melbourne shows would be hard to beat anywhere.

Draught horses

Pure bred heavy horses were first imported to Australia in about 1826. They were originally so few in number that they made an insignificant impact on the farming scene.

Many settlers brought farm implements and equipment with them to Australia, but the transport of livestock was far too costly and difficult. In Tasmania, for instance, few horses were working on farms before 1850, but by 1867 in South Australia it was estimated that 350,000 acres (140,000 hectares) of cereals had been harvested by horse-drawn reapers.

Wool was hauled on huge wagons from inland properties to ports on the rivers and railheads. An eyewitness in 1870 wrote of seeing over 400 horses unharnessed at one time in the yards at a railhead, after having unloaded their wool bales at the stores.

The "teamsters", who drove these teams of up to 23 horses in threes with a pair in the shafts, became a legend in the country and outstanding individuals are remembered in poem and song.

The horses were seldom pure bred. Draught stallions were used on mares of suitable type to produce a strong, clean-legged, hard-footed muscular animal that would stand up to the long dusty days in the heat of the outback.

It was only on the small arable farms that the true draught breeds were to be seen. Clydesdales, Shires, Suffolks and Percherons were early imports, and by 1830 there were recognised studs of these heavy horses.

The Clydesdale has always been the predominent heavy farm horse in Australia, not only because of the large number of Scottish farmers who brought their preference for the breed from their homeland, but also for the breeds adaptability, endurance, response to handling and natural adaptability to the often harsh Australian farm conditions. So well have the blood lines been maintained that in 1975 a team of four Australian bred Clydesdales was considered by international Scottish judges to be the best of its kind in the world.

Suffolks, Shires and Percherons never achieved the same prominence or numbers as the Clydesdales. They were mainly limited to haulage work in towns.

It is unlikely that draught horses will ever again be the main source of power on Australian farms, but there has recently been a revival of interest, particularly in Clydesdales. Rising fuel prices, transport strikes making fuel supplies short, and a change of attitude to some types of machinery has brought this about. Today, the sight of heavy horses working on the land is not as unusual as it used to be.

Part Two:
Saddlery

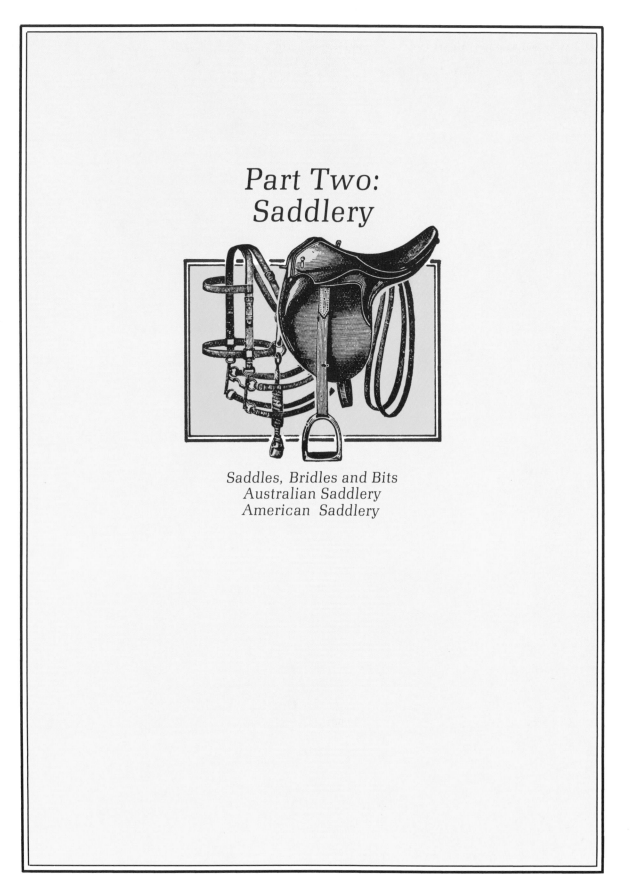

Saddles, Bridles and Bits
Australian Saddlery
American Saddlery

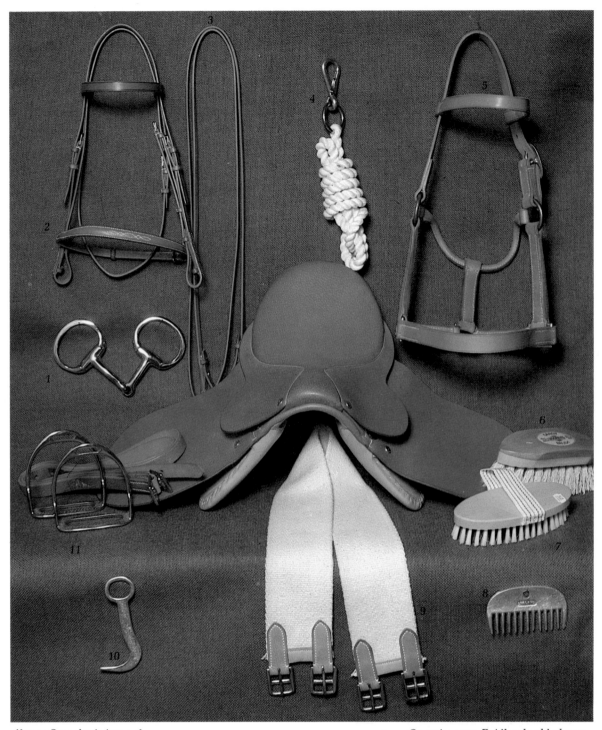

*Above: Some basic items of
equipment.
1, 2 & 3. The component parts of a
complete eggbutt snaffle bridle.
4. Rope and spring hook.
5. Headcollar. 6. Dandy brush.
7. Body brush. 8. Large mane comb.
9. Webbing girth. 10. Hoof pick.
11. Stirrup irons and leathers.
12. General purpose saddle.*

*Opposite, top: Bridles should always
be hung from their racks with the
reins being looped through the
nosebands.*

*Right: Saddle cleaning is an essential
stable chore involving a little warm
water, some saddle soap and a lot of
elbow grease.*

Saddles, Bridles and Bits

by Elwyn Hartley Edwards

Although every rider would admit the necessity of a saddle and bridle, not all appreciate the importance of a correctly designed and fitted saddle as a prime factor in their performance and that of their horse. Similarly, a very large number of horsemen are not as conversant with the action and subsequent effects of the various bridles and bitting combinations as might be expected.

The use of items of "tack" directly related to specific riding purposes is, none the less, essential, particularly in today's highly competitive equestrian climate.

Saddles

The principles of saddle design are common to all riding disciplines from dressage to race-riding, the differences in the shapes of saddles being caused by the shifts of emphasis made necessary by the special requirements of individual sports.

The prime consideration in saddle design is that the saddle should position the rider's weight as nearly as possible over the centre of gravity, or the point of balance, of the horse. It should fulfil this requirement, and contribute positively to the rider's security, without the rider having to make any pronounced physical effort. Finally, the saddle must afford maximum comfort to the horse, being constructed so that it cannot impede the animal's natural movement; and, of course, it has to be supremely comfortable for the rider, since if the rider is uncomfortable he is less likely to be secure.

The centre of gravity in the horse at rest has been determined as being a point in the centre of the body-mass formed by the junction of two imaginary lines: the first a vertical line running from some 6–8 inches (15–20cm) behind the wither to the ground, the second a horizontal line drawn to the rear from the point of the shoulder. This centre of gravity is not, however, static. It shifts in accordance with the movement and posture of the horse. When a horse stretches out at full gallop, extending the head and neck, which are the balancing agents for the body mass, the centre of gravity moves to the front. Conversely, in the highly collected movements of piaffe and passage, where head and neck are raised, the former assuming a near vertical carriage in relation to the ground, and where the croup is, indeed, lowered, the centre of gravity moves slightly to the rear in accordance with the shift of the body weight to the quarters.

If we accept that the weight of the rider is most easily carried when it is positioned, or balanced, over and in relation to the horse's centre of balance, it follows that a racing saddle will be constructed to encourage the carrying of the rider's weight well to the front; the dressage saddle, on the other hand, will be made to place the rider centrally on the horse's back.

The racing saddle is an extreme example, in which consideration of comfort, particularly in respect of the rider, are not relevant. None the less its shape, involving very forward cut flaps, does conform to the principle of placing the rider "in balance" with the horse's movement. (The rider is said to be "in balance" when his weight is balanced over the horse's centre of gravity. He is said to be "behind the movement"

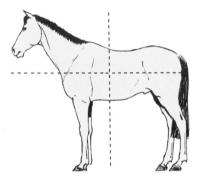

The centre of gravity, or balance, of the horse at rest is taken to be at the intersection of the two broken lines. In movement the point moves forward in accordance with the speed of the pace.

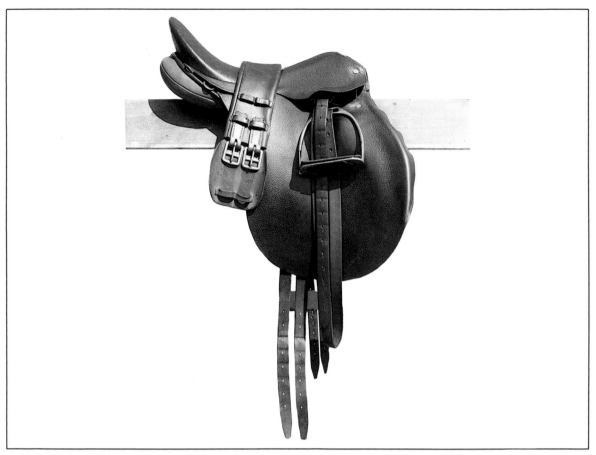

Above: A type of all- or general-purpose saddle fitted with extended girth straps and a short girth.

Below: The side-saddle for women riders came into general use in the 14th century, although ladies had ridden in this fashion from very early

times. The balance strap, running from the rear of the saddle on the offside of the horse assists in keeping the saddle firmly in place.

when the weight is carried to the rear of that point and "in advance of the movement" when the opposite occurs).

In general terms the bulk of modern saddles are constructed to conform to the needs of today's major disciplines of show jumping, eventing and dressage. The saddle most frequently used for eventing, at least for the speed and endurance phase and the jumping, is the "general-purpose" saddle and this is the type most used for hunting, endurance riding and for ordinary hacking.

"Show" saddles, in reality skeleton versions of the dressage saddle, designed to show off a horse's "front" to best advantage, are still made and used, and the same applies, to a very much lesser degree, to the old-fashioned "English hunting saddle", a few of which are still to be seen. There are, of course, saddles made for specialist use, like those used on the American Saddle Horse (the Saddlebred). These saddles are notable for the exaggerated "cut-back" head of the tree (they are, often referred to as "cow-mouth" saddles); the very straight-cut flap and the exceptionally flat seat. They are best regarded as the exception which proves the rule, since they do not conform to the usual principles of saddle design – for that matter the Saddle Horse seat conforms to no accepted principle of equitation, so it may well be a case of the one deserving the other!

The difference between the three major types of saddle is governed largely by the shape of the "tree", the foundation upon which the saddle is built and the decisive element in the shape of the finished article.

In all three cases the "waist" or "twist" of the tree is made deliberately narrow so as to give the rider a "narrow grip" and avoid spreading his thighs. In all cases, too, the tree is made with a characteristic central dip so that the rider must sit in the lowest part of the finished seat, while the panel, the leather-covered cushion between the tree and the back, is made with a swelled roll to support the rider's knee and lower thigh. The difference occurs in the "head" of the tree or the "pommel". The head, of course, incorporates the projections below the body of the tree which are called the "points" and to which are attached the stirrup bars on which hang the leathers and irons.

In the dressage saddle the head is vertical in relation to the remainder of the tree; in the "general-purpose" saddle the "points" are advanced, giving the impression that the head itself is sloped to the rear, although this is not, in fact, the case; in the jumping saddle the "points" are still further advanced.

The effect of these departures from the vertical are, obviously, to position the stirrup bars farther forward. In turn, this will cause the rider's weight to be held farther to the front and over the bars. Additionally, since the line of the flap is governed, or should be governed, by the line of the point, the flaps in a jumping saddle, where the rider uses a shorter leather and needs to get well forward, will be cut farther to the front to accomodate the lower thigh and knee. The flaps in a general-purpose saddle will be somewhat less inclined to the front thus allowing the use of the somewhat longer leather advisable for cross-country riding, while those in the dressage saddle will be straight, or just swelled forward, to conform with the dressage position, which is not concerned with an advancing body weight to the same extent. There are, of course, exceptions. Many German saddles, for instance, are made with "cut-back" heads which are thought to accomodate high withers more satisfactorily, but which are inclined to place the rider's seat behind the movement.

Today, most saddle trees are made of strips of plywood bonded under heat and produced in a mould, a process which ensures a total consistency in shape and size. Fibre-glass is used increasingly in the manufacture of trees and so far appears to be satisfactory for the purpose. For the most part jumping and general saddles will be made on "spring" trees and dressage saddles on a "rigid" tree.

A spring tree, as the name implies, has a particular resilience, which is made possible by two lengths of tempered steel laid, basically, from

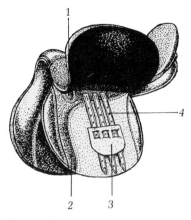

Above: The raised saddle flap shows the position of the girth straps.
1. *Pocket for point of tree*
2. *Panel*
3. *Buckle guard*
4. *Girth straps*

Right: The all-purpose saddle.
A. *The tree; the framework of the saddle. Traditionally made from beech wood, nowadays it is generally made from layers of bonded wood and sometimes from fibre glass.*

B. *The panel is important; it is stuffed with wool and acts as a cushion between the tree and the horse's back. The channel dividing the panel prevents the rider's weight from pressing directly on the horse's spine.*
1. *Saddle flap*
2. *Half panel*
3. *Girth straps*
4. *Panel*
5. *Channel*
6. *Lining*
7. *Cantle*

C. *The parts of the saddle.*
1. *Pommel*
2. *Skirt*
3. *Twist or waist*
4. *Seat*
5. *Panel*
6. *Cantle*
7. *Stirrup leather*
8. *Surcingle loop*
9. *Girth*
10. *Saddle flap*

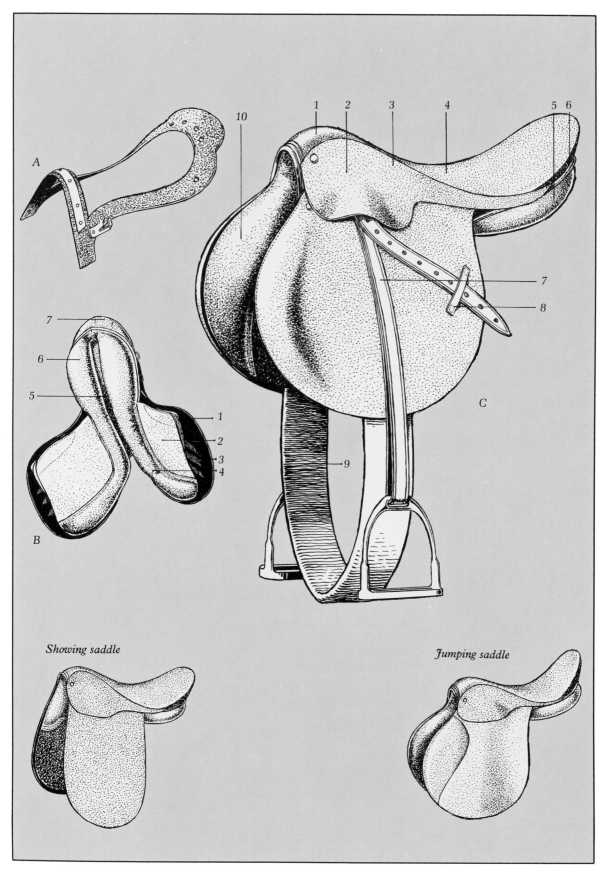

A

B

C

10

1 2 3 4 5 6

7

8

7

6

5

1

2

3

4

9

Showing saddle

Jumping saddle

the head to the cantle. The advantages of such an arrangement are first, the resilience given to the seat, which adds to the comfort of the rider and "gives", as it were, to the movement of the horse's back. Secondly, the "spring" allows the drive exerted by the rider's seat to be transmitted more directly to the horse than would be the case if the tree was of the rigid variety, i.e. without springs.

A spring tree is not often considered to be necessary in a dressage saddle, although very few logical arguments are put forward in support of the practice.

Saddle accessories

A saddle is said to be "mounted' when equipped with leathers, irons and girth.

Stirrup leathers are cut from oak-bark cowhide butts (oak-bark describing the dressing process and a butt referring to the portions of hide on either side of the backbone excluding the shoulders and belly leather); or they are made from rawhide or from what has come to be known as "red buffalo hide" which is claimed to be unbreakable. All leathers stretch in wear, the last two rather more than the first. It is, therefore, advisable for leathers to be switched from side to side in the initial period of use so as to ensure that both stretch equally – it is a sad fact that *all* horsemen and women sit more strongly to one side than to the other, the degree of one-sidedness decreasing in direct ratio to the rider's level of equestrian education.

A point of interest about stirrup leathers is that, in the case of cowhide and rawhide, the "grain" side of the leather (i.e. the outside, which is the tougher) faces inwards so as to receive the friction caused by the eye of the iron. The "flesh" (or inside) of these leathers is more fibrous and would not stand up so well to the wear. The "buffalo" hide is so tough as to make this precaution unnecessary.

Stirrup irons are best made of good quality stainless steel. Nickel irons, usually dignified by the misleading prefix "solid", are liable to bend, break and become discoloured. Irons should be heavy and a size or two larger than one's boot to ensure that they will release the foot in the event of a fall. In the past "safety" irons were very much in favour, but today very few are seen beyond the Peacock iron, which has a rubber ring forming the outside of the iron between eye and tread, and the more practical Simplex, or Australian, iron which has the outside curved forward to facilitate the freeing of the foot in the event of a fall (see page 71).

A popular iron in days gone by was the Kournakoff, invented by a Russian cavalry officer of that name. This iron had the eye offset and the tread sloped so that the foot was held in a heels down position with the outside of the sole higher than the inside – a position giving very considerable security when jumping, for instance.

Girths are made from a variety of materials and in a number of patterns. At one end of the scale there are the popular and very practical nylon cord girths; the soft lampwicks, so useful for thin-skinned horses, and the more old-fashioned web girths: at the other, the more expensive leather girths like the soft three-fold baghide kind; the anti-gall Balding, which is cut away at the elbow, and the similarly shaped Atherstone.

Whatever girth is chosen the point to remember is that it should be of a length which, while being sufficient to fasten without effort, does not cause the buckles to lie directly under the rider's knee. This problem is removed, of course, in the case of many of the dressage saddles which are made with extended girth straps to which is attached a special short girth that obviates any bulk under the leg.

Numnahs may also be termed as saddle accessories. There are horses who appreciate the comfort afforded by such articles, but for the most part they are used either for no very good reason or because their presence mitigates the effect of an ill-fitting saddle. All too often they are a source of soreness because they generate enough heat to scald the back.

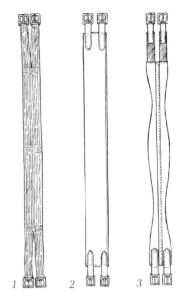

Three types of girth.
1. The very popular nylon cord girth.
2. A 3-fold leather girth made from soft baghide.
3. An all-leather Atherstone girth with elastic insets so as not to restrict breathing.

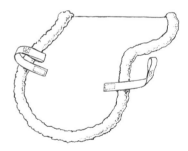

A sheepskin numnah which is placed under the saddle to give greater comfort to the horse's back.

Bridles

A complete bridle comprises head and cheekpieces, reins, a noseband and a bit or bits.

In general there are five principal groups of bridles, each acting upon one or more of seven parts of the horse's head to achieve its effects.

Those parts of the head upon which the bridle acts are (1) the corners of the lips, (2) the bars of the mouth, (3) the tongue, (4) the curb groove, (5) the nose, (6) the poll and, if only very infrequently, (7) the roof of the mouth.

The principal bridle groups are (1) the Snaffle, (2) the Weymouth or double bridle, (3) the Pelham, (4) the Gag and, (5) the bitless bridle commonly called a Hackamore (derivation – *jaquima*, a noseband). Of these the snaffle constitutes the simplest form of control, whilst the Weymouth is the most sophisticated in its action and effect.

The Snaffle group of bridles is a large one, but for most practical purposes can be divided conveniently into bits employing a jointed mouthpiece and those with a half-moon, or mullen, mouth. Further sub-divisions are between fixed and loose rings, the former being exemplified by the eggbutt.

Of the two mouthpieces the mullen can be considered the mildest, particularly when made in rubber. The jointed mouthpiece has a stronger effect and can operate in a squeezing action either across the bars of the lower jaw when the head and neck are carried reasonably high with the nose just slightly in advance of the vertical, or upwards and more against the corners of the lips when the head is held low and stretched out, as might be the case with a horse in the early stages of training.

The advantage of a loose ring is thought to lie in allowing the bit to be "mouthed" by the horse, the mouth being kept moist and the flexion of the lower jaw being encouraged in consequence.

The eggbutt cheek fixes the bit in the mouth and, according to its supporters, prevents the horse from making undue movements with his head.

The Weymouth bridle employs two bits, a snaffle (usually referred to as the "bradoon") and a curb bit. In this bridle the action of the bradoon, fitted above the curb, tends to act upwards to raise the head. The curb, on the other hand, lowers the head and causes a retraction of

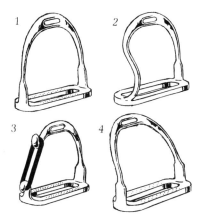

Above: Saddle irons.
1. A plain hunting iron.
2. Australian Simplex safety iron.
3. Peacock iron, a safety iron. (Note the attached rubber band forming the outside of the stirrup.)
4. A bent top iron.

Below: Bridles.
A. The snaffle bridle is the simplest.
B. The Double bridle, or Weymouth, with bit and bradoon is the most complex.
C. The parts of the Double bridle.
1. Browband 2. Headpiece 3. Noseband 4. Cheekpieces 5. Bradoon bit 6. Weymouth (curb) bit 7. Lip strap 8. Bradoon cheek and sliphead 9. Snaffle reins 10. Curb reins 11. Curb chain

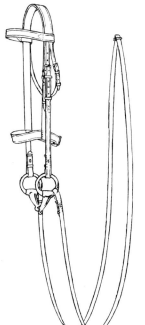

A

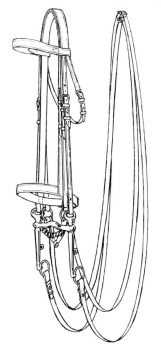

B

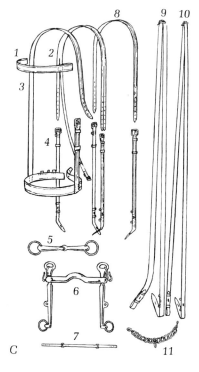

C

the nose by exerting pressure directly on the bars (an action made possible by the tongue port in the centre of the mouthpiece which accommodates a portion of the tongue and prevents it from lying over the bars). Additionally, the action of the curb bit is intensified by pressure on the curb groove, brought about by the tightening of the curb chain when the bit assumes an angle of 45 degrees or more in the mouth, and by exerting a downward pressure on the poll through the eye of the bit. This latter is achieved when the eye of the bit moves forward in response to rein pressure and exerts a downward influence, first on the cheekpiece and subsequently upon the bridle head and, therefore, the poll.

In general the leverage of the bit is increased according to the length of the cheek below the mouthpiece, while the possibility of poll pressure increases according to the length of the cheek above the mouthpiece.

When the bradoon rein is held outside the little finger (in the English manner), the influence of the bradoon predominates. Conversely, if the curb rein were to be held on the outside the bit action would predominate.

Pelham bridles, like the Weymouth, employ two reins but they operate in this instance on only one mouthpiece. Usually, but not necessarily, the mouthpiece is of the mullen variety without a tongue port and much of the pressure is taken on the tongue rather than the bars, an action which is appreciated by some horses. In theory, the bradoon action is brought into play through the bradoon rein and curb action by operating the curb rein. In practice, the action is at best indefinite, but it does appear to suit some horses and is a useful bit for the cobby sort of horse who has little length to his mouth. Horses with these short jaw formations cannot physically accommodate the bit and bradoon of a double bridle and are better suited by a Pelham. On the other hand, a Pelham is not suitable for horses with a long jaw formation (such as will often be found in Thoroughbreds), for the reason that when the bit is adjusted correctly in the mouth i.e. wrinkling the lips, the curb chain is bound to ride out of the curb groove and to bear upon the virtually unprotected jawbones.

A gag bridle, in which a rounded cheekpiece passes through holes in the centre of the bit rings and is thence joined to a rein, accentuates the upward action of the snaffle and is considered to be a means of raising the head. It could, of course, be argued that the upward pressure exerted on the corners of the lips is largely negated by the opposite downward pressure which must be exerted on the poll. The gag, none the less, is used when a fairly strong bitting arrangement is required and often, quite illogically, is combined with a standing martingale.

It is often thought that the so-called Hackamore is a humane and mild bridle. Nothing, in fact, could be further from the truth. The Hackamore, which exerts pressure on the nose, can be very severe in its effects in anything but the best of hands. The strong action can impede the breathing momentarily, and unless continual alterations are made to the adjustment of the bridle on the nose the area will become sore and then calloused.

The last of the seven parts of the head affected by the action of the bridle is the roof of the mouth. Pressure can only be brought to bear on this area when a curb bit is fitted with an exceptionally high port, a practice that cannot be regarded as either legitimate or humane.

Bitting auxiliaries

Auxiliaries which strengthen the action of bits include such items as nosebands, martingales and the various forms of running reins. The most common of these is the ubiquitous drop noseband employed with a snaffle bit. The nosepiece is fitted so as to lie some 3 inches (7.5cm) above the nostrils, while the back strap passes *under* the bit and is fastened sufficiently tight to effect an almost complete closure of the mouth. This prevents the horse evading the bit by either sliding it through the mouth or opening the mouth in resistance. More

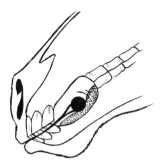

The mouthpiece of the bit bears upon the bars of the mouth, the area of gum between the molar and incisor teeth.

Below: 1. A straight-bar Pelham bit. 2. The "Fulmer" cheek snaffle. 3. The single-rein Kimblewick bit, sometimes called "Spanish jumping bit".

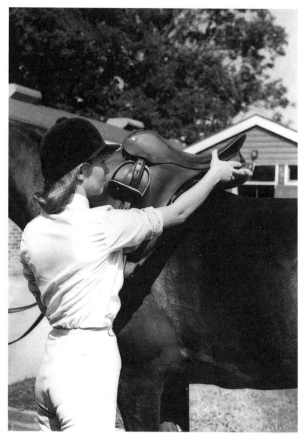

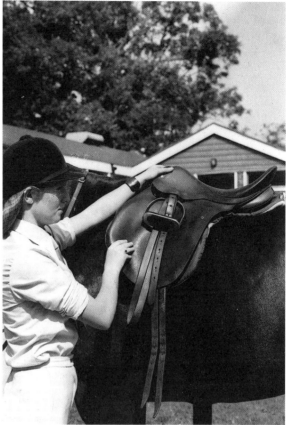

The proper way to put on a saddle is first to place it well forward of the wither and then to slide it back into position, after which the girth straps can be adjusted fairly loosely, only being tightened when the rider is in the saddle.

The importance of a well-fitting saddle, which spreads the weight evenly over its bearing surface and in no way restricts the backbone, cannot be over-emphasised. Badly fitting saddles, which pinch, press, or rub, restrict the action of the horse and will detract from his performance potential.

Note that this saddle is fitted with extended girth straps and a short girth in place of the more common fastening arrangement.

importantly, pressure on the rein transmits a pressure to the nose and may, indeed, on occasions cause a momentary restriction to the breathing. The effect is to cause the horse to drop his nose, in which position his mouth will be below the hand and the bit in consequence will be rendered more effective.

The purpose of either the standing or running martingale is to prevent the horse raising his head above an acceptable level and thus evading the action of the bit. In the former instance pressure is exerted on the nose via the cavesson noseband to which the martingale is attached, and in the second the action is against the mouth itself, since the branches of the running martingale are attached to the rein by the rings through which the latter is passed.

Fitting saddles and bridles

In both instances the object should be to ensure the comfort of the horse. The rules of saddle fitting are these:

1. In the first place the tree itself must fit the horse's back. Unless the tree fits the finished saddle cannot do so. Too narrow a tree will pinch below the withers, too broad a tree will bear upon the top of the withers.

2. The finished saddle should stand clear of the backbone along its length and across its width. This involves a clearance of some three fingers width at the pommel when the rider is mounted and complete clearance from that point to the cantle. Clearance across the width of the backbone is concerned with the "channel", which divides the panel on either side of the backbone, being made sufficiently wide. Channels which become closed cause pressure on the backbone and restrict the horse's movement in consequence.

3. The panel (the cushion between the tree and the horse's back) must be regulated, or stuffed, so that the weight of the rider is spread evenly over the whole of the panel's bearing surface. A saddle that is stuffed unevenly causes the rider's weight to be concentrated in one area of the horse's back thus causing a pressure point and once more restricting the horse's action.

4. The bearing surface of the panel, for obvious reasons, must be free from any irregularity which could cause a point of pressure. It must, also, and for equally obvious reasons, be clean.

While fulfilling all these requirements the saddle has to fit as closely as possible. A saddle standing too high off the back will roll and cause soreness by the ensuing friction.

A well-fitting bridle should observe the following:

1. The bit, in the case of a snaffle or Pelham, should be adjusted so that the corners of the lips are slightly wrinkled, otherwise it will lie too low and knock against the molar teeth. It should project about ½ inch (1.5cm) either side of the mouth. A curb bit, fitted below the bradoon, should lie in the centre of the bars, not so high as to touch the molars nor so low as to be in contact with the incisor teeth.

2. The cheekpieces should be adjusted to exactly an equal length.

3. Where a curb bit or Pelham is used a lipstrap should be employed to keep the curb chain in place and to prevent the bit becoming reversed in the mouth, an unlikely happening but not an impossible one.

4. The browband should be large enough to allow the headpiece to rest on the poll without it being pulled forward on to the back of the ears. The discomfort that is caused by a bridle rubbing on the ears can be the cause of head-tossing and general irritability.

5. When fastened, a cavesson noseband should permit the entry of at least two fingers between it and the jawbones.

6. The throatlatch should permit the entry of three fingers between it and the throat. A tight throatlatch discourages the horse from flexing at the poll.

1. First stage in putting on the bridle. The horse is secured by the headcollar slipped round his neck and the rein has been put over his head.

2. The fingers of the left hand open the mouth and guide in the bit without knocking the teeth.

3. The headpiece is passed gently over the ears, and the throatlatch is fastened so that it will permit the insertion of three fingers between it and the throat.

Points to note in bridle fitting are that the browband is not too tight and pulling the headpiece onto the ears, that the throatlatch is fastened loosely enough and that the bit is level in the mouth.

Tack cleaning

Tack should be cleaned not only for the sake of appearance but also to preserve the leather.

Leather has an outside, known as the "grain", and an inside, called the "flesh". The thickness of a piece of leather is referred to as the "substance". The grain side of the leather is dressed to provide a waterproofed surface and in the process the pores of the leather are virtually sealed. On the flesh side the pores are still capable of absorption and like the pores of our own skin will open in warm conditions and be closed when drops in temperature occur. In the dressing of leather grease is applied through the pores on the flesh side and it follows that the greater the substance of the leather the greater will be its grease content, which can be regarded as its life blood. Once the grease content is lost, the leather becomes brittle and will crack and break. The cleaning of leather, therefore, involves not only the removal of surface dirt but the regular replacement of the grease content lost in normal wear. Grease will be lost through the body heat of the horse, through washing the leather with too much water, particularly hot water, and by the injudicious drying of leather over heat i.e. on a radiator or over a fire. In the last two instances the leather can become so dry as to be of no further use.

To clean a bridle it must first be dismantled and then each piece cleaned with a damp, not wet, sponge and saddle soap. Particular attention must be paid to removing sweat deposits on the flesh side which will block the pores. At least once a week one or other of the proprietary greases or oils should be applied to the flesh side to replace any loss of grease which may have occurred.

Saddles should be cleaned thoroughly with saddle soap in the same manner and grease applied to the flesh side of the flaps where it can penetrate through the pores. Grease applied to the outside of the saddle will be largely expended on the rider's breeches.

Where tack has to be washed to remove mud or in instances where it has become wet from rain, it should be dried off with a cloth and left to dry in a warm, but not hot, atmosphere before being soaped and greased.

A snaffle bridle employing an ordinary cavesson noseband instead of the ubiquitous drop noseband, which closes the mouth and can give greater control to the rider.

2. The left hand supports the bit and ensures it does not bang the teeth as it is removed from the mouth, while the right hand eases the headpiece over the ears.

1. Before removing the bridle the throatlatch and noseband must be unfastened.

3. The final stage in removing the bridle.

Australian Saddlery

by E. A. Weiss

The horses that came to Australia in the mid-19th century brought with them their furniture – "bits, bridles, saddles, cart harness and haulage traces". But inevitably the demands of a new country and conditions far removed from those of their country of origin, resulted in modifications suitable for Australian conditions. Where there are no fences stock must be herded, and to meet the specialised demands of the riders who carried out these tasks, many changes were made in the original equipment. Stock Horses had to be fast, sure footed, change direction abruptly, and their tack had to suit these demands. Bits, bridles and reins had to be repaired on outback stations, or in the paddock with a few unspecialised tools. Reliability and simplicity became the keynote of design, and for the riders, the jackeroos, large comfortable saddles.

The basic design of the bridle changed but little. The addition of a short strap between cheek strap and throat lash, which was often much wider and thicker than on a normal bridle, or a double cheek strap were most common. Double bridles are normally never used when working stock, and a well trained cutting horse can be worked in a halter only.

Nosebands of various types were common, and given regional names, but all were in fact well-known types. The Australian checker was one of these, it stopped the horse getting its tongue over the bit and applied pressure on the nose to restrain a very hard puller. Not an uncommon type on outback stations where riders were often heavy rather than light handed, and horses hard-mouthed goers.

Bits were normally some kind of snaffle, either jointed or bar, with large rings or long cheek pieces. These cheek pieces were necessary to stop the bit being pulled through the mouth when turning sharply. One of the most common is the Long Bar Stockman's snaffle, also known as the Tom Thumb or New Zealand full-spoon snaffle. The jointed bit had long cheek bars fixed so that they were outside the horse's mouth but inside the bit rings.

Rings were usually round, large and loose; but round fixed, and oval loose and fixed were available to suit district preferences. The cheek pieces varied in length, and in the half-spoon snaffles, were below the bit only. Extra large rings also served the same purpose as cheek pieces, and one such came to be known as the Australian Loose Ringed or Fulmer Snaffle. A variation of the long cheek piece snaffle, the heavy side-bar, was adopted by the late Frans Mairinger in the teaching of dressage, and is now known as the F. M. Dressage bit.

Reins were often made on the stations from locally tanned hides, and were knotted, not buckled to the bit rings with a Kimberly knot. This knot was made by forming a series of loops, usually three, at the end of the reins; by passing them through the snaffle ring, and each other, formed a secure fastening. Reins were long, often not fastened together, so that if a horse got away from its rider, it would tread on the reins and be easier to catch.

Stockman's saddle

The Stockman's Saddle had a high cantle and deep seat, with knee and thigh pads for comfort and stability when working stock for long hours over rough country. A few had high pommels, but the American style with its hitching post for a lasso is absent. (Lassos were not an integral part of an Australian jackeroos gear as they were of the cowboys). Saddles were stuffed to make them sit high, and once ridden-in, seldom gave a horse a sore back. When relined on a station, curled cows tails were used. Breastplates were common but cruppers very rarely used. It is believed in Australia that Count Toptani adapted the general design of the Australian Stock Saddle with its high cantle to produce his deep seated jumping saddle.

To ensure that leathers were quickly released from the saddle, if a rider was unhorsed, the Simplex safety iron was developed. The lower of the two bars under the saddle flap was extended beyond the upper, to the back of the saddle, and bent upward in a curve. This design stopped the leather slipping out accidentally, as could happen if the bars were straight. It also removed the danger of the common spring-loaded clip closing the gap between the bars, from becoming rusted in place during the "big wet". For additional comfort when working stock, the four-bar Stock Saddle stirrup iron was developed. This gave a much broader surface for the boot to rest upon, having twice the area of a normal iron.

The last essential item for any jackeroo was a stockwhip. The finest were plaited from 16 strands of well-tanned kangaroo hide, and were virtually indestructible. The best types had heavy removable handles, sometimes bound with a metal band carrying the owner's name or brand. When fitted with a cord cracker, the reports echoed through the bush.

Today most saddlery and other horse tack has become standardised, and there is little variation from that seen in other countries, especially in the show ring.

An Australian cattleman treating his horses to a soak near Keiwa, Victoria. Notice the wide four-bar Stock Saddle stirrup iron with its broad surface for the boot to rest on. A heavy stock-whip rests against the horse's left shoulder.

American Saddlery

by Robin Serfass

Most saddlery and equipment used on show-jumping horses in the United States is quite similar to that found in Great Britain and on the Continent. Of course, there are regional preferences in the brands of saddles, etc., but basically show-jumping riders use "flat" saddles and snaffle bit bridles with a standing martingale.

Saddles seem to be a matter of personal preference, but most riders of jumping horses use a type of saddle modelled after the Hermes saddle designed by the veteran USET (United States Equestrian Team) rider William Steinkraus. This saddle is called a "flat" saddle because it has absolutely no knee roll and a very low seat, enabling the rider to keep a close feel of the horse beneath him. There are numerous variations on the basic flat saddle, including models by Crosby, Barnsby, Crump, Surrey and Blue Ribbon. Only occasionally will one see a show-jumping rider in the United States using a Pariani, Stuebben or other forward seat saddle with knee rolls and a fairly deep seat. The American Western saddle is never used for jumping, except perhaps over very small obstacles in a trail horse class at a show or over a small log on a trail ride cross country. The Western saddle is used for pleasure riding as well as for stock and working cow horse routines.

Bits and bitting are popular topics of conversation among American horsemen. Most riders prefer to use a snaffle bit of some type combined with a standing martingale on both hunters and jumpers. It must be remembered that hunters in the United States compete primarily over fences, being judged on style of jumping and pace between the jumps; therefore, most hunters are shown in bits and

A typical American Show Hunter wearing a "flat" saddle and a full-cheek snaffle. He is wearing a breast-plate with no martingale. Notice the plaited mane, tail and forelock.

bridles similar to that worn by show jumpers. A hunter cannot wear a hackamore (a bridle with no bit that controls the horse through pressure on his nose and chin), or any other "artificial" bit in which a jumper can be shown, so one usually sees the hunter in a snaffle or a pelham bridle. Very seldom does one see a full bridle used in the United States at horse shows – most riders prefer to use a pelham, if they desire both curb and snaffle action in the horse's bridle.

It would be fair to say, however, that snaffle bits predominate in the United States. The least severe snaffle is the rubber dee-ring snaffle, often used on green horses just being taught to yield to the bit, while the next least severe is the "fat" German or hollow-mouth snaffle that is usually an egg-butt bit. Following this snaffle bit in terms of severity, one finds an assortment of smaller snaffle bits, from a copper-wrapped dee snaffle to a full-cheek thin snaffle. The most severe category of snaffle bits is the wire snaffle – a double twisted wire is less strong than a single wire with regard to control. Most professional trainers in the United States prefer to have their horses show in a moderate snaffle, such as a full-cheek or copper-wrapped snaffle, using a wire snaffle on a horse that might want to get strong on the bit.

Despite the type of bit utilised, most who take part in hunting and jumping employ the standing martingale. Like the question of bits and bitting, the controversy between the benefits and detriments incurred by the standing martingale remains a favourite topic. George Morris, the most prominent and successful instructor of hunter-jumper riders in the United States today, had the following comments on the merits of the standing martingale versus the running martingale:

"A running martingale can interfere with a horse really as much or more than a standing; it can hit a horse in the bars of his mouth. There are pictures and movies of horses, such as that horse of Benny O'Meara's Untouchable, jumping a 7ft 4in. (2.23m) wall in Rotterdam; his standing martingale was very short and he never hit it. So the problem with the standing martingale is a myth. It's a good aid and it doesn't restrict a horse."

The standing martingale is held in high favour by United States' horsemen because it simply limits the degree to which a horse can escape the action of the bit by raising up his head. The standing martingale does not actually have to tie down the horse's head; rather, it restricts his ability to throw his head up and thus escape the effects of the bit and the rider's hands.

Above left: A Hunter wearing a "Chambon" or "Chambois". The bit the "Chambon" is attached to is a dee-ring rubber snaffle, a very moderate bit.

Above right: The "Elevator" bit. The bit itself is a smooth broken snaffle.

Of course, in jumping competitions recognised by the FEI, horses are not allowed to wear a standing martingale, so riders either use a running martingale or try to develop a good head carriage without any martingale. Naturally, the ultimate goal of any horseman surely is to train a horse to accept the bit and set his head properly without a martingale, regardless of whether the horse is a show jumper or a hunter.

This magnificent Western saddle will grace the back of a show horse. One can only admire the embroidered hide seat and tooled leather saddle flaps.

Artificial aids

Most professional trainers in the United States at some point utilise artificial devices in order to establish a good head carriage on a horse. Draw reins and side reins are two auxiliary reins most commonly used to help the rider fix the horse's head into a flexed position. Leading professional trainer Rodney Jenkins states: "I usually start a horse with a plain snaffle and then go on up the range of severity required … I also use draw reins to help place a horse's head, and to help some horses that don't use their necks well."

Draw reins, like side reins, act as a "second" rein and are usually held on the inside, much like a curb rein on a double bridle. Draw reins go through the snaffle bit and hook to the front of the breastplate, or they go between the front legs and are attached to the girth. Side reins go through the snaffle and are attached to the girth near the billets of the saddle. Both reins cause the horse to pull his nose in and bend his head down, arching the poll of the head and neck. Horses can be shown in jumper events with draw or side reins, but hunters cannot wear any artificial device except a martingale.

An American Palomino seen here on show. Notice the heavy silver saddle.

Another bitting aid that is used to help set a horse's head is the chambon or chambois, which is most commonly seen on the West Coast. The chambon attaches to the girth underneath, runs up between the horse's legs, through rings on either side of the crown piece of the bridle, and back down the face, clipping to the rings of the bit. If the horse puts its head up or nose out, the chambon applies pressure to both the mouth and the head. The only way the horse can escape this pressure is to put its head down and tuck its nose in. It is similar to the effect caused by draw reins, except that the rider exerts no direct pressure – the horse corrects himself. In order to relieve the pressure caused by his improper head position, the horse must flex his head and neck.

Horsemen have developed numerous other bitting devices to achieve a proper head set, including the "gag" bit and the "elevator" snaffle. The latter was invented by the well-known and successful trainer from California, Jimmy A. Williams. The "elevator" bit is a smooth, broken snaffle bit that has a long shank; the bit thus has a snaffle rein and a curb rein, so the rider is able to elevate the horse's head with the snaffle rein and tuck in the horse's nose with the curb rein – all using a smooth snaffle!

As long as horsemen continue to train horses and try to best their peers in competition, new and imaginative devices will be developed. Conventional tack definitely has its time and place in training the hunter or jumper, and the subject of what a horse "goes in" will doubtless be a source of controversy forever. However, as George Morris succinctly said, "... in the long run, you'll probably discover that the rider's ability and control over his aids greatly outweighs a 'bag of bits!'"

A typical American Quarter Horse. Here it is being used as a Stock horse in a show. Notice that the horse is turning the cow with his shoulder, a natural instinct.

Part Three:
Breaking-in and Schooling

The Young Horse
The Horse's Health
Learning to Ride
International Riding Styles
Dressage in Schooling
Learning to Jump
Show Jumping in Australia

Right: A class of novice riders working with an instructress.

Right below: A horse being worked on the lunge line (together with side-reins).

Below: A foal having a lesson in being led.

A pleasant picture of a foal, its mother and a human being enjoying each other's company.

A young horse working on the lunge-line.

The Young Horse

by Sylvia Stanier

A foal with a head-slip on and with a stable rubber round his neck for safer handling.

To understand a horse it is important to know about its natural instincts. Very often it behaves out of obedience to these instincts. The horse is a gregarious or herd animal; he reacts in varying degrees to fear and fear of pain; but he is the most willing of creatures once he understands what is wanted of him. As he has a small brain and little reasoning power, it is essential that the instructions that are given to him are simple and clear. The horse has a phenomenal memory; once something is established in his mind it is almost impossible for him to unlearn or forget. So it is most important that he is taught the right things, but taught them quietly and slowly yet definitely and without ever giving him a bad fright. A horse may have great difficulty in forgetting a fright.

From the very first the foal should learn to accept man as his friend. Very much of a horse's future behaviour can be formed during its first year. From its earliest days it should be stroked and talked to gently. Then, gradually, it should get used to being led, groomed, having his feet picked up and even having a soft piece of stocking held round his middle. All this makes training at a later stage much simpler for the handler, to say nothing of the horse which, if not used to being handled, is likely to be nervous and so take much longer to train.

When he is only a day or two old, a foal should have a slip (a small foal headcollar) put on and be taught to be lead around the stable. Later he can be lead out alongside his dam. It may be advisable to put the lead rope through the underside of the noseband rather than clipping it on. Foals are lively and, if they get away, it is better that the rope comes free rather than trailing along which can frighten a foal into hurting himself. The natural instinct of a horse when frightened is to run away; a very frightened foal or yearling can crash into something and cause both himself and others serious injury.

Sixteen-week programme

The actual backing and breaking-in of a horse usually takes 16 weeks. That is the old cavalry way. This period is divided into fortnightly sections from the time you lead the horse in hand to the time you consider him fit to be both useful and safe to ride outside. This may sound a long time but there are no short cuts.

Breaking-in to the saddle should take place when the horse is three and a half years old. Some people put the tack on at two years and then let the horse out to grass again and re-saddle him at three and a half years. As this preliminary work will probably not be really established in the horse's mind it would be inadvisable to ride a horse that has only had the tack on a few times as a youngster. A proper programme and routine is necessary.

After leading in hand, the next stage is lungeing. Start on the left rein, and use a cavesson headcollar, the type with a metal inlay on the noseband. (The noseband should be padded.) Carry a lungeing whip – but take care that your horse is not frightened by it. Also see that the lungeing rein is not upsetting the horse by coming up near his eye. If your horse seems to be disliking the lunge-line on the point of the cavasson, then try working him off an ordinary headcollar from beneath the jaw. But remember that the ordinary headcollar does not provide as much control as a cavesson.

Lungeing should take place in an enclosed space; there is nothing worse than a horse getting loose in a big field with a line dragging behind him. Out of doors there is also too much to distract the horse's attention from the handler. It is sound advice to stable the horse most

A horse being schooled on the lunge-line; this is a fully broken-in horse, wearing all the accoutrements necessary for training.

of the time when it is being broken-in. To prevent it from becoming over fresh and annoyed it should be allowed an hour or two in the paddock. But a stabled horse for breaking-in is far easier to civilise and to get to know. He should have a diet that is not too high in protein; but he needs plenty of bulk – that is hay.

Start with 50 to 60 minutes of quiet lungeing, walking followed by a little trotting – all geared to making the horse calm and confident. After 20 to 30 minutes take a break and lead the horse in hand to see the sights around him. Then start lungeing again. If you lunge young horses non-stop for the full 50 to 60 minutes on a small circle, you are likely to have a very lame horse, probably with swollen joints. On this subject of feet, it is probably better not to shoe very young horses, but keep their feet well trimmed. This helps to prevent the horse developing splints as well as lessening any injury resulting from the horse hitting himself. But a shod horse should usually wear boots when lungeing. Whether an unshod horse should wear them is a matter of opinion.

The value of lungeing is not only to control the horse but also to develop muscles and paces. Start on a circle of about 65ft (20 metres) in diameter. Once the horse will go quietly to the left, teach him to go to the right. Next, let an assistant lead the horse while you position yourself some three metres behind the horse's inside hip. Encourage the horse with your voice, and remember that your own body position is most important. If you are too near his head or shoulders he will probably stop – for this is the aid to slow the horse down. So do not use it by mistake!

In training a horse always take things slowly and establish one thing before going on to the next. Establish your walk to trot and back again nicely as soon as you can. Remember every horse is a little different in temperament so get to know how much urging on or not your horse may need. Find out his level of acceptance and understanding. The development of a *rapport* at this stage is of the utmost importance. And always remember to stick to the important principle of never surprising a horse.

Some sections of the work the young horse does, overlap. Bitting, putting on a roller or saddle or backing all overlap or coincide with lungeing and long-reining. It is probably advisable to put a bit in a horse's mouth during the lungeing period. A thick but comfortable jointed snaffle is a fair one to start with, although some people advocate the straight bar "keys" bit. Keep the bit well up in the horse's mouth so he does not develop the tiresome and hard-to-cure habit of getting his tongue over the bit. If a horse's tongue is over the bit there is no feeling on the bars of his mouth and all control is lost.

When the roller is put on for the first time, it should not be done up too tightly. There should be a breast girth round the shoulders and chest to prevent the roller slipping back – and frightening the horse.

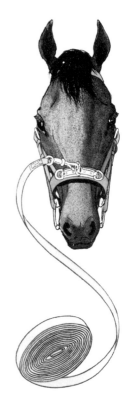

The breaking cavesson, which has a metal noseband, covered with soft padding. It is used to control a horse without using a bit. The lunge-line is attached to the front of the noseband, so pressure is brought onto the horse's nose.

The backing process

The backing process should take place at about the third or fourth week – when the horse has completed the lungeing stage.

The best place to start backing a young horse is either in the riding school or in a big stable with a high roof (should the horse rear up no one's head will hit the roof!). See the place is quiet; for it is no good trying to back a horse with a lot of disturbance around.

Start by having an assistant (and you must have one at this stage) lie against the horse's near side, putting his weight against the horse's shoulder and patting the horse on the neck and back. The handler holds the horse fairly close by the lungeing rein with the left hand and (discarding his whip) takes the assistant's left leg and gives him a slight lift. The assistant puts some weight on his arms and places them across the horse's neck. Provided the horse accepts this the action can be repeated several times.

The horse now having got used to someone clambering on to him, the next stage – after a day or two – is to repeat the same action but now

This horse is working at the walk, on the lunge-line, to develop his muscles correctly and also his outline. His well-rounded outline is nicely demonstrated in this sequence.

The "English" method of long-reining, which is used to obtain a degree of control over the young horse before mounting. It also develops muscles and strengthens ligaments.

lying across the saddle, first from one side then from the other. Next the rider can be allowed to sit on the horse, but in a crouched-forward position as it may take some time for a horse to get used to a person's head being above his own. When mounting the horse for the first few times, it is most important not to hit the top of his back with your foot. This will easily frighten an already apprehensive horse. Sit quietly, and, very important, remember to remove the stirrups the first time you mount.

At this stage the rider is simply a passenger; the horse is still under the command of the lunge-rein handler. The handler should now lead the horse on the lunge-line (and equipped with a neck strap) round to the left for a pace or two. If the horse accepts this, proceed to longer periods. Gradually, as the horse shows that he is accepting what is asked of him, more control can be handed over to the rider, until the horse can be let off the lunge-line.

When you introduce trotting, start with the sitting trot then after a couple of days move on to the rising trot. Most of a young horse's work is done at a rising trot. This is because his back is delicate and his muscles undeveloped. The way the muscles develop can be either helped or hindered according to the way the rider sits on the horse when it is green and undeveloped. At this stage a soft numnah under the saddle can be recommended.

Once the horse is well established in the walk and trot, canter work will follow quite easily. Allow the horse to go into the canter on a large

circle – perhaps on the outside track of your *manège*. At first the horse may be unbalanced and canter disunited – a result of his starting off into the canter on the wrong leg. He should immediately be brought back to the trot. If the corner is used to come out of into canter, it is most likely that the horse will automatically lead with the correct leg. In the beginning never punish a young horse for making a mistake in the canter. Do it again and position him correctly, and use a definite outside leg aid.

Once the horse has got thoroughly used to being lunged during the first two to three weeks of work, you can then move on to long-rein work. Some people leave out the long-reining stage and go straight on to mounted work, which is getting the horse accustomed to carrying a heavy weight.

If long-reining is to be left out, it is important to make sure that the horse understands why he has a bit in his mouth. You can start by lungeing him dismounted but with a saddle and bit. Allow the bridle reins to stretch back to the saddle and lie under the stirrup leathers. The reins should be of good length so as not to pull on the horse's mouth – just to accustom him to the feel and sight of reins flapping against his neck. To produce some feeling on the bit, it is allowable to attach a very slack pair of side reins – preferably those with a rubber or elastic inset – simply to let the horse know the bit is there.

To mount a horse which knows nothing about stopping is foolhardy, so a horse should be taught the rudiments of stopping and

Backing a horse. Persuasion is needed before a horse accepts a mount. Before sitting on him, you should lie across the saddle making sure you do not kick him. Once he is used to this, you can mount him.

Top: Side-view of a cavesson noseband. Note its position, under the cheekpiece.

Above: The lunge whip is never used to hit the horse. A crack of it is usually enough to correct the horse.

starting by means of the lunge-line or long-reins. The more work the horse does dis-mounted the stronger the muscles will become and the easier it will be for him to carry a rider.

Long-reining

The best known way of long-reining is the English method. Here the reins go from the cavasson along the horse's sides through the stirrups, which are tied together under the horse's stomach to stop them swaying about. The reins then continue past the horse's hocks and are held by the handler some 6 to 10 feet (2 to 3 metres) behind the horse. The horse can then be driven forwards, stopped, turned and so on at the handler's command. The snag to this method is that the horse may learn to over-bend his neck and head due to the low position of the reins and the strong contact that is built up along the reins. This is the main reason why long-reining has become unpopular among certain trainers. The Danish method of long-reining is often preferred. Here the reins come though the terretts situated on a driving pad on the horse's back. This allows a more natural position for the horse's head and neck and consequently a much lighter rein contact.

People often wonder how the horse learns about leg aids. It is more than likely that if he understands the simple rein aids and the voice, once mounted, it is relatively easy to teach the horse to move from the leg by using the voice plus the leg and, if necessary, touching the horse behind the girth with a light schooling stick.

After about six to eight weeks the horse will have been lunged, long-reined and quietly mounted. The dis-mounted work will have been gradually reduced until in the 10th to 12th week of training, he can be mounted normally and start working with a school-master – an older, or at any rate quiet horse. Work should start first in the *manège* with walking and trotting and then move out of doors. It should now learn manners, which means going quietly, standing still when required and seeing traffic, as well as being patient and having good sense. By about the fourth month of training the horse should be able to go cubbing or to a small horse show. It should also be able to proceed with whatever special training the owner may have in mind – as an eventer, hunter, or show jumper, or simply a well-mannered horse for riding round the countryside.

Four months training may seem a long time, but there are no short cuts. It is very important to lay solid foundations. As the horse has little capacity to unlearn, what it is taught in the first instance is most important.

The importance of the proper care of the horse can not be emphasised enough. Teeth are particularly important to look after. Teething troubles may lead to pain and thus resistance. Wolf teeth, the small extra teeth on the upper gum can be a particular source of trouble. Remember, too, that the young horse's skin is sensitive and girth galls are easily caused, and if saddlery is not fitted properly rubs can occur under the saddle and around the nose (under the cavesson).

If a horse is frightened of something, take him quietly to look at the cause. Do not hustle the horse. Let him see, and then he will probably accept the problem. Give him time to think. Most faults and difficulties arise because the horse has been hurried through his training and is asked to do something he does not understand or is incapable physically of carrying out. Or the horse may be in pain – perhaps a sore mouth caused by teething, or a sore leg perhaps caused by a splint.

Remember that some horses have more lethargic temperaments than others, some are quicker to learn than others and that some, by hereditary breeding, are suspicious and take a lot of convincing. That is why it is so important to handle foals and young horses so as to instill into them that man is their friend, not their enemy.

Mr Rarey, the famous horse trainer with "Cruiser" a horse previously thought to be un-controllable. Mr Rarey, came to London in the mid-19th century to demonstrate his talents as a horse tamer.

A young horse being ridden, probably for the first time on the lunge-line. Note how the whip is handled by the trainer to keep the horse moving forward but not upsetting him by over-use.

The Horse's Health

by Jill Ogden

Those who have a horse or pony to work, who have spent hours or weeks schooling and getting it fit, preparing for an Event or Show, will share one fear – that it will go lame or be ill just when everything else is ready. Lameness may be trivial or serious, curable or the start of a permanent disability. Its first signs must not be neglected. Unless the cause is very obvious and correction straightforward, a vet should be called in to determine the exact seat of lameness, assess its significance and the likely course it will take, to arrange an X-ray if necessary, or perhaps in difficult or obscure cases to allocate final responsibility for diagnosis to an appropriate specialist.

"No foot, no horse" is an old truism but also a healthy reminder, with any lame horse, to examine the foot first. This assumes that you have already been able to establish which is the lame leg. A conscientious owner will want to determine this himself. Have the horse trotted towards you on a loose rein and note which leg he drops his head on i.e. which leg he puts most weight on. This will be the sound leg in a front limb lameness; in a hind limb lameness, as he trots away, the weight will be taken on the sound limb and the lame hock or hip will jerk up higher. Tests should always be carried out on a hard level road, when an even beat will also help diagnosis. A slight lameness may show up better with the weight of a rider on the back, provided the head is left alone.

Once the lame leg has been ascertained, the foot should be examined for heat, abnormal shape and for any area of sensitivity – the latter by using hoof pincers or by striking with a hammer. If the foot is found to be the source of trouble, the shoe must be removed and the foot searched. Some lesions will be found straight away, others will only appear after the foot has been poulticed for several days and the sole or horn softened so that paring is easier. The examiner should look for a bruised sole; for a prick, possibly a deep narrow prick with pus at its tip; for a wide area of pus under-running the sole; or for a corn under the heel of the shoe (more probably in a forefoot). Sometimes a nail prick into the sensitive laminae, occurring accidentally at shoeing, will lead to heat and pain.

Puncture wounds of the foot require poulticing to draw out the pus and soften the sole, and paring to establish and ensure adequate drainage. In addition, the horse should have injections against tetanus and, where appropriate, antibiotics to check the spread and control any infection. The hind foot is as susceptible as the front to injury or pricks but less susceptible to corns or laminitis.

Laminitis

Laminitis can cause very considerable fever in the feet, with sudden acute lameness in front on both sides. The horse, desperate to take his weight off them, will stick both feet forward, transferring weight to his heels and move with a paddling gait. Changes in the shape of his feet and ridges in the growing hoof, the so called laminitic rings, may indicate he has suffered this type of lameness before. It is a congestion and inflammation of those same sensitive laminae, underlying the hoof, that can be pricked by a misdirected shoe nail. Firmly encased by the hoof, there is no room for the swelling associated with inflammation in softer tissues and the resultant pressure causes extreme pain. In severe cases, rotation of the pedal bone will often follow as well as changes in the shape of the foot.

The cause of this generalised inflammation of the laminae is not precisely known, but organic toxins from food are often named. Certainly it occurs when horses, or more particularly ponies, are

It is important to keep the teeth in good condition. Filing may be necessary because overlong teeth prevent older horses from eating and sharp edges make it painful for a horse to accept the bit when ridden.

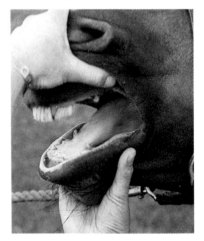

Below: The horse's left fore leg.
1. Flexor carpi radialis muscle.
2. Humeral head of flexor carpi ulnaris muscle. 3. Radius. 4. Check ligament. 5. Metacarpal bones.
6. Flexor tendons. 7. Sesamoid bones.
8. Flexor tendons.

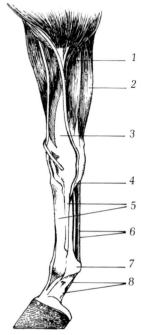

allowed too much rich grass or get an excess of grain. Laminitis has been known to be caused by other stresses to the gut or body, e.g. overheated horses drinking an excess of cold water; bacterial infections, as in mares retaining the placenta after foaling, or following severe systemic infections; concussion from trotting too hard or too long on made-up roads, particularly in unfit horses; and hormonal imbalances in mares.

Treatment of laminitis involves ridding the gut of toxic substances with laxatives, the use of anti-histaminics and anti-inflammatory agents, a strict control of the diet (often virtual starvation for one to two weeks), local cold to the feet and, where possible, enforced exercise.

Horses are very sensitive to pain and, even when the pain comes from the foot, the whole leg may quiver, muscles bunch and tendons fill, making a false assumption possible that the primary trouble is in these swollen tendon sheaths or in the fetlock and not in the foot.

Intermittent lameness, or gradually increasing lameness, may be caused by changes in the deep bony structures of the foot – the navicular or pedal bones, the hidden coffin joint or lateral cartilages. Suspicion of these deep bony changes may be confirmed by X-ray.

If the foot is cleared as the site of trouble the examiner should then look for heat, swelling or sensitivity to pressure over the heel, pastern and fetlock joint; examine the little sesamoid bones behind the joint for fractures and the heels for soreness; then examine the two layers of flexor tendons, the suspensory, and check ligaments for sprain and finally feel the cannon and splint bones for developing splints or for general soreness from concussion. A firm swelling in front or behind the knee could result from trauma (wound) or fracture, and a fluid distension here could be a sign of wear and tear, strain or a knock.

To check for hind leg lameness the horse is trotted away from the observer. In a lame horse there is an inequality in the movement of the quarters. The quarter tends to sink on the sound side and rise when the lame foot comes to the ground. Generally, front foot lameness is associated with the foot; hind leg lameness with the hock.

The lame foot and hock being examined for heat, abnormal shape and sensitive areas.

The elbow and shoulder joints should be similarly examined for pain, fluid or crepitus (crackling sound), and the muscles of forearm and shoulder checked.

In active horses, using their hind legs for great propulsive effort, there is more strain on the tendons and ligaments of fetlock joints, hock and stifle. The forelimbs are more subject to concussion and the flexor tendons to tearing and strain.

Lameness in the hock could be curb developing or the start of arthritis, as in bone spavin. Bog spavins, thoroughpin and capped hocks are less likely to cause lameness. Injuries to the stifle joint are less common though stretching of the ligaments supporting the patella (knee cap) do occur particularly in young horses with straight hind legs. Usually the lateral patella ligament is stretched and the patella gets caught up on the medial trochlear of the femur. If this is only very slight in a young horse, it may right itself in time with correct feeding and vitamin and mineral supplements. If the locking occurs often so that the ligament is overstretched, surgical treatment is indicated. The current technique is severance of the medial patella ligament.

When the site of lameness cannot be detected, it may be necessary to use local anaesthetics to block off the nerve supply to various areas of foot and leg selectively, so that when the injured area is blocked the horse goes sound and thus the injured point is localised. Confirmation of lesions in the lower limb, as with the foot, may be made on most portable X-ray machines.

Lameness caused by back injury

Lameness caused by back injuries can be acutely painful and diagnosis and differential diagnosis may be extremely difficult. Sudden acute lumbar pain with muscle spasm could be caused by damaged muscle, or by injury to the ligaments supporting the lumbar spine and sacrum, or injury to the spine or pelvis.

Ligament and bone damage. Damage to the bony structure of the spine or pelvis, dislocations at the sacroliliac junction, overlapping of the thoracic and/or dorsal spinous processes could all be factors in back lameness acute or chronic, and would have to be ascertained by X-ray. X-rays of such deep and massive structures can usually be undertaken only at the colleges, equine centres and hospitals.

Muscle damage can occur when muscle is torn by over-exertion, or in a condition called Azoturea, or in muscle cramping called the "tying up syndrome" which is similar to Azoturea; and also when blood supply to muscle is impaired. All these conditions can be acute and painful, but as they have to be very differently treated diagnosis will have to separate them.

Azoturea, also called myoglobinurea, is a severe destruction of muscle fibres. Muscle pigment or myoglobin is broken down and passed in the urine which becomes discoloured, the breakdown leading to acute spasm of the lumbar muscles. It commonly comes on within fifteen minutes of the start of exercise, more usually in animals on a high protein diet and after a couple of days of enforced rest. It is very painful and the horse may be unable to move. In this case the horse should be returned home by box and never forced to walk when further muscle damage would occur. Treatment is aimed at reducing the inflammation and acidity of the muscle. Cortisone and anti-histaminics are used, possibly sodium bicarbonate by mouth and injection, and Vitamin E by both routes. Many cases respond quickly to one injection of cortisone, others will not and kidney damage may follow. In all cases protein and carbohydrate foods must be stopped.

Confirmation of Azoturea is made by finding the muscle pigments myoglobin in the urine. Confirmation of muscle damage and an assessment of the degree of damage can be accurately determined by the level of muscle specific enzymes in a blood sample. These readings will be high in all muscle damage but correlated with the presence or absence of myoglobin in the urine can differentiate Azoturea from other muscle injuries.

The cramping of muscle or cording up of muscle in the tying up syndrome occurs in horses on high protein rations, but the onset of pain in the muscles of loins and quarters occurs after exertion. Treatment is similar to that for Azoturea.

Severe muscle injury may show the same symptoms of pain shortly after the start of exercise. Treatment involves the use of anti-inflammatory agents such as phenylbutazone and cortisone, the application of anti-phlogistine packs, liniments and warmth, and prolonged rest with subsequent checking by blood samples.

Muscle damage occurring when blood supply to the muscle is reduced could be caused by a fragment of a clot from a verminous aneurism in the wall of a main vessel, breaking off and being carried in the blood stream until it blocks an artery supplying the lumbar muscles. Treatment is aimed at reducing the clot.

Another disease called Shivering also affects the muscles of the loins and quarters, but its origins lie in a degenerative change of the nerve supply to these muscles. It is gradual and occurs in older animals.

Treatment of all lameness is aimed at reducing inflammation, controlling any infection and promoting the healing process.

Sprained tendons, strained ligaments and bruised tendons need the application of cold and pressure support for the first 24 hours. This may be followed by alternating hot fomentations with cold compresses. Heat is well retained in Kaolin poultices, or packs such as Animalintex which exerts osmotic pressure as well as retaining heat. There is also a gelatine-filled plastic pack (Tendon Eze) which can be strapped on hot or cold.

Ultrasound therapy can be very valuable. Ultrasonic vibrations provide deep stimulation and improve the blood supply to injured tendon or muscle and quicken healing. The use of systemic cortisone and anti-inflammatory agents may also be useful.

Any further treatment will depend on the severity of the sprain or strain, but very often the most important need will be rest. In a severe sprain this will need to be really prolonged i.e. turning out for six months. This may be heartbreaking for those who have put in all the effort, but it is imperative if you are to avoid repeated disappointments.

Treatment of inflammatory lesions on bone, the splints, sore shins or bruises follow a similar pattern – poultices or anti-phlogistine packs or cold compresses, and rest.

Just as the owner wants to understand a little more about his horse going lame, he will also want to know what to do if there is an accident, and how to recognise the commonest illnesses.

Minor cuts and grazes need to be cleaned if there is dirt or grit in them and then dressed with a wound powder, (in the summer a powder containing fly repellant should be used). If the cut is clean, it is better not to wash away the serous exudate that has brought repairing blood cells, but simply to dress the wound. Deep cuts may need stitching or supporting, and certainly antibiotics and tetanus anti-toxin need to be administered. A horse immunised with tetanus toxoid may require a booster.

The *risk of tetanus* is so well recognised that protection following cuts and injuries is always quickly sought. Consequently, tetanus is not a disease the horse owner is now likely to meet: however, it does occur. The cause is a bacterium, called *Clostridium Tetani*, gaining entry to the body through a wound. There may be several weeks delay between the wound and the onset of symptoms. In fact the wound may have healed, or the portal of entry may not be obvious at all – e.g. a deep prick in the foot or even a mouth lesion. It is a painful and alarming disease and is almost invariably fatal. The onset of symptoms is sudden – there is intermittent spasm of skeletal muscle so that the neck and body become stiff and the animal may fall if moved over. The tail may be erect and quivering, ears flickering. Soon swallowing becomes impossible and the jaw locks. Treatment, even if started early, has only rarely known to be successful.

Colic

If a horse should show signs of colicky abdominal pain, kicking up at his belly, restlessness, sweating, perhaps blowing, he should be rugged up and moved quietly about until he can be examined. There are several causes of colic and consequently a varying clinical picture. It can be mild with a quick recovery, may need protracted treatment or may even be fatal.

Spasmodic Colic Horses are very sensitive to spasm of the muscle of the gut following ingestion of unsuitable substances or from imperfect mastication of food, or eating while nervous or hurried. Usually this type of colic will respond quickly to injections of anti-spasmodics and a suitable laxative drench.

Impacted Colic is an impaction of the colon due to too much coarse fibrous feed, imperfect mastication because of irregular teeth, or getting at finely ground barley or a cattle mix and gobbling it down quickly. The impaction needs extensive softening up with quantities of laxative salts and oils, such as liquid paraffin given as a drench or better still via a stomach tube.

Flatulent colic is caused by substances that ferment and cause the rapid formation of gas. If in the stomach, the resultant gastric tympany must be relieved quickly by a stomach tube or there may be a risk of rupture of the stomach. Fortunately, this is comparatively rare. Flatulence in the lower gut can be helped by injections and laxatives.

There are two types of *Verminous Colic*. They occur more commonly in young animals. One is simple impaction with ascarids (round worms) which can be relieved with correct worm treatment. In the other case red worm larvae may settle in a vessel wall supplying a length of gut and the resultant aneurism may block the blood supply to the bowel. Painful intermittent spasmodic colic will follow and, if the blood supply is not re-established, gangrene will develop. Surgery to remove the injured loop of bowel can be attempted.

Similarly in the case of a *twisted gut* (when the horse rolling has caused a loop of bowel to twist through a rent in its mesenteric support) the horse can only be saved by rapid surgery. Where this is not practicable, it is better to destroy it.

An incurable colic occurs with degeneration of the neuro-muscular junctions of the nerve supply to the alimentary tract resulting in atony of the bowel. It is difficult to differentiate clinically from a twist, but fortunately these serious cases are unusual.

Colic can be avoided by following simple rules such as:
(a) avoid giving cold water to an over-heated horse.
(b) do not feed a tired horse, wait for him to recover.
(c) always water before feeding.
(d) check teeth periodically.
(e) worm him regularly.

Grass sickness, in its acute form, initially resembles colic because of the accompanying acute constipation, pain and apparent gastric tympany, often with stomach contents dribbling down the nostrils. The disease tends to occur in certain localities and even in certain fields. The cause is unknown, though allergy, bacterial and plant toxins are thought to be factors. The nerve supply to the gut degenerates, resulting in stricture of the pyloric sphincter of the stomach. This is a comparatively rare disease. There is no known cure.

Coughs caused by virus, like the Equine Influenza virus, are highly infectious diseases with a hard dry cough, a nasal discharge and systemic febrile reaction (high temperature). A horse developing a sudden cough should be isolated and examined. The milder strains of the virus may cause laryngitis only, but virulent strains involve the lymph nodes and chest and may affect the blood cell picture and heart. Secondary infection will prolong the illness. Treatment is symphomatic. Viruses do not respond specifically to antibiotics and it is wiser to protect against the disease by routine vaccination.

Coughs can accompany infection by the bacteria *Streptococcus Equi*, causing the disease called Strangles. It is highly infectious and spread

One week

4–6 months

2 years

4 years

7 years

15 years

25 years

Age and the horse's teeth
A. Longitudinal section of an incisor.
B. Cross-section of the same tooth at
5–6 years, 8–9 years, 11–12 years
and 13–14 years.
1. Front surface
2. Pulp cavity
3. Infundibulum
4. Dentine
5. Peripheral enamel
6. Cement
7. Dental star
A horse's age can be judged from the
growth of its incisors, which, up to the
age of eight, change recognisably each
year. Thereafter, the change is enough
to guess its age to within a year.

by direct contact. Symptoms include fever and swollen glands of the neck and throat. The outcome of the disease depends on the severity of infection and whether the glands come to a head, burst and discharge or whether the lesions remain as chronic infections or spread inwardly to other glands in the body – Bastard Strangles. Treatment with antibiotics is effective, but the timing of treatment should be decided according to each case. Poulticing and inhalations can be useful.

Young horses teething or horses subjected to the stress of a long journey and getting chilled may develop a nasal discharge and a cough, simulating Strangles, but without the generalised swelling of lymph glands and rise in temperature. They will recover with warmth, fresh air, correct feeding and simple expectorant mixtures.

The upper respiratory tract of some horses is easily irritated by dust and such animals may cough when they trot round with others in a covered school or when schooling in a dry field. A horse giving an odd cough should be checked by the vet for infection.

Allergic chest and laryngeal conditions leading to coughing may be controlled if the causative agent is known. Some horses are allergic to straw bedding, for example, but other allergies cannot be identified and constant coughing renders the horse unusable. Allergy to fertilisers on grass and hay have been incriminated.

Bronchitis, following any respiratory tract infection or accompanying impaired circulation, will result in a chronic moist cough which is helped by expectorant mixtures and luteolytic agents, but may not be permanently curable. It may be followed by loss of elasticity of lung tissue, leading to alveolar emphysema or "broken wind". Breathing is short on exertion and there is a double expiratory effort and a cough. Eventually the cough becomes continuous and the animal distressed.

Finally coughing in horses has been caused by the lung worm *Dictyocaulus Arnfeldii*, commonly transmitted by the donkey host. If this is suspected, faecal samples should be examined for larvae.

Various *skin diseases* will be met by most horse owners and should not be too difficult to recognise and confirm. Hair loss over neck, withers and base of tail accompanied by irritation, occurring towards the end of the winter and early spring, is likely to be caused by lice. Lice can be controlled but may return at yearly intervals.

Mud fever, really an exhudative eczema, may develop on sensitive skins at the heels, over the back and belly. This usually responds to dressing with cortisone creams and systemic cortisone. Zinc oxide, castor oil ointment or coal tar ointments are all useful.

Ringworm is not always as characteristic a ring as it is in cattle, so it may be hard to diagnose. There are several causative fungi in horses. It usually responds to systemic treatment with Fulcin Feed Supplement and dressings. It is highly contagious.

The Medicine Cupboard in the stableyard can only be built up as it is needed. However surgical requirements should be there:
antibiotic powders
cotton wool
crepe and stable bandages
a tin of Kaolin poultice
Animalintex
methylated spirits for hardening skin
cooling lotion
roll of Gamgee tissue to go under bandages during treatment or for warmth
Epsom salts
a colic drench, provided it is recommended by your vet.
worming preparations
hoof preparations, such as Stockholm Tar

Sweet itch, or summer eczema, is a skin condition which develops in early summer and continues through to the autumn in a select number of susceptible animals, usually ponies. Itchy, scabby areas develop on mane, and tail, sometimes on the flank and round the ears. Mane and tail, sometimes on the flank and round the ears. Mane and tail may be virtually rubbed away. The cause is basically an individual allergy, possibly to the bite of the midge culicoides – and the susceptibility to this allergy appears to be hereditary. Deficiencies of minerals and allergies to over-rich pastures are also incriminated. Systemic cortisone, mineral supplements, the regular use of fly repellants and eczema preparations help considerably.

Disease from *internal parasites* must be briefly mentioned. Foals suffer from roundworms (ascarids), which can cause diarrhoea, poor condition, colic and broncho-pneumonia. Red worms are the cause of strongylosis in horses of all age groups, causing loss of condition, diarrhoea, anaemia and the formation of aneurisms in arterial walls which can lead to colic or to severance of blood supply to muscle. Ship worms may lodge up the rectum and cause irritation at the tail base. Horse Bot Fly maggots, lodge in the wall of the stomach causing indigestion and colic, and can lead to rupture of the stomach.

Learning to Ride

by Sylvia Stanier

Left: The correct position of the hands and the legs.

When learning, a rider must first of all gain confidence and then learn to use the aids correctly. A correct basic seat is a priority. When this has been established, which may take some time, then, and only then, should the rider decide what type of riding he or she may wish to specialise in, or what particular school to study.

In all traditional riding establishments (by which is meant such places as Saumur, Vienna, Strömsholm, Warendorf and so on) there is a set period of time and lessons on which the future training is based. Most of the time is devoted to building up the proper muscles for riding and learning the rudiments of the aids by which to influence the horse. Most of these schools teach riders on good school-master type horses. This means that the teacher does not have to worry too much about the horse and so can concentrate on dealing with the rider.

To learn to ride efficiently – to a standard of being able to control a reasonably well-mannered horse and go for pleasant rides out of doors – takes a number of lessons. Some people have a natural ability, but unless this ability is educated and developed it can not proceed beyond a certain point. Equally, someone with little ability can, with good teaching, be improved considerably.

One of the attributes of a good teacher is to be able to assess the type of horse a rider will do best with. For instance, it is no good putting a nervous beginner on a very hot-tempered Thoroughbred. However, later on in training riders should learn to ride a variety of horses – but never to the degree of dangerous situations being allowed to arise. And

A good way to carry a saddle and bridle, so that you have a free hand.

Left below: A class of riders being worked at the trot on a circle. (Note the leading horse is wearing a Hackamore.)

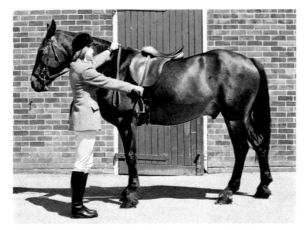

The rider in position to be ready to mount. Facing the saddle, and holding the reins in the left hand.

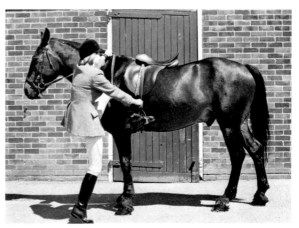

The left foot is in the left stirrup, which is held by the right hand.

so teaching people to ride is as much an art as teaching the young horse. It needs kindness, patience and expert knowledge.

Before mounting a horse for the first time, it is a good idea to look at some diagrams showing the names of the various parts of the horse and its accoutrements (see page 14). Pictures can tell one a great deal. The first few times a rider is given mounted lessons they should not last too long. This is because stiffness can set in. Some people like to do a few exercises each day to work-in the different muscles used in riding. There is no doubt that giving the novice rider exercises to do while having the riding lesson is an important part of the development of a good basic position. You can start the lesson with a few minutes of exercises. These exercises should be carried out slowly but thoroughly with the object of relaxing and suppling the muscles. Fingers and wrists, ankles and toes and the neck are the places to start with. Work must be geared to easing muscle tension in the beginner. But always remember that each person can only take a certain amount of concentrated work and that each person's reflexes are different – some react very quickly, others rather slowly. As a teacher try never to be impatient, yet have the courage and confidence to know when to go on to the next lesson. The instructor must study this progression of training thoroughly to be able to put it into practice efficiently.

One of the most important lessons a beginner can learn is when mounting for the first time. Reins and stick (if carried) should be in the left hand, the right on the back end of the saddle, the left foot placed in the centre of the stirrup on the left or "near side". On making the effort to get up high enough to place one's right leg over the top of the saddle it is a great temptation to land quickly and, in many cases, heavily in the saddle. This is not only disturbing for the horse – whose back is very vulnerable to injury – but is a sign of an unsympathetic rider. So the rule is: place yourself quietly in the saddle.

There are various ways of dismounting. The simplest is to take both feet out of the stirrups and take the right leg quietly across the saddle thus allowing oneself to slide to the ground, just bending the knees enough to take the body weight on landing. Keep hold of the reins; if you intend to lead the horse take the reins over his head and put your right hand near his chin and take the loop of the reins in the left hand. Run up the stirrups and put the leathers through them for safety. Always walk beside a horse when leading him; do not try to drag him along. If the horse is lazy, a little tap with the stick just behind the girth should encourage him to walk on.

The rider is now poised over the horse's back ready to arrive in the saddle, (which must be done very lightly).

The rider now happily sitting on the horse.

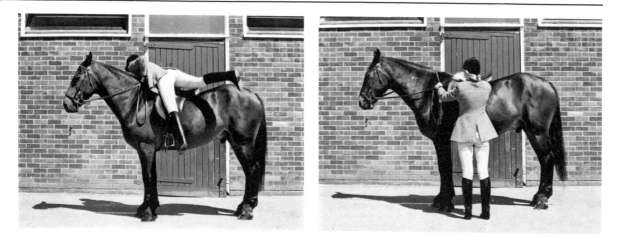

To dismount, both feet are removed from the stirrups, but the reins are still held. The right leg is about to come over to the left side of the horse.

Above right: The rider is now on the ground, having put both feet on the ground lightly and quietly, and still holding the reins.

The rider's seat

Once in the saddle, the rider should sit straight with the spine at right angles to the horse's spine. Most saddles today are well made, fairly deep seated and comfortable. It is best, for a variety of reasons, to sit in the deepest part of the saddle. The thighs and legs then cover the maximum part of the horse (later it will be explained how big a role the thighs play in controlling the horse). And in this position the rider is sitting over the centre of gravity of the horse, which, when the horse is moving, it is most important to be able to feel. It is the point of balance of two living things and so should be synchronised as much as possible. So sit central and in balance; sit softly; and lastly, sit deep, but not so deep that you start gripping upwards. This is a fault common with beginners who try to develop too deep a seat too early, are unable to maintain, thus stiffening themselves in their efforts to stay put. They are, in fact, doing the exact opposite of what the teacher really requires – a supple and relaxed rider.

The "independent" seat is one that is independent of the hands in regard to staying on the horse. This independence should be built up gradually through the exercises, through actual hours in the saddle and sensible teaching – which consists in establishing a basic seat before any specialisation. A neck strap is a valuable piece of equipment for the beginner. Besides being a psychological extra help it also stops

97

the horse from being pulled in the mouth when security is lacking. So never be too proud to use one.

The rider's legs create the impulsion; the hands guide and control this impulsion. Forward movement is a very important part of equitation. The rider's legs should be used in conjunction with the horse's hind legs. This means an alternating leg movement – right, left, right, left and vice versa. So try to build up the feel of the horse's legs. As you feel his ribs bulge out, it means his leg is coming up under his body and you apply your leg; as the ribs flutter out so you ease that leg and apply the opposite one. Obviously this takes time to achieve. For the harmony of this movement the hands also make an alternating movement, taking up the slack of the reins as the horse's shoulder comes back, following with the shoulder as it goes forward. The timing of these movements will vary according to whether the horse is walking, trotting or cantering. The trot is the easiest of these paces at which to feel this synchronisation and build the harmony, because it is a pace of two time. The walk is much slower and is four time.

Sit softly in the saddle, taking the body's weight through the thigh and knee (*through* and not on) and down into the ankle joint which acts like a lever. When pressed down, the muscles tense and harden and so stimulate the horse; when the ankle is not pressing down, the muscles

The rider conforming to the correct principles of a "good position".

relax and the rider disturbs the horse much less. The best position for the ankle is just a little down with the toe a little up. A soft knee position leads to a better rider – the weight of the rider really needs to go into the top half of the calf. To establish this the rider can practise pressing the heels down and then relaxing them and then taking a middle position. Standing in the stirrups for a few paces to encourage balance is good too. Such little exercises help to relax the very strong lumbar muscles in the rider's back. Stiff and hollowed-back riders are never attractive to look at and are seldom particularly successful, as they cannot follow the movement of their horses and are therefore limited as to how far they can go in higher equitation.

The foot position is akin to that when one is walking – a little weight on the inside of the sole and the toes just a little outwards, but not too much, as this stiffens the whole leg. The ankle must be very supple so as to act as a lever. The legs must give a firm base of support to encourage the independent seat. A rider with very long legs may achieve this fairly early with a longish leather, whereas a short-legged rider needs a shorter leather. Again a rider with short arms has a problem; he may need to adjust shoulders and body position ever so slightly forward. The horse must always know where the rider's hands are, and the length of rein is therefore of paramount importance. Too long a rein leads to far greater problems than too short a rein. If the reins are too long a jerky contact with the arms can happen; with a short rein the contact is usually even, and need not be too severe. The best contact with the reins on a really well-trained horse is that which is simply the weight of the reins. But at all times an even contact is important.

Beginners often find it hard to hold on to the reins; which may be too thick and thus uncomfortable; or they may hold them too tight and try to pull themselves into position via the reins – a very bad fault. Continual assessment by a good teacher is the best way to improve. The teacher may ask the pupil to do some riding with the reins in one hand, for instance; and when cantering (or jumping) the teacher may ask the pupil to put one hand on the neck strap to remove this fault, until the rider's leg and seat position is strong enough.

Lungeing the rider
Lungeing the rider used to be thought of as rather a punishing ordeal. Nowadays, the methods used have been sophisticated to suit the needs of civilian riders and considerable results can be achieved really very quickly. The most important thing to start with is to have a suitable horse. He should be one with good paces, comfortable and with a nice temperament. A suitable saddle is also important; it should be one that puts the rider into the correct position without exaggerating.

The horse is under the complete control of the handler. This gives the rider time to think of his or her own position without having to bother about the horse. The horse should be well versed in lungeing and know what is required of him. The ideal is an older – trained horse who is perhaps retired from competition work. Since the horse being used for lungeing work travels a considerable distance round and round, the handler should be careful not to tire him out. The biggest danger with lungeing the rider is straining muscles and causing stiffness. The horse should wear side reins, which should be attached after the rider has mounted, and the lunge-line should be attached to a cavesson head collar.

There are basically two types of work to be carried out in lungeing. One is the various physical exercises designed to improve a rider's position; the other is the various "feels". These "feels" involve the rider feeling transitions and different paces. It is a matter of opinion as to the exact exercises to be carried out, and whether riders should or should not have their stirrups, but there is no doubt that the most important factor should be safety and, in the beginner, the building up of confidence. A few minutes on the lunge – 10 to 15 minutes to start with – followed by half-an-hour's private lesson is probably all that a

A rider being schooled through gymnastic exercises on the lunge-line.

Here the instructor is looking to see if the rider's spine is immediately over that of the horse.

This exercise is designed to improve balance and the use of the arm and shoulder muscles.

beginner could take. An adult who is already fit could do quite hard exercises for 30 minutes. Particular care must always be taken with children; nothing is worse than a child being hurt or losing its confidence. Jumping is not to be recommended, especially not if the horse is wearing side reins. Teaching the rider to improve his position via the lunge-line is strictly for the flat, and a very great deal can be achieved even at the walk.

The work can be divided into three categories: exercises; feeling the paces and transitions; and feeling the effect of the rider's correct position in influencing the way the horse is going.

Certainly, riders even in the higher levels, need continual assessment. A good lesson with a good instructor every now and again is a must for all riders. Never be too proud to learn. There are also many improved techniques available today. One is the video-tape. In the old days a good mirror was the only thing available for pupils to study themselves. The video-tape has the advantage of being studied quietly and in comfortable surroundings and the instructor can then both point out the faults and give advice on solving them.

Sound fundamental training is the foundation of all future success.

Balance and Collection

Balance is a very important word in equitation parlance. Balance in the horse and balance in the rider. Synchronisation of horse and rider is the ultimate aim.

A horse is said to be balanced when the weight of the rider is evenly distributed and carried by the horse's legs. The horse's head and neck will be raised in proportion to his age and training; his hocks will be carried well under his body, giving good thrust. The horse propels himself mostly with his hind legs; the fore-legs, although giving the impression of moving well forwards do so in order to carry the body which is already being propelled from behind. A horse can be naturally well balanced. He need not be collected to be naturally balanced. However, to be "collected" the horse must be correctly balanced first.

continued

A horse at the halt, listening to his rider and awaiting his instructions.

Right: Artificial aids.
1. Standing martingale.
2. Running martingale with hunting breast plate attachment.
3. A good pair of spurs with blunt edges – suitable for most schooling work.
4. Various whips, including the long Dressage whip and the racing or cutting whips.

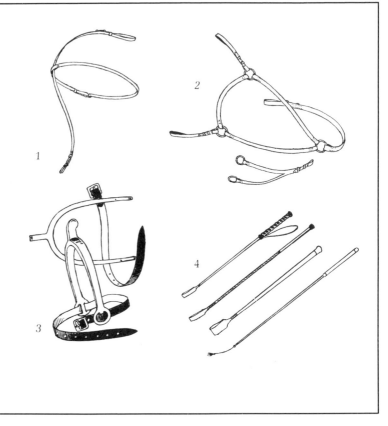

Conformation plays quite a big part in how far, or how early, a horse can be collected. The work the horse is required to do will also determine the degree of collection he needs and how it is used. Obviously a horse with heavy shoulders and weak quarters will be very difficult to collect, as his balance will be all wrong to start with. A well balanced horse, easy to collect, should have a well set on head and neck, well sloped shoulders and fairly powerful quarters with good hocks. This is because the idea of collection is to put more weight on to the quarters and instill a carrying effect as well as the propelling effect on the hindquarters. Slightly bent hocks sometimes do this with less strain than the more fashionable straight ones. A horse whose croup is higher than his withers is also a problem, as the aim of collection is to lower the quarters with a flexion of the hip joints. In fact there are two well-known rules about collection. One is that the horse should carry his muzzle as high as his withers with the flexion at the poll. The other is that, if you run a horizontal line from the hip joint through the shoulder blade, the lower down the shoulder blade this line comes, the better the horse's balance. The horse balances himself with his head and neck and so, in true collection, he needs a high neck carriage which, of course, he can only achieve when the weight is properly put on to the quarters. The action will then be higher and full of energy. Collection can be obtained in all three gaits – walk, trot and canter. Usually the horse should have had at least two years' training before beginning the proper collection, and it will probably take about four to six years to obtain the highest results.

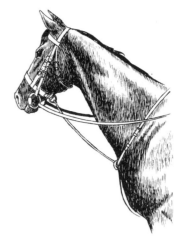

A standing martingale, used to keep the horse's head within the angle of control. This martingale is attached to the noseband and the girth.

Aids

There are two general types of aids, the natural and the artificial. The former consists of the rider's body weight, the legs, the hands and the voice. The artificial ones consist of the whip, the spurs and such things as martingales and running reins.

We have seen how important it is for the rider to be balanced and one with the horse. Having achieved this, the rider should study the aids and their application. In general the legs create the impulsion; the hands channel this impulsion. But there is more to it than that; because not only is there the light and shade of the degree of application, which must vary from horse to horse, but there is also the effect the aid will have. For instance, if a rider applies his leg close to the girth, he should expect the horse to move forwards, whereas if applied a little farther back the horse may well move sideways. So it is very important to make things clear to the horse when applying an aid and know exactly where and when to apply it. The rider's leg aids should be applied when the horse's hind leg is in the air – i.e. the rider's left leg should be applied as the horse's left leg is in the air, and vice versa. So it will be seen at once that there is an alternative application of the leg aids. The same applies to the hands.

Running martingale also used to keep the horse's head in the correct position but attached to the reins instead of the noseband.

The seat bone aids or back aids are always controversial. The main thing is to sit straight with the hips supple. The pelvis should be tilted or rolled slightly under the rider's upper body so as to have the upper body weight behind it; this will act as a forward-driving influence on the horse. It is this position which sometimes causes confusion and makes the rider sit too stiffly and to lean backwards. As well as being a forward influence on the horse, the seat bone aids can ask for the canter. But there are some schools of thought which disapprove of this particular aid, but nevertheless such a one exists. What all teachers want to avoid is for the rider to sit too heavily on the seat bones, in a downward direction (or even a backwards one). There should really be a slightly sliding motion which, of course, can only be achieved by a very light seat. For canter, which is where the seat bone aid can be used satisfactorily, if one presses on the right seat bone, followed up by the left one and one has a slight left tension on both reins, it is very likely the horse will canter on the left lead. This is, the diagonal aid, starting at the seat bone instead of at a lower part of the rider's leg. The canter aids are very varied.

continued

Hands (fingers and wrists) should always be sympathetic. There should be no backward tension. To stop the horse, close the knees and thighs and then close the fingers on the reins. On a well-schooled horse this should be quite enough. Sit perhaps just a little straighter. On circles or in changes of direction, with a young horse the rider's hand can lead the forehand round by using the open rein. This means carrying the inside, or leading hand, slightly out towards the rider's knee. At the same time the outside hand should come in closer to the neck of the horse, but never over it. Later (as we have already seen) the inside seat bone can slide forward and the inside shoulder back, so as to turn the horse. To collect the horse, alternate pressure of the legs and hands – just resisting the horse from lengthening himself – so as to contain the balance the impulsion has created from behind. In extension, the hand allows the lengthening, but is never slack, which would unbalance the horse. In all movements the legs should act before the hands.

If the horse does not answer the leg immediately, you may use a spur, an artificial aid. But only use a spur when absolutely necessary, for a rider should learn to use his legs correctly without a spur. The spur is used in the same way as the lower leg, but more subtly. The same applies to the stick, which is always carried when jumping, but not always allowed in dressage tests. In schooling, a stick is an important aid to back up the leg, either on the ribs or on the hocks (using the long dressage whip). Never should either spur or whip be used in anger. If you want to punish a horse with a stick, do so immediately he has done wrong by one sharp smack on the ribs. The voice is a most useful aid in schooling, but is never allowed in dressage tests. However, to encourage or to calm, or even to discipline a horse being broken-in or schooled, this natural aid has no equal.

Running reins and martingales – both artificial aids – are mainly used to keep the horse's head in the correct place. Some riders only use the running rein to ask a horse to relax his lower jaw; others use it to lower the whole neck, which, of course, leads to over bending (when the horse has his nose tucked in towards his chest).

The use of aids is a subject about which many books have been written. The signals by which one gets through to a horse are varied. When you find an aid that suits you and your horse, use it and do not give it up until you find a much better one.

A class of children out hacking with an instructress leading a beginner. An excellent example of imparting confidence to young riders.

International Riding Styles

by Sylvia Stanier

The large and fascinating subject of riding techniques embraces a span of history of well over 2,000 years. Fashions in riding have changed over the years, and the quest for better ways of achieving perfection continues.

The earliest form of educated horsemanship is usually associated with the Greek historian, philosopher and soldier, Xenophon (c.430 BC – c.354 BC). There is no doubt that he was a kindly master and also a practical one. Many of his ideas still hold today. The Greeks were sophisticated people and Xenophon's horses were trained along well thought-out methods.

The Chinese emperors of the Ming dynasty (1368–1644) were also highly sophisticated; their famous horses (which appear to have come from Arabia) were magnificent, and their silken saddles and golden stirrups were truly beautiful. The mongol conquerer Genghis Khan (1162–1227) was far less sophisticated. He used small tough ponies and simple saddlery for his cavalrymen. Although all these horsemen have a place in history, it is really to the great Renaissance courts of Europe that we should look in order to relate riding techniques of the past to those we value today.

During the Renaissance – that great intellectual movement which spread from Italy throughout Europe from the 14th to the 16th century – the nobility not only used horses as modes of transport, but were beginning to use them for pleasures other than hunting. Young gentlemen were expected to ride elegantly on the finely bred Spanish-type horses which were so fashionable. These horses were magnificent to look at, very comfortable to sit on, good-tempered and easy to collect with their very high action. The 16th and 17th centuries was the time when the art of collection was being studied and performed in great detail. The Spanish Riding School in Vienna was formed at that time. The Portuguese school of Marialva dates from about the same time. Both are now considered the Classical Schools. So, too, was the French school which was formed at Versailles and which was later moved to the town of Saumur. In Germany schools were formed in the different principalities, each with its own individuality. During the 17th century cavalry training was taken more seriously and the various countries began to cater for training horses and men. It is the combination of these methods that today forms the basis for the rules of the Fédération Equestre Internationale (FEI).

German and French schools

The techniques used by the different countries were originally designed to fit in with the particular needs of that country. And so national characteristics were seen very clearly in the methods. Perhaps the best example of this is the German school which looked for complete discipline, while the French school looked for a lighter, more artistic approach. Today, the methods used are much more integrated, although the precision and obedience of German horses to their riders' demands is particularly successful in the exacting world of international competition. The breed of horse used is also developed so as to be suitable to stand up to this precision, in both temperament, soundness and power. The German stud masters are always looking to improve their breeds.

Above: Major Raimondo D'Inzeo one of the most famous exponents of the Italian style of jumping.

Patrick Le Rolland on "Cramique". This picture shows the tremendous lightness and collection sought after by the French school.

Below: The Spanish Riding School in Vienna. The horses used at the school are the specially bred Lipizzaners which can be trained to a very high degree of collection.

The German classical style, as developed by the 19th-century veterinary surgeon, Gustav Steinbrecht, and so brilliantly produced by the great Otto Lörke, is a very pure, logical form of training. It consists of a certain set of gymnastic exercises through which the horse is put over a period of time. Much thought is given to the development of muscles – the neck and the back coming in for particular attention. Every qualified horse-trainer must go through these exercises and be trained both in theory and practice by a senior instructor before gaining his badge as a trainer.

The training centre for German equitation is at Warendorf, a town near Münster. Briefly, the German technique consists mainly of training the horses via the lunge-line to accept the bit correctly, with side reins to help. Then the riders are taught to sit very deep, use their seats and legs correctly and to keep the horse on the bit with a steady hand. The riders are taught these techniques on trained horses so as to learn the correct feel; and only when this is firmly established are they considered competent to pass this on to either a young horse or a young rider.

Much the same sort of routine is in use at Saumur, although riders are required to study a slightly different theory. French riders have always thought more about the rein aids than their German counterparts, who rely so much on the seat to influence their horses. Impulsion is important in both schools – powerful impulsion in Germany, on their horses bred from the old carriage breeds of Europe. French horses, often having much Arab blood, are hot-blooded and need careful handling. These horses suit the French idea of attaining great lightness of action and lightness to the aids. The French school requires a more horizontal balance in the horses than either the Germans or the Spanish School of Vienna.

The Spanish School, using their specially bred Lipizzaner horses, can, and do, ask for a considerable lowering of the quarters in collection. These horses, being powerfully built behind, have a special facility for this work. The Spanish school differs somewhat from the French in that the rein aids required at Saumur are not used in quite the same way at Vienna. At Vienna very little hand aids are used, and the riders who have been worked very systematically on the lunge-line are able to do most of the work with their very strong supple positions. The horses are required to perform certain sets of movements in sequences which lead up over a period of years to the highest and most difficult dressage movements. After a certain length of training, horses with particular abilities are trained to develop the movements they are best at. So horses at Vienna become specialists in their own right.

In Germany and France all sorts of horses of differing breeds are trained, some for dressage, some for jumping as well as Three-Day Events, to say nothing of the now very popular driving events. In Vienna stallions are traditionally only trained in dressage, and just some of the mares are broken to light harness work. So the techniques used in Germany and France embrace a lot more than just dressage, while at Vienna the accent is on pure classical dressage as laid down by de la Guerinière in the 18th century.

Scandinavian and Italian systems

Two other very important schools of thought are the Scandinavian and the Italian systems of Caprilli. Strömsholm, a lovely wooded park about 100 miles (160km) from Stockholm has been the centre of equitation in Sweden since the 17th century. The Swedes have over the years developed a system based on gymnastic exercises for horse and rider. Due to the varied types of horses used in Sweden (many of which have won medals in Olympic competition) there is a vast reservoir of exercises designed to cure nearly every fault to be found during horse training. It is an adaptable system compared with the very clear-cut rules of some of the other Continental schools which deal in horses suitable to their own traditions. Leg yielding is a speciality of the Scandinavian school.

When it comes to English or Irish Thoroughbred type horses, what really counts is the degree of application of exercises, whether German or Swedish. For there is no doubt that the more Thoroughbred the blood the less room there is for error. So, however good the gymnastic exercise, it is only as good as the rider allows it to be. The Scandinavian school is cavalry orientated, based on the Swedish Army Manual, even though Strömsholm is now a civilian establishment.

The Italian jumping system as laid down by Federico Caprilli is the great innovation of 20th-century equitation. Due to the influence of the forward seat, the whole jumping and eventing scene has gone from strength to strength. By watching horses jump loose, Caprilli observed that they needed to use their heads and necks to be able to jump and hardly ever fell or hit fences if left to jump naturally and freely.

What then are the techniques used in the Italian system? Firstly, rhythm and stride. Then there is the rider sitting on a horse with its balance much more forward than the highly collected dressage horse. So, the horse will be in a long low outline, yet using his hocks properly and with a rounded top line, which will allow him to use himself correctly over the jump. With a horse in this position the rider must of necessity sit farther forward and with the seat just a fraction out of the saddle. Thus more weight comes down the rider's legs and on to the stirrups. In this method the rein contact should be even, and for jumping one should normally use a snaffle bridle. The curb rein in classical work – dressage – is for the collecting effect only, not a brake.

The Italian-trained jumping horse should be trained to go with an even rhythm and pace and in the correct jumping outline. If so-schooled, the horse will be able to approach the jump calmly and gather himself to jump. And this is very much the crux of the technique – helping the horse to help itself. The rider sits still when necessary, yet when the horse needs encouragement to lengthen his stride or steady it, he must answer the rider immediately.

To school a horse through the "Italian" method he will start by learning to jump with no help from the rider. When the horse has learned to look after himself, he will be further schooled to listen to his rider, yet retain the ability or initiative to look after himself. In this, as

The steady hands low over the withers and the very deep seat with the characteristic long stirrups, exemplifies the German dressage technique, here demonstrated by Frau Lisselot Linsenhoff on "Adular".

Implementing the Scandinavian riding technique depends on a sequence of gymnastic exercises for the horse. Olympic medallist Major Boltenstern on "Krest" demonstrates the rein-back.

in any method of riding, the rider's body-weight is used and the point of balance must be found. The horse will follow the rider's weight in turning, for instance. The rider's lower leg and heel does quite a lot of work and can only come in contact with the horse's sides by being fairly close to the girth. If the lower leg is too far back, balance is lost; and if too far forward, no useful purpose is achieved. The rider must have a relatively short leather, so as to close the angle between the heel, the hip and the shoulders. The knees will of necessity be a little farther forward, but the rider's weight must be pushing downwards in a supple manner. The rider's hips and back should be supple, so as to keep balance and lower the seat into the saddle in order to drive a sticky horse forwards if he hesitates approaching a fence.

In all the techniques we have looked at – whether for dressage or jumping – split-second timing is the real criterion. Aids that are too late are of no value; and often actually harmful.

To put all these methods into perspective for the rider of today is rather difficult. Dressage riders still go for their own particular school of thought (see page 111) and, although the rules of the FEI are very clear as to what is required, the way this is achieved is rather varied. This is partly because of the different types of horses used and partly because of the great traditions of the old European establishments.

For jumping the techniques do not vary so much, though some people say that there is no correct technique for jumping, because, compared with dressage, it is a much newer sport. Yet, it must be stressed that the forward seat and good balance plus split-second reflexes are of vital importance and that they must be developed in both horse and man. German horses probably need a good deal more working than the more fussy British Thoroughbreds. The United States show-jumping team is nearly always mounted on Thoroughbreds. These horses are trained to be supreme athletes with lots of gymnastic work, and their riders are equally supple. But the degree of application of the work may have to be lessened for the Thoroughbreds.

So what are the points you would expect to see in riders of different schools? From France you would expect to see a supple rider on a horse full of impulsion. The rider would use more rein aids than his German counterpart. In dressage he would have a very deep seat, use his seat and legs to influence a very powerful horse, but keep his hands steady. The German rider, whether in dressage or jumping, would use a lot of gymnastic exercises to work in their horses. The Viennese rider would have a deep seat, work with great sophistication and his horse would perform various patterns, and lead up to the specialist horses working in various ways. (When worked from the ground very often two people will work the horse). The great Quadrille of the Spanish School is a sophisticated ride to music with the precision of the patterns of the movements forming the basis, to which elegance and beauty are added.

At the other end of the scale – the Caprilli style jumping – you would expect riders to work their horses a lot in canter in forward seat and ask their horses to lower, and to some degree round, their necks, thus allowing the hocks to come under the body ready for a correct bascule over the fence.

The traditional European schools like to turn their riders out to a certain pattern. But, of course, so often the really brilliant rider is an individualist and, although he may have had his basic training at a particular school, he later launches out and develops a style of his own. These people are very hard to copy. Many of the English jumping riders are very individual in their ideas and so there is a considerable variation of style between them. This suits the British temperament, and as varied types of horses are used, methods have to vary a little to get the best out of these horses.

The fact that techniques are so varied is part of the fascination of equestrianism.

Dressage in Schooling

by Sylvia Stanier

Dressage, for many trainers, has a big place in the schooling of horses. The word dressage is frequently misunderstood. In the original French, *dresser* means to raise which, translated into horse language, would mean to lighten the forehand. In the world of the 18th-century trainer de la Guerinière this definition was good sense because of the type of horse then used – the Andalusian. (The use of the Andalusian is one reason why most gentlemen riders were interested in collected riding.) With the coming of the faster-moving era of the 19th century, the Thoroughbred horse became fashionable to ride and the likes of James Fillis began to exhibit them in France at the circus. At that time the circus was the only place where the private or civilian rider could show off his horses. Most of the other trained horses belonged to the cavalry and were not therefore for public display. But 19th-century circus riding was somewhat different from the present day exhibitions which really come under the heading of tricks. They are, of course no part of dressage proper.

Fillis's book on dressage training is still a classic on the art. Yet it was François Baucher, who lived a little earlier than Fillis (at the beginning of the 18th century) who, starting out on the Andalusian, the over-collected, high-stepping horse of the Renaissance, changed over to the Thoroughbred.

In modern dressage the first thing to study is a programme of systematic schooling exercises. After the horse has been broken-in (see page 81) the trainer is always looking to improve the natural paces, once the rider disrupts things by being in the saddle. So if one regards dressage as the gymnastic schooling of the horse, then it is a matter of sorting out the sequence of exercises and carrying them out. Of course, it is not quite so easy as that, particularly with British horses which carry a lot of Thoroughbred blood. Thoroughbred blood means quickness, but also lack of concentration and little margin for error on the trainer's part. Nevertheless, all horses can be improved in gymnastic work at a level consistent with their ability. It is rather like physiotherapy: you cannot suddenly make a muscle do something it has never done before.

With dressage, what we are really talking about is the physical training of a horse in order to improve performance. It also involves training the rider. The rider at the highest level must have complete control of temper, muscles and reflexes. The horse, being the willing creature it is, will then respond to the degree we expect. So how do we go about achieving this?

The stages in dressage are first the Basic Training level which includes the Preliminary Dressage test and on up to the Three Day Event level; then we move into the more advanced level of Medium Tests, then on to the Prix St Georges, with the final stage being the Intermediate and Grand Prix of Olympic standard. To arrive at Intermediate and Olympic standard requires at least four to six years' training for the horse and much ability and patience from horse, rider and trainer.

There are now a variety of types of pace. These are included in the "repertoire", bringing the tests and the levels of training into line. Nowadays, top-class trainers are less available and certainly more expensive than ever before, so more people are inclined to do their training at home. So the tests they are asked to perform are in some respects training tests designed to help the horse on the road to higher things. Dressage tests should never be thought of as an end in themselves – certainly not until the Grand Prix – but rather as milestones in schooling.

For horses of first year's training after the breaking-in period, one is looking for the Working Paces. These are simply the beginning of balance, rhythm and forward movement with the horse on the bit. It involves tracking up correctly and, in the old-fashioned parlance, showing a good swinging back. In fact the horse will be moving as one unit all through, with the back slightly rounded and the whole outline perhaps on the long, low side, but well co-ordinated. The pace will not be hurried, yet show good activity. These Working Paces are the basis of all good gymnastic training. The criteria are that the hind feet shall place themselves into the foot-print of the front feet but with the important proviso that the shoulders and front feet are moving well forwards. What is required of the horse is to work all his muscles.

The phrase "on the bit" is often misunderstood in the context of how the horse takes the bit. What it means is that the horse should accept the bit, but not lean on it or try to drop it. To do this he needs to have a supple jaw. One should look for this suppleness and acceptance with the horse's mouth gently closed, not clamped shut or wide open. There should also be a little froth showing at the sides of his lips which shows that he is working the bit quietly. These points, plus the correct paces, rhythm and swing of the back all go towards developing a nice working pace both on straight lines and large circles of at least 20 metres (65 feet).

The trot is the pace at which the horse actually works, but to introduce him to some new movement or position it is often best to do so at the walk. The canter comes later, although this pace often makes the horse use muscles he would not otherwise use – and this helps when returning to the trot. The walk is a difficult pace; it is slow and the horse has a tendency to lose balance and either run or get behind the aids.

Having to some extent established the Working Paces during the first year's training, the horse should be fairly familiar with circles, changes of rein and possibly large loops at serpentine. These are the very beginning of the introduction of lateral suppleness. We start with the forward impulsion on straight lines and then introduce the lateral bends, first of all on a large circle of about 20 metres (65 feet) and being sure that the hind feet follow correctly in the track of the forefeet. Over a period of time, these circles can be reduced. In the top degree of schooling a really supple horse can perform a "volte", a circle of eight metres (26 feet). But the horse needs great elasticity to perform such a movement gracefully. This in itself is a good illustration of the object of dressage – to improve the horse's abilities and to bring out and develop his work.

If training is made easier for the horse, he should last longer. By a slow mental build-up and gradual gymnastic development the result could be a long-lasting animal which is supremely good at his work. Two good examples of such training are the stallions used at the Spanish School in Vienna who often go on working easily well into their twenties; and the horses used by Mounted Police forces in Britain. These horses go through a slow and patient training and offer continual work for years. The whole object of the cavalry training was really to produce horses that remained economically useful for as long as possible.

One of the things that is often done in error is to fix or place a horse's head as a priority of dressage training. The French have a word – *ramener* – which means the preliminary placing of the horse's head. This word, analysed in context with the parts of training, really means the acceptance of the bit by the horse plus a suppleness of his jaw, and not the absolute fixing of the whole head into a certain position. If you look at the highly schooled dressage horses, it is their necks that take

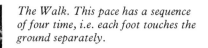

The Walk. This pace has a sequence of four time, i.e. each foot touches the ground separately.

The Trot. A pace of two time – when the horse has a hind and a foreleg off the ground at the same time – the two limbs involved are each on opposite sides of the horse.

The Canter. A pace of three time, in which the limbs come off the ground and touch it with a distinct three time beat.

A horse coming round a corner; influenced by the rider's position and aids to curve his body in the direction of the circle.

on a higher and therefore different position; their heads are in a reasonable position on the neck with a nice flexed poll and soft jaw. If you place the horse's head without organising where his hind legs go and how his back moves (swings), then the training will be limited in scope and may even be harmful. A horse's vertebrae work by being interlinked and swivelling within each other. If the horse swings his back with a rounded outline, these vertebrae have more room to move freely; whereas if the back is hollow, they are inclined to become restricted and can pinch nerves. With a hollow back the horse's hind feet are away behind the body and so not in position to carry weight evenly for good balance or thrust. So development of the back is of supreme importance.

Rhythm, allowing the horse to stretch his neck forwards into the bit, and the rider sitting softly in balance help develop the horse's back.

The proper establishment of the Working Paces, with nice transitions both upwards and downwards on straight lines and with the next movements as large circles (not less than 20 metres, 65 feet) are the Preliminary requirements. Then come the changes of pace, from *working* into *medium*, the more energetic and more developed pace that prepares for the *collected* and *fully extended* paces of the advanced levels.

Lateral work

Lateral work – often referred to as Work on Two Tracks – is also used to supple the horse's muscles, bringing more elasticity and balance. In fact lateral work covers much more than work simply on two tracks. General Decarpentry named the circle as the first lateral movement. It actually requires the horse's feet to follow a single track. The *shoulder-in* in its preliminary form is performed on three tracks. *Leg yielding* is often used as the basis of lateral work, and that again can be performed in various degrees of difficulty, aimed at suppling either shoulders or quarters and asking the horse to move away from the rider's inside leg. The best known of the lateral movements is possibly the *half-pass*, which is the most advanced of the lateral movements. It can be performed at either walk, trot, or canter, and if you have a horse with enough ability and training the half-pass can be performed in passage too. For ordinary purposes the half-pass is usually carried out in the trot, although as a Preliminary it may be taught via the walk.

The real criterion of the half-pass is that it is a collected movement and therefore ought only to be introduced when the horse is ready for some collection (usually at about 18 months or two years training). But trainers differ on this timing. In the half-pass the horse should be very well balanced, able to show a nice crossing over of both the hind and front legs; rhythm is also important; and the rider should just be able to see the eyelashes on the side of the horse's head in the direction of movement. This is an elegant movement when well performed – and a very uncomfortable one when poorly executed. The aids for this movement are diagonal, as opposed to the lateral aids used for leg yielding and shoulder-in.

These are just some of the basic exercises – and it is well to stress *some* – which are used in the dressage training of any horse. It will be seen that in the training of any horse there are several areas which ought to be pin-pointed. They are the patience and common sense required to produce and look after the young horse, followed by the breaking-in period, in which one gains control of the horse and rides him. Once these things are established, then the so-called dressage schooling proper can start. Dressage should be regarded as the gymnastic training which goes towards the better performance of a horse as well as prolonging his working life. So dressage exercises take a high place in schooling.

Remember that, above all, in the training of any horse or pony a love and understanding of animals is a real necessity. It is not what you do that counts in the end, but how you do it.

Continental Dressage riders parading at a Horse Show. Note the distinct and deep position of the leading rider.

Learning to Jump

by Julie Richardson

It is not natural for horses to jump. Horses jump because they are trained to do so. A youngster running loose in a field will go round a fence rather than jump it – and so will many older horses.

But if the horse is obedient to early training on the flat, there is no reason why he should not then be obedient to training over fences, provided common sense and sympathy are used. A lot of good horsemanship is done on the ground and nowhere near a horse. It is in the head and involves being always one step ahead, thinking out what you want and planning the best way of achieving it with your particular horse.

There is no reason for jumping to be something out of the ordinary. It should not be treated as a separate stage in the life of a young horse, but as part of his overall education. A rider who becomes tense at the thought of jumping and rides accordingly will soon have a horse that does the same.

An oval jumping lane is better than a straight one, because it will help to stop him rushing. It is better, for this reason, to school mainly on a curve; it will also help to supple him. Also, work him on both reins to develop the muscles equally and avoid giving him a hard side.

Start loose jumping, lungeing and long-reining with no fences up. Get the horse going calmly and then introduce a low fence. Make it a solid, heavy round pole with a ground line. Flimsy poles throughout training encourage careless jumping and only the most chicken-hearted horse will continue to clear fences that do not hurt when he knocks them. A ground line is essential because the horse judges the height he must clear by measuring from the ground to the top of the fence. If there is no ground line, it is difficult for him to gauge the height. If he is jumping well he will look down at the fence, slightly lowering his head. This is one of the reasons why a horse who approaches a fence with his head in the air is quite likely to knock it down, particularly if it is an upright. Always use round poles to begin with. Flat-edged poles will hurt his legs more if he knocks them.

When he is going calmly, raise the fences as necessary, but make sure you also include a spread, say from about two feet to four and a half feet ($\frac{1}{2}$m to $1\frac{1}{2}$m) wide. This will teach him to bascule over fences from the start.

Before beginning, the horse should physically obey the aids, be obedient and have well-developed muscles. More, he should be calm and relaxed and in an attentive and observant frame of mind. Horses learn quickly and forget little; this works both ways. For while they will not forget a good lesson, well taught, neither will they forget a bad, ill-tempered one. If you help a horse to jump quietly and calmly, you will be well rewarded.

To achieve this, the horse must be started correctly from the beginning. (Whether you are leading him in from the field or lungeing him or, later, riding him.) From his earliest stages in training he should be walked over poles and through shallow water.

Loose jumping and lungeing and long-reining over fences will improve the horse's natural balance and obedience, give him confidence and teach him to be athletic and to move forward freely. Loose jumping is also a lot of fun for a young horse, but accidents can happen so it is far better to take the trouble to use brushing boots or bandages all round and over-reach boots in front, to avoid injury to his legs. Contrary to the opinion of many, boots will not make the horse

careless – he will still feel any knock to his legs – but they will protect him from injury that could put back his training by a few weeks at least. Using a saddle with a breastplate and surcingle to prevent it flapping, but no stirrups, will get the animal used to jumping with tack on. A headcollar can be used. If you are using a bridle, fit it with a breaking bit – one with keys – but no reins.

Walking poles. Use a forward seat, allowing the horse enough rein to stretch his neck and achieve the balance aimed at in this gymnastic exercise.

In long-reining, particularly, make sure you are capable on the flat before you ask the horse to jump, or it will be easy to get him tangled in the reins and frighten him. When jumping, always have the inside long-rein coming directly to hand and not through the stirrup iron, as normal. This will allow him more freedom to stretch both his head and neck.

Cavaletti and grid work

Start riding your horse over fences as if he has never jumped before. He has your weight to contend with now and there is no one on the ground to give him moral support!

Begin with a single pole on the ground and, when he is walking quietly over it, add on one at a time until you have five or six. Lengthen them to trotting distances and ride over them again, using a forward seat, with a light contact on the reins but no backward pull at all. He will probably be clumsy and trip up. Be patient; gradually his balance and rhythm will improve.

In any of this work, do not ride monotonously round and round over the poles or turn at the end of the line and go back. Keeping a forward rhythm, take him over the poles and then school in circles elsewhere in the field, particularly if he gets upset; or school around the poles, crossing between them, changing rein and varying the angle of approach. You need not start from the beginning of the line, but can trot over your grid (sequence of poles) when the circle you are riding meets it. Never think that because you are having a jumping session,

you can jump only. You will have a calmer, more obedient animal if you keep him thinking about what you want him to do next, and not allow him to anticipate it.

A word here, too, about impulsion. Do not mistake speed for impulsion. The horse should, of course, still be moving freely forward, but impulsion means that this forward energy is controlled. This will enable the horse to jump easily off his hocks, rather than rushing unbalanced to a fence and either making a bad jump off his forehand – and usually then not getting the height – or stopping. A horse's impulsion is increased by strong use of the back and seat and this neither shortens his stride, nor increases his speed. If he should ever stop at any fence, remember that the time to hit him is straight away, not when you have already turned away from the fence. If it is low enough, or can easily be knocked down, make him either take it from a standstill or walk over it. Do not allow stopping to continue. Find out the reasons for it and put an end to them.

Introduce cavaletti to the grid singly, keeping them low so he will first walk and then trot over them, at the correct distances. A couple placed at the diagonal and in other parts of the field are good variations.

School over cavaletti, grids and other small fences by using a forward seat position. Sitting and rising trots over them distribute the rider's weight wrongly, the body starting upright and then bending suddenly forward. This immediately unbalances the horse on to his forehand. Also, do not sit back in the saddle during the landing stage. It disturbs the horse's balance and can cause jumping faults with the hind legs.

When the horse is going calmly and fluidly over the grid, you can begin to ask him to make a proper jump. Have a raised cavaletto, complete with ground line, about three yards (3m) away from the last trotting pole. Add more as you go along. Do not discard the grid. Grids steady a horse and build up his approach to a fence by condensing him, keeping him level and creating a rhythm and slight elevation. They

Top: Cavaletti work. The cavaletti are here adjusted for the canter stride. The last cavaletti will gradually built up to become a single fence.

Above: When taking the first single fence, do not discard the grid. Adjust it so that the horse always meets the fence right and therefore gains confidence.

also teach him to go forward into his fences and not hang back. Do not rush your cavaletti and grid work. It is the basis of all jumping and should last about three months.

First fences

You can now go on to jump single fences, preferably keeping the grid to begin with and varying the fence or fences behind. Adjusting the spreads of these rather than the height will make the horse jump roundly. It is a good time now to introduce coloured poles, always using ground lines and filling in the spaces between them and the top poles, which will make the fences more inviting and the horse use himself more. You can now put two or three fences after the grid – for instance, a low three foot by three foot parallel (1m by 1m), followed by an upright, followed by another parallel or crossed poles. Crossed poles are an excellent school because they lead a horse's eye to the centre of the fence, the place where he should be jumping.

When starting to canter into fences without a cavaletto or a grid in front, it is a good idea to canter a few circles round the fence until you feel that he is balanced. Then straighten him up and pop him over. It is much easier for him, and less fuss, than attempting to make him adjust his stride at this stage.

It is worthwhile to note that it can take as much as 40 yards (36.5m) before a young horse can balance himself after a fence. So, if he seems to be accelerating on landing, do not pull back at him, but wait. As he gets back in balance you will feel him also slow down. As his work progresses, so will this balancing time shorten. If you start by pulling on his mouth, he will begin to associate this pain with jumping and will also pull back. This leads to all sorts of problems that are completely unnecessary.

Remember never to move too quickly on to another stage of training. Be sure that he is happy with what has gone before. If he does not feel secure now, it will come out as stops and nappiness later.

When all before has been mastered it is time to adjust the stride at the canter. You can, over small fences, get away with not doing so, especially if the horse is bold and has a lot of ability and can jump himself out of trouble. But leaving him to it can badly frighten him if he makes a mistake and lands in the middle of a big fence because he has stood too far off. And he could fall if he attempts to do this over a fixed fence such as those in a British Horse Society Horse Trial.

Practice for jumping a complete course can be achieved by using two or three fences at home. Space the fences differently so that you will have to ask for both extended and shortened strides. If you have the horse on the bit and ask for a series of half-halts, it will be easy for him

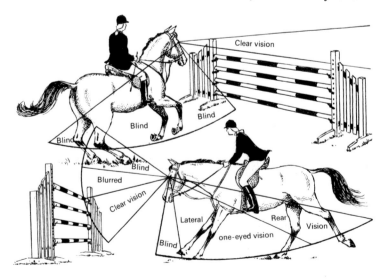

Upper: Head up four feet (1 metre) from the jump.
Lower: Head carried low on the approach to the jump.
The horse's vision is such that he can only see the groundline when his head is lowered. When the horse jumps his head is upright, so the horse has had to lower his head on the approach to assess the jump. Because of this need to move his head freely, it is important that the rider does not restrict the horse if he is to clear the jump.

Typical fences at a novice Show Jumping event. From the top: a wall and rails; a spread; a rustic gate; a combination of upright jumps; and parallel bars.

to produce either of the strides, either by checking or by pushing on. Make the stride tests easy at first, then more complicated – but always at the end of a lesson go back to something that he knows and does well. In the same way, if you come out and he jumps as well as you can expect him to, that is the time to finish, even if he has jumped only three times. To go on invites mistakes, which then have to be corrected before the session ends. He will also learn by this that good behaviour has quick rewards.

Types of fences

Although course builders spend hours planning and preparing varieties of fences, in both show jumping and cross country, there are really only four types of fence – the upright, the spread, the parallel and the hog's back.

Uprights are probably the hardest of all single fences to jump. To clear a three-foot upright, the horse has a take-off range of anywhere from three feet (1m) from the fence bottom to nine feet (3m). But as the fence gets bigger, so does the take-off range get proportionately smaller.

To jump a big upright successfully requires great impulsion and precision. You must be able to lengthen or shorten the stride to put the horse exactly on the take-off target. It is preferable, especially with a horse that is inclined to be on the forehand, to shorten the stride into an upright to keep him back on his hocks. If he is on his forehand, he is likely to hit the fence on the way up.

Spreads can be ridden as uprights up to a spread of four foot (1.5m). The natural parabola of the jump will take him over. A wider jump than this needs more impulsion – not speed – generated by the back, seat and legs, and more precision. Above all with a young horse, do not allow him to take off too early. He would get a nasty, damaging shock at a bigger fence if he could not make the distance and fell into it.

In novice competitions, it is best if the wall is built with "wings". Even when the wall is low the horse should, as with all jumps, be allowed maximum use of its neck.

Jumping a low spread is a good school, teaching a horse to bascule and develop good style. Test the horse by making the fence wider, not always higher.

You will probably find that a young horse will jump bigger than necessary when first asked to take a spread. Be prepared and do not get left behind the movement – even if it means using a neck strap.

Combinations – doubles and trebles combining any of the four types of fence – are a real test of how well a horse has been schooled to jump. Refusals usually come from a bad balance between speed and impulsion, resulting in bad strides. So the most important thing is to jump the first part correctly, bearing in mind what is to follow. Should the horse lose impulsion before the first part, he may still clear it but he will land slightly too far from the second element and need pushing on in the middle to regain enough impulsion to reach the next fence and jump properly.

The opposite is true if the horse flattens over the first part after a too-fast approach. Always approach combinations straight, and not on an angle, which alters the stride that has been allowed. Do not ride in on a circle either for that will encourage running out. Horses, creatures of habit as they are, usually run out to the left.

The easiest combination to jump is one that has a spread fence as the first element, letting the horse jump in with enough impulsion to be then either hooked back or pushed on to the next.

If there is a vertical start to the combination, you will arrive to face the second part with less forward movement. If you bring your weight slightly farther back than usual, it will lighten his forehand to help him take it cleanly.

Water is in a class of its own. Horses have the idea from birth that holes in the ground – wet or not – are horse-traps. And this tendency to take a good, suspicious look at water encourages them either to stop, or to make a bad corkscrew-type jump. Begin teaching the young horse by taking him over a small, dry ditch, preferably with a pole above it. Ride at it hard – but not fast – and use a strong seat, keeping a firm contact with his mouth in case he tries to run out. The aim is to jump *high* and not just wide. You want stronger, longer strides, ending in at least one shorter, bouncy stride to get the height. Galloping at the fence makes the horse flatten. He is therefore unable to get height by rounding over the water and he will probably land in it. Aim to take off as near to the front tape as possible. Water jumping is another time when it is strongly advised to use brushing and over-reach boots.

Fred Walsh jumping clear over the third element of a combination.

It is easy to talk about "seeing a stride". A good horseman will also make it look easy. But it is something that needs working out – and not really on a novice horse. If you keep getting a young horse wrong at his fences so that he hits himself or gets pulled in the mouth as he screws over, unless he is very stupid he will decide jumping is painful and not for him. A talented horse may be able to get you out of trouble – but he may not be willing to do so for long.

Your first show
The first show in which you ask your young horse to compete is a vital stage in his development, and it should be well thought out.

It is advisable to have already taken him out to shows without actually participating in any competition, simply to allow him to get used to travelling and to the novelty of the showground. He may play up and it is far better to let him get this out of his system before you ask for total obedience in the ring.

The actual build of the show-jumping fences must weigh considerably in your decision to go to any particular show. Do not make the mistake of thinking that a small unaffiliated show using small fences will be a better school. These shows often build fences with flimsy and easily knocked down poles, have haphazard and unrelated spacing between the combination elements and have badly designed courses. There may also not be room for you to school quietly before your round; nothing will upset him more than a melée of animals rushing backwards and forwards about him.

You may be wiser to become a member of the national organisation, the British Showjumping Association and to stick to those shows affiliated to it. For instance, in a Wing Newcomers class – the one with the smallest fences for seniors at an affiliated show – the course will be properly constructed and range from 3 feet 3 inches (1m) to 3 feet 6 inches (1.1m) in the preliminary rounds.

On the day of your horse's first show, a plan of the course, stating the speed allowed, will have been posted in the collecting ring. Use it, noting any sharp turns or anything that may either unbalance him or cause difficulties.

Walk the course. That does not mean walk the fences, but the whole "track" – the route to be taken – taking note of the amount of space that is in the arena for you to use. You will want to know exactly how you are going to jump each fence before you start. You will have enough to do later, trying to translate that into action on a probably excited and wide-eyed young horse.

Check the distances between combination fences and from the place where you will turn to come in to the water, if there is one. Calculate how many strides that means to your particular horse. Try to imagine the aim of the course builder. A solitary hanging gate in a lonely end of the arena may look simple, but be warned that it will probably be the most difficult fence on the course.

The time needed to warm up before your round depends entirely upon the individual animal. It will do little good if you then have to stand around waiting to be called into the ring, so time it so that you are ready to jump as the person before you begins their round – a round takes an average of two minutes to complete. Do not overjump the practice fence so that the horse gets stale. Six or seven times is enough to have him going smoothly and the fence need not be high – certainly not higher than those in the ring.

Entering the ring

When you enter the ring, ride off on the opposite rein to that on which the first fence will be, then make a smooth change of rein before the bell to start. It may sound pedantic and unnecessary, but wait for the bell or horn. Starting before means elimination, as many have found to their cost. Once the bell has been rung, you have 45 seconds to begin. Wherever you are in the ring, do not abruptly turn and head for the start. The horse will soon learn his cue and start doing it for you.

A word about finishing a round: it is a terrible practice to ride straight through the finishing line and out of the ring exit. If you do this (when a fence takes you past the exit,) you are asking for the horse to whip round and cart you off through it. Cantering into the collecting ring is also highly dangerous both for you and for everyone else. Ride through the finish, turn in the opposite direction, slow down and walk.

Once the young horse has begun to compete regularly, the need to jump at home becomes precisely that – need. If he is making mistakes, correct them (mistakes in finding the right take-off point can be corrected by unmounted practice in a jumping lane). If not, then jump him as little as possible. Now he really needs to go on to more advanced dressage work – which will of necessity improve his jumping – and hacking to strengthen his legs and develop his muscles.

A major part of jumping – and riding in general – is to be *positive*. Know what you want and be quick to realise when you get it. Remember that you have the distinct advantage over your horse of knowing what you are asking him for. Unless you tell him clearly, he cannot hope to oblige.

When people speak of "forward riding" it does not mean riding with your nose sticking out one way and your seat the other. It simply means using your seat, back and legs clearly and putting the horse in no doubt that you mean business – forward business.

You need to be determined and disciplined – and, at times, courageous. Even a bold, kind horse, when saddled with a weak, hesitant rider will sooner or later either become hesitant, or so unmanageable that he is a menace to his rider and himself, through no fault of his own.

Carol Harrison (New Zealand) on Topic jumping at Lexington in 1978.

Alvin Schokemohle (West Germany) winning the Butlins Championship at the 1976 Horse of the Year Show.

Show Jumping in Australia

by E. A. Weiss

Show jumping under FEI rules was introduced to Australia in 1951, under the direction of the Equestrian Federation of Australia, (EFA), formed in 1950. Slow progress was made initially in persuading the majority of State and regional shows either to adopt the rules or stage events under them. A basic problem was the layout and construction of suitable courses. The older style jumping events had used a variety of jumps, and there were no standards for either these or the judges to follow. This lack of uniformity led to controversy, and arguments between competitors and officials. The first course built to the "new" rules, then known as Olympic Jumping, caused consternation, with riders and owners threatening to go on strike rather than jump them! Experience told in the end, and course builders, riders and owners accepted the new, uniform regulations.

When Melbourne was awarded the 1956 Olympic Games, this gave a great impetus to EFA standards, and events under their rules were staged at all major and State shows. However, due to the Australian

Jeff McVean (Australia) on D'Inzeo jumping in Australia.

Federal Government's strict rules regarding the importation of horses, the equestrian events could not take place in Melbourne, and were awarded to Stockholm, Sweden. Australia sent only one entry. Dumbell ridden by Bert Jacobs, who was unplaced. But Dumbell was later sold to an English owner, and ridden by Ted Williams.

It was to be 1964 before Australia entered an Olympic Team, in Tokyo, finishing seventh. Individual riders have, however, consistently proved better performers than the team collectively, winning medals in many events. During 1976–77 the EFA sponsored teams of four young riders to compete in the jumping events of the Official International Teams Events in the USA. In 1976 the Australian team won both team and individual events, and was placed and won individual medals in 1977.

During the last few years the EFA has introduced a national grading system, which has greatly assisted in the administration of show jumping.

That Australian horses and riders are equal to any show jumpers in the world was demonstrated in August 1978, at the Royal International Horse Show at Wembley, London. Jeff McVean riding Claret won the King George V Gold Cup, and Di Dawson was beaten into second place by only half a second in the equally prestigious Queen Elizabeth Cup. Interestingly, neither of the horses used by the two riders proved particularly impressive in Australia, probably due to the differences in the type and layout of the courses.

Show jumping at all levels is flourishing in Australia as never before. There are some 2,000 registered and graded horses in the State of Victoria alone, and many thousands more in the other States.

One basic difference between competing in shows in Britain or Europe and Australia is distance. Distance to the shows, and distance between shows. It is possible in Britain to compete in London one day and Edinburgh the next. But to compete in Sydney, then in Perth entails a journey of 2,000 miles (3,200km). One local enthusiast works hard on his property until late on Friday night, regularly drives an average of 150 miles (240km) to a show on Saturday, then the same distance home on Sunday morning. Not on nice smooth tarmac, but over outback roads rough and potholed or thick with mud. All this severely restricts the opportunities for competing against other top-class riders and horses, either nationally or internationally. Such experience is essential to establish confidence and improve ability, and allow selection of teams for overseas competition. However, all local shows have jumping events, and such is the enthusiasm at all ages and levels of experience that most are over filled. For show secretaries they are a boon. With an entry fee of A$5 to A$10 (£3 to £7) according to grade, there may be between 60 and 80 entries per class.

Australia's relatively mild climate in the south, and semi-tropical and tropical north, allow shows to be staged throughout the year. There is one practically every week-end, and several a week during the school summer holidays in January and February. Many will be very local or pony club events, similar to any village gymkhana.

The surroundings are very different. In the south the rolling hills and blue gums round the paddocks holding the show, contrasts with the burnt brown grass, dust and flies of Queensland. Yellow crested cockatoos and bright red and green rosellas flash among the dull greeny-blue of the gums. Yellow-legged mynas hop cheekily round the refreshment tent, and the crow-sized magpies miss no chance to steal the unguarded sandwich or pie! The jumping itself is best described as brilliantly erratic, for everyone has a go on mounts of all shapes and sizes. It is a day out for all, and not taken at all seriously as are the well organised events under recognised rules and judges.

Although the horse no longer reigns supreme in the outback, where jackeroos now use motorcycles and helicopters for mustering, there is no lack of enthusiasm for show jumping, eventing and endurance riding. The future looks good.

Above: Bruce Davidson (USA) on Might Tango at Lexington in 1978.

Right: Juliet Bishop (Canada) on Sumatra at Lexington in 1978.

Part Four:
Care of the Horse

The Stable-kept Horse
The Grass-kept Horse
Feeding and Watering
Grooming
The Horse's Feet
Clipping and Trimming
Rugs, Bandages and Clothing
Travelling

Top: Grass-kept horses need some
form of shelter to protect them from
the flies on a hot day.

Above: Catching your horse can
sometimes be a problem. Entice him
with a bowl of oats.

Right, top: Horses in the stable yard
quickly become bored, so they should
be able to see what is going on outside.

Right: Dressed for travelling.

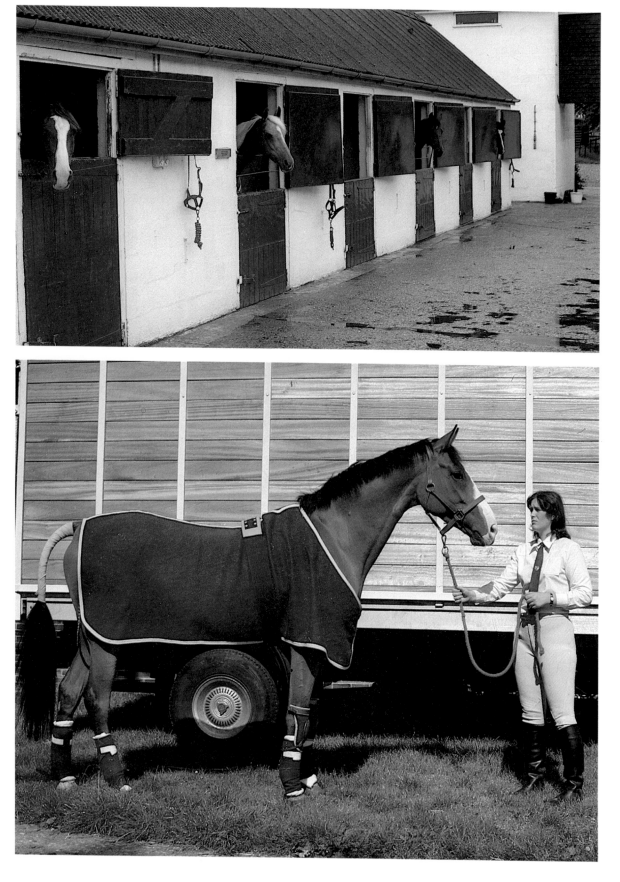

The Stable-kept Horse

by Jennifer Baker

The ball, known as a log, and rope is used to tie up stall-kept horses. It gives some freedom of movement and enables the horse to lie down without difficulty.

The decision to keep a horse or pony stabled is not one that should be taken lightly and without giving the matter great thought. Ponies with the exception of the very well bred ones, or those whose owners require them to be kept at peak fitness, are on the whole happier, healthier and more contented living out. A lot of horses, too, particularly the more plebeian varieties not doing a great deal of work, will live out quite happily either for the whole or part of the year. But if circumstances in the form of facilities, time and money permit, and the horse is in regular work, keeping a horse stabled does have numerous advantages.

Certainly the horse can be kept fitter, and therefore able to work regularly as opposed to being exercised, if he is stabled provided that regular exercise related to energy food is available. The horse can, of course, be clipped out for the winter season and so maintain condition while working. All horses and ponies in hard work (that is hunting regularly, showing, competing in cross-country events, show jumping, long distance rides and so on) will need to be stabled for at least part of the time. Also, of course, the problems involved in catching up a wet, muddy unco-operative animal in the pouring rain are avoided. However, the stabled horse requires a great deal of attention in the way of mucking out, bedding down, grooming, feeding at the very least twice a day, watering, and exercising for at least an hour a day. These duties have to be performed every day and not just when it is convenient, if he is to be kept happy, healthy and fit.

It is unnatural for horses to live confined to their boxes for the greater part of each day instead of grazing freely with other horses. For a horse to learn to adapt to being stable-kept he must be treated firmly but with kindness and understanding.

Combatting boredom

Boredom is one of the greatest enemies of the stabled horse. This can be combatted to a large degree if the horse is kept on the combined system, that is being kept stabled at night and turned out for a few hours each day in a paddock. Apart from benefitting from the odd bite of grass, especially in the spring, this period of freedom gives him the opportunity to relax and unwind which he will need to be able to do, particularly if he is being "kept up" for regular competition work.

The degree and type of fitness required depends upon the activities to be undertaken. The hunting horse, for instance, needs to be able to go all day but does not necessarily need to possess a fast turn of speed since sustained effort is what is required. The same applies to a horse required for long distance riding where he may be expected to cover anything up to 50 miles (80km) a day at a minimum average speed of 6 or 7 mph (10 or 11kph). The event horse, on the other hand, will need to be fit enough to gallop four miles (6.5km) and jump perhaps 30 cross-country fences in the fastest possible time, so here speed as well as stamina has to be considered. Dressage, show and show-jumping horses, other than those "doing the circuit", when they need to be mentally as well as physically resilient and conditioned to withstand the rigours (and boredom) of continual ring competition and the constant travelling involved, do not need to be so fit. But if they are in too "soft" condition, they will be liable to sprains and strains.

The "ordinary" horse which is ridden for an hour or two each day, perhaps hunts for several days throughout the season, and competes in the odd hunter trial, dressage or show-jumping event at local level, will not need to be "super fit". He will need to be stabled and to receive an energy ration and regular grooming and exercise.

The stabled horse, being unable to wander at large and feed himself, requires food to maintain the correct body temperature and replace natural wastage, to build up condition and to supply energy. So, within reason, the more energy the horse is asked to expend the more energy-producing food he will require, if he is not to lose condition. If he receives too much food without expending any or very little energy, he will become too fat, so a careful balance has to be worked out between food in-put and energy out-put. The principal energy-producing foods (and those which are rich in protein and starch) are oats, barley and maize. As the horse requires a balanced diet, bulk foods such as hay, nuts, and to a degree bran, and auxiliary foods such as bran, grass, carrots, linseed, molassine and the mineral and vitamin supplements now on the market, are also necessary. Most important, there must be a fresh and readily available supply of water without which the horse is unable to digest solid food. A reasonable diet for the stabled horse would consist of oats, preferably rolled or bruised, and bran, which is highly digestible as well as containing a high percentage of salt. If he is a little on the thin side, give him additionally flaked maize, which is heating but which puts on condition, or perhaps, a little boiled barley, which is excellent for putting on weight. Most horses like linseed; it has a very high fat and protein content and so will put on condition and produce a nice shine on the coat. Linseed must be well soaked and boiled before being added to the feed in the normal way, or allowed to cool and be fed as a jelly.

Since in many places crops, and the land growing them, are deficient in one or more of the necessary vitamins or minerals, it is a good idea to add to the feed one of the combined vitamin and mineral supplements, or a seaweed supplement which contains all the necessary trace elements and is particularly rich in protein. Ponies will frequently get too full of themselves if fed oats, and so small amounts of bruised barley, which has a less excitable effect on them, is often fed instead. Horse and Pony nuts, virtually a complete food in themselves (although rather a dull one if fed alone) are also a very useful feed for ponies and horses, especially for those in light work. They are less heating than either oats or barley. Both horses and ponies will benefit from an occasional bran mash, which is usually fed after a day's hunting or competition.

Hay, the largest portion of which should be fed at night, will supply the bulk ration, but it must be of good quality to be of any value. Meadow hay is perfectly adequate for all horses and ponies who are not in really hard work, and is, in any case, much better for ponies, being less heating than seed hay. A mixture of chopped hay and oat straw (chaff) may be added to the ordinary feed ration to supply extra bulk and to ensure that the horse does not "bolt" his food.

To ensure, as far as possible, that this expensive food is actually being utilised by the horse and not being wasted, two important points must be checked regularly: the horse's teeth and the worm situation. If the teeth are allowed to become sharp due to uneven wear, they are likely to cut the mouth or tongue, causing ulcers or, at any rate, considerable discomfort, and poor mastication and digestion will result. So as a matter of routine, the vet should be called in to inspect the teeth annually, and if necessary file them down, after the horse has reached the age of nine.

Regular worming

All domestic equines harbour worms. They are virtually impossible to eliminate entirely. They can be kept down to an acceptable level by administering a worming powder or paste at approximately six-week intervals. This frequency is necessary because the horse can be completely re-infested within eight weeks, particularly if he is grazing for a time with other horses on a small acreage, as one infected horse

The quick-release knot should be used when tying up horses; it can quickly be undone should the horse pull back.

can re-infect the others. The stabled horse can be infected through soiled bedding.

There are three types of worm common to horses; the white worm or ascaris, the red worm and the stomach bot (which is not really a worm but can conveniently be dealt with here). Of these the white worm is the most common and, being anything up to 10ins. (25cm) in length and the thickness of a pencil, can easily be seen in the droppings. However, by the time they can be seen, they will have become well established and the horse will have lost condition, have a staring coat and possibly bouts of colic, and although harmless in small quantities prevention is better than cure, and regular worming will ensure that the worms do not get a hold.

The red worm is far more dangerous. In severe cases of infestation they can cause death, since the larvae develop in the gut wall and pass through the organs and blood vessels feeding on the blood as they go, and can cause a stoppage of the blood stream. Signs of infestation are anaemia, when the eye membranes will be very pale yellowy-pink, a dry and staring coat, a distended belly, poor condition and diarrhoea. Here again regular worming will prevent the red worm burden getting out of hand.

Stomach bots only usually affect horses at grass when the bot fly lays her small yellow eggs, usually on the horse's forelegs, the horse by licking the affected area transfers the bots to his stomach. They are harmless, however, except in very large quantities (when they will cause lack of condition), and can easily be picked off the legs by hand, or if in large numbers clipped off or removed with a razor blade.

Exercise

Apart from food the other main requirements of the stabled horse are exercise and grooming and so through a combination of these three the horse will reach a state of fitness.

Exercise strengthens and hardens the horse's limbs and tendons, reduces the amount of fat he carries, conditions and tones his muscles and clears his wind. Slow, steady road exercise is a particularly good way to harden the legs and tendons. Not until these are fairly hard and sound can faster work be undertaken, if the tendons are not to suffer strains and sprains. Work up and down hills, especially at a steady trot, is a particularly good way to remove surplus fat and to start to get the wind in order, which a short sharp gallop should clear. Exercise should be progressive, if the horse is unfit or semi-fit, and should start slowly for short periods working up to faster paces of longer duration gradually, until the horse has gained a certain degree of fitness.

The stabled horse must be exercised every day, if he is to maintain his state of fitness and is not to become bored and resort to those stable vices of wind sucking and crib biting to keep himself amused. In both these infuriating habits the horse deliberately gulps and swallows air, in the latter case catching hold of a door, fence or solid object before swallowing. It is very difficult to keep flesh on these horses, and it is almost impossible to cure crib biters and wind suckers once the habit has caught a hold. It is also a habit that tends to be copied by other horses in the stable. If you can turn the horse out in a paddock for the odd hour or so, this will help to overcome the problem of boredom to a large degree.

Clipping is dealt with elsewhere (see page 158), but suffice to say that the stabled horse, who is working during the winter months is usually given a full clip or a hunter clip when the winter coat is "set", usually about October, and he will then probably need clipping again about December.

Stabling

Having decided to keep the horse stabled, either entirely or on the combined system, consideration must be given to suitable accommodation and siting. Ideally, the box should face south so as to be out of the worst of the wind and at the same time catch as much sun as

Horses leaving the stable. Stable-kept horses must be exercised every day if they are to remain fit and healthy.

Stabled horses sometimes develop vices.
Top: Weaving. The horse swings its head from side to side.
Above: Crib-biting. Crib-biters are difficult to keep in condition, since they tend to lose weight.
Both are annoying habits which tend to be copied by horses stabled nearby. Boredom is usually the cause, so horses should be kept happy and occupied as far as possible.

Right: Mucking out should be done first thing in the morning. The droppings and soiled bedding must be removed, and clean straw added to the bed for the following evening.

The largest portion of a horse's hay ration should be given fairly late in the evening.

possible. It should, in addition, be sited so that the horse can see as much as possible of what is going on around him, for instance, not too far away from the house so that he can watch the comings and goings of humans and other animals.

There are a number of firms who specialise in "ready-made" wooden loose box stabling – either individual boxes or a whole row of them including tack and feed rooms. If wooden stabling is used, it should be lined, both for warmth and for added strength. In most cases these firms will lay the concrete base for the box. Loose boxes must be of a good size to enable the horse to move about and get comfortable and to lessen the possibility of him getting cast in his box. If possible the loose box should be 14ft × 12ft (4m × 3.5m) for a horse and 12ft × 10ft (3.5m × 3m) for a pony, although two foot (0.50m) smaller than these sizes is acceptable. It must also be high enough so that plenty of fresh air can circulate freely, the bottom door should be high enough to stop him jumping over it, but low enough for him to be able to put his head over easily. It must also be wide enough, so that there is no danger of him knocking his hips against the sides as he comes in and out of the box. If there is an overhang of the roof over the door so much the better, since he will be able to look out of his box in the rain without getting too wet. Most of the ready-made boxes have roofs made of asbestos sheeting. This is perfectly satisfactory. Another kind of roofing frequently seen, corrugated iron, is not to be recommended since it tends to keep the box hot in summer and cold in winter – the exact opposite of what is wanted. (It also tends to make a great deal of noise when it rains.) There should be two bolts on the bottom half of the door, one at the top and one at the bottom. Two bolts provide extra security but they also discourage the horse who bangs his door for food or attention, since with a bottom bolt the door will not rattle so much. The top door should always be kept open to allow plenty of fresh air into the box. The window should be on the same side of the box as the door, and it should open inwards, being hinged at the bottom rather than the side. One or more bars should be fixed horizontally across the window on the inside so that the horse cannot stick his head through the window. The light switch should be on the outside of the box, so that there is no danger of the horse switching it on or electrocuting himself.

The concrete base of the box should be laid with a shallow slope of about two inches (0.50cm) towards the door, and for preference there should be a drain just outside the box to one side of the door. Any wet from the box can then be swept straight from the box and down the drain. Many older type stables had drains in the middle of the box floor and although they seemed satisfactory enough, there must have been blockage problems. The important thing is that the boxes must be kept clean and regularly mucked out.

Stable fittings

The only fittings necessary in the box are a manger or other container in which to put his food, buckets for water, and a ring screwed fairly high in the wall from which to tie up the haynet and to which to tie the horse when grooming.

A convenient and easily cleaned manger is one of the heavy plastic or polythene variety which fits into the corner of a box and is held in place by a simple bar of wood across the corner. Failing a manger, horses can be fed from bowls on the floor, but these stand more chance of being knocked over and the food spilt.

Unless the very expensive but very useful self-filling water bowls are installed in the stables, rubber or heavy plastic buckets serve as adequate water containers, but they, like the mangers or bowls, must be scrubbed regularly to keep them clean. Some old stables may be fitted with a hay rack on the wall. These racks are not very satisfactory since the hay seeds are likely to fall into the horse's eyes as he cranes his neck to reach the hay. A more satisfactory way of feeding hay is in a haynet which can be suspended from the ring set fairly high in the

The haynet shoud be secured to a ring fairly high on the stable wall.

Far left: Light switches should be outside the stable and high up. This is a special type designed to prevent electrocution should a horse bite it.

Left: Lights should be out of the horse's reach with the wire running up the wall.

The bucket or manger may be fitted to the wall to prevent the horse kicking it over.

wall. If it is hung up too low, there is a danger of the horse catching a foot in it when it is empty.

Having correctly sited the box, consideration must be given to the rest of the facilities required in the yard and their positioning. It is obviously convenient to have the feed room and water supply as near to the rest of the boxes as possible. Inter-locking prefabricated structures for both feed and tack rooms can be obtained to match the boxes. Feed must, of course, be stored in damp-proof and vermin-proof containers, and the heavy duty plastic type of dustbin fills the bill adequately. The other principal consideration must be given to the placing of the muck heap, since it must be in an area not too close to the house, for hygienic reasons, nor too far away to be easily accessible to the stable, and conveniently placed so that it can be collected and removed regularly by the muck man. Hay and straw should be stored under cover and raised off the ground if possible to allow the air to circulate underneath.

With the stable suitably sited and the horse in residence, various routine stable jobs must be undertaken every day, if the horse is to remain happy and healthy. To start the day right the horse will expect his breakfast of oats, bran and whatever else has been selected as regular feed. His bucket must be re-filled with fresh clean water and he must be checked over to see that he has not damaged himself during the night and received any cuts and scratches as a result. In winter his rugs should be removed to give him a quick strapping (brushing over), his mane and tail brushed out and the coat polished off with a stable rubber, and he should have his feet picked out. His rugs should then be replaced.

He must then be mucked out, i.e. the droppings and wet section of his bed sorted out and removed to the muck heap, the dry bedding put on one side while the floor is swept and the clean bedding put back down again. He will then be ready for his daily exercise and will enjoy a ride of a couple of hours round the lanes, along bridle tracks, over the fields or wherever convenient. Since horses get just as bored as humans, he will appreciate a change of route as often as possible. On returning from his ride he will be ready for his lunch, after which he could be turned out in his paddock for a couple of hours before coming in for his afternoon grooming session. While he is out in the paddock it will give you a chance to make his bed.

The most widely used (and probably the best) form of bedding is straw. Choose wheat straw as horses are less likely to eat it than oat or barley straw. But for confirmed bed-eaters, wood shavings, sawdust or peat moss make acceptable alternative forms of bedding. Shavings,

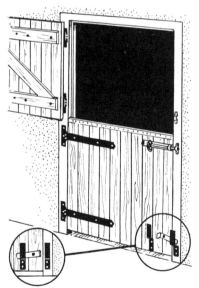

Above: Loose box doors should have two bolts or latches on the bottom door to prevent the horse opening the door himself. The bottom latch can easily be kicked into place by the handler.

however, are not absorbent and sawdust packs hard together when wet and tends to get hot. Peat does not get hot, but wet patches should be removed quickly or they are liable to lead to foot troubles, notably thrush. Peat, too, tends to make the horses dirty and is not to be recommended for greys. All these three beddings are difficult to get rid of and usually have to be burnt.

All beds, regardless of the materials used, must be thick since this encourages the horse to lie down and, if he gets cast in his box, he is not so likely to hurt himself if there is a thick covering over the floor. Also, a nice, clean thick bed gives added warmth especially if built up around the sides of the box to give walls, as they keep out any draughts. The deep litter system is, in fact, a very warm way of bedding horses down because the process involved of removing the droppings and just adding more clean straw on top builds up a considerable amount of heat. This method can work quite effectively if the box is not left for too long without being mucked out properly, and it is a quite useful, time-saving operation if done weekly.

Once the horse has come in, been groomed and had his feed he will be all right for a few hours until he has his hay fairly late in the evening. If he has it too early, he will eat it quickly and be bored for the rest of the night. The largest proportion of his hay ration should be given at this time. His water bucket must be checked to see that it is full and some horses need two buckets to last them through the night. The horse should be checked last thing at night to see that he can be safely left until the morning when the whole procedure starts again.

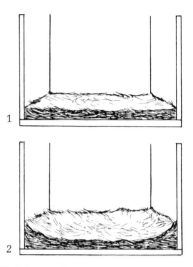

Bedding. 1. Incorrectly laid.
2. Straw should be banked up around the walls of the box to prevent injury to the horse and to make the box more warm and comfortable.

Pile up the clean straw in a corner. Put the dirty bedding into a barrow and take it to the muck heap.

The Grass-kept Horse

by Judith Draper

Many people new to horse ownership imagine that when keeping a horse at grass they are recreating for him his natural environment, one in which he will be able to fend for himself, thrive and be happy without assistance from man. Such an assumption is very wide of the mark for the management of the grass-kept horse or pony is, in many ways, as complex as that of the stabled animal. Of course, the problems and pitfalls are of a rather different nature, but unless measures are taken to avoid them, no horse or pony will remain in good health for very long.

The horse is by nature a nomad and to confine him, be it in a loose box or in several acres of pastureland, is to subject him to the considerable restrictions of domesticity. In the wild he roams freely over wide areas in his constant search for more and better food and his need for natural exercise; by wandering at will he can vary his diet, seek out the most nutritious grazing and by so doing avoid such hazards as mineral deficiencies and excessive worm infestation. When food is plentiful, he can build up his reserves against the leaner months of winter. In the confines of a paddock he is dependent upon man to recognise and make up for the deficiencies that will inevitably occur in his food, in both quantity and quality; and so careful management is essential.

Not only is it unnatural for a horse to be kept in a confined space, it is also unnatural for him to have to work, and a diet of grass does not produce sufficient energy for him to do so. By feeding a carefully balanced diet and giving regular and progressive exercise it is possible to bring a stabled horse to the high degree of fitness required for such sports as hunting, eventing, show jumping and racing. With the grass-kept horse it is impossible to achieve such "hard" condition, partly because grass of itself produces soft condition in horses. Nonetheless a horse kept entirely at grass or one kept on the combined system (that is, out by day, in by night) can, with proper care, be kept reasonably fit, certainly fit enough to go hacking, do a short day's hunting from time to time or compete occasionally at not too ambitious a level at shows or across country.

Horses are kept at grass for various reasons, the most usual one being that of economy – of both time and money. A great many of today's horse-owners have full-time jobs; those who have stabling facilities – and many one-horse owners do not – cannot spare the time to attend to the needs of a stabled horse. Very often, too, the horse will be ridden merely at week-ends and turning him out during the week is the only way to ensure he gets enough exercise.

On the other hand there are horses that are in hard work during many months of the year for a specific purpose – hunters for instance – and they need to be turned out for a few months in the summer to rest and relax. A period of rest may also be prescribed by the vet for a horse that has recently had an illness or injury and cannot be ridden for a while. Then again there are ponies, much hardier creatures than horses, that will generally do better and be more easily managed (an important point if they are to be ridden by the very young) if kept at grass all the year round.

Good sound fences, plenty of fresh water and good grazing are essential if a horse is to live out.

Supplementing food

Whatever the reasons for keeping a horse or pony at grass, there are certain principles which must be observed, the most vital being the need to supplement the food value of grass as and when necessary. Provided it is of good quality and available in sufficient quantity, grass will provide sufficient nutrition for a horse from about April to September (the growth period), provided the horse is not expected to work. At all other times of the year – and sometimes during the summer, too, when grass may become parched during a prolonged dry spell – supplementary food must be given regardless of whether the horse is in work or not. Horses, like humans, vary in their needs, and any guide to feeding can only be approximate, but the following figures can be taken as a rough estimate of the quantities of food intake required daily by animals of various heights: under 12 hands: 14–16lb (6.5–7.5kg); 12–13 hands: 16–18lb (7.5–8.5kg); 13–14 hands: 20–22lb (9–10kg); 14–15 hands: 22–24lb (10–11kg); 15–16 hands: 24–26lb (11–12kg); over 16 hands: 26–28lb (12–13kg).

Supplementary feed will comprise bulk (hay and bran) and energy-giving food (oats, barley, maize, nuts, which also include some bulk, etc.). The proportion of energy and bulk foods given will vary according to the amount of work expected of the horse. A grass-kept horse of, say, 15.2 hands, doing no work during the winter months would do well enough on one small "short" feed daily – 3lb (1.5kg) of oats or nuts plus 1lb (0.50kg) of bran perhaps – provided he has plenty of good quality hay to make up his bulk requirements. The grass during winter time will be too poor to afford him a significant amount of nutriment. On the other hand, should the horse be used for hacking at weekends and perhaps during the week too, the quantity of hay would need to be decreased and replaced with hard feed consisting, perhaps, of 3–4lb (1.5–2kg) oats, 3lb (1.5kg) nuts and 1lb (0.50kg) bran (divided into two feeds) daily. If the horse is to do an occasional half-day's hunting the quantity of energy-giving foods would need to be stepped up still further for a few days prior to the hunting day.

Adjusting to requirements

The only way to know whether the quantities are correct for a particular horse is to keep a close watch on him, his appearance and his behaviour. If he becomes hot and spooky when ridden, then he is having too many oats; if he is sluggish and lazy, his energy food intake must be increased; if he becomes over-fat, he is eating too much; if he is a poor doer and tends to look "ribby", his rations should be increased, and boiled linseed or boiled barley should be fed two or three times a week in addition to his normal feed. Like humans, some horses feel the cold more than others and burn up more of their food ration simply in keeping warm. Their feed must be adjusted accordingly.

There is always the danger of the grass-kept horse or pony (especially the latter) becoming too fat if turned out on lush spring or summer pasture. If he is required to work, some energy-giving food will have to be supplied and since he will already be exceeding his daily bulk needs by gorging himself on grass, any additional food will simply serve to make him even grosser. Not only will the horse become indolent, his health will suffer and there will be the danger of his developing laminitis. Consequently, some method of restricting his grass intake must be devised.

To restrict his grass intake an area of his grazing should be fenced off so that he no longer has free access to limitless quantities of grass. Alternatively, if some poorer quality grazing is available, he should be turned out there for part, at least, of each day. If a stable is available he can also be brought in for a number of hours each day. In hot weather he will appreciate coming in during the day when the flies are at their most troublesome; if it is cold he should be kept in overnight. If he is receiving a ration of energy-giving food this can be fed while he is in and will help relieve boredom. Since prevention is better than cure, a horse with a known tendency to laminitis should have his grass intake carefully restricted as soon as the spring grass comes through.

Remember all horses carry a worm burden and need regular treatment to prevent loss of condition. Grass-kept horses – especially those on small areas – are particularly vulnerable and should be given a worm powder, as supplied by the vet, every two or three months. The commonest worms are the white worm (ascaris) and the dangerous red worm (strongyle) which lay their eggs in the small and large intestines respectively. The eggs are passed out with the droppings, hatch on the pasture and re-enter the horse as he grazes, thus beginning the whole cycle again. The smaller the area of grazing, the more vital it is to remove the droppings regularly to prevent a heavy worm infestation. Larger paddocks are less of a problem since the horse will tend to use the less good patches of growth as a "toilet area", restricting his grazing to the better areas. Nonetheless, care must be taken and droppings cleared whenever possible. Where several horses are grazed together it is useless for some to be wormed and not the others, for the worm-infested animals will quickly re-infect the others.

All grass-kept horses should be visited at least once a day. They should be inspected daily for cuts, abrasions, lumps and bumps; their feet should be cleaned out and their shoes checked or, if they are resting, and have had their shoes removed, should have their feet inspected for cracks. During a long lay-off the feet must, of course, be trimmed regularly by the blacksmith. If a horse is being fed, his hard food should be divided into two feeds, one to be given in the morning, followed by some of his hay ration, and the other in the evening. The bulk of the hay ration should be given after the evening feed. Horses are creatures of habit and appreciate their meals at regular times, so it is advisable to work out a convenient schedule and try to stick to it fairly strictly each day.

Where a stable can be used, the horse may be caught, brought in and fed in the manger. Otherwise, he can be fed in the paddock, either in a manger in a field shelter, if there is one, or on the ground in a galvanised bin or solid box, one deep enough to prevent the horse from spilling his feed over the sides as he eats.

The best and most natural way to feed hay is on the ground. However, horses can be very wasteful, and if quantities of hay are being trampled underfoot and rendered inedible a haynet can be used. When ground feeding a number of horses – and horses should, if possible, be turned out in company with others – one or two extra piles of hay should always be allowed to prevent fighting. A salt lick or lump of rock salt should also be provided and can best be kept in the field shelter.

Fresh water must be constantly available and, if there is no natural supply, must be piped to the field, ideally to a purpose-built water trough with a ballcock for regulating the supply. Ponds are never very satisfactory since they all too often become stagnant, while ditches may be contaminated with harmful household waste. If there is any doubt as to the purity of such water, it is better to fence it off and provide an artificial supply. Where a spring-fed stream flows through the field the problem does not arise and, provided there is safe and easy access, the horse will be able to drink at will. However, care should be taken to note whether, in the summer, there is a danger of the stream drying up. In winter, troughs must be kept free of ice, and care should be taken to see that taps and exposed pipes are adequately lagged. Troughs and other containers should be emptied and cleaned out every week, especially during the autumn when leaves will collect and start to rot.

Unlike the stabled horse, who benefits from thorough grooming and from being clipped, the grass-kept horse needs the accumulated dirt and grease in his coat to keep him warm and dry. So grooming should be kept to a minimum, particularly in winter. For appearance sake the worst of the mud, when dry, can be brushed off with a dandy brush, particularly in the saddle and girth area; the mane and tail can be kept trimmed and neat. In winter, or very wet weather, a horse or pony's heels should be left untrimmed since the hair which nature provides will help protect them from the mud and wet, thereby preventing cracked heels and mud fever.

When riding the grass-kept horse, the same basic rules apply as for the stabled animal. He must always be given time to digest his food – a minimum of 1–1½ hours – before being saddled up. Because of his relatively soft condition, special care must be taken with the fitting of his saddle and girth to eliminate the possibility of galling, and he should be brought back to his field as dry as possible.

If he grows a thick coat and is inclined to sweat up badly when ridden, the possibility of giving him a trace clip and a New Zealand rug should be considered. Excessive sweating will quickly cause loss of condition. At the opposite extreme are the thin-skinned horses, usually the more highly-bred variety, who will suffer badly from the cold if required to live out the year round. If they cannot be brought in overnight, then they too must be fitted with rugs. A well-fitting New Zealand rug will keep a horse warm and dry, but it must be straightened and adjusted night and morning to afford maximum comfort and protection.

Quality of grazing

Ideally, each horse should be allocated a minimum of two to three acres of grazing. While it is possible to keep a horse on less, a paddock of, say, one acre can be considered as no more than an exercise area and will in no way provide any sustenance once the top grass has been grazed off. On the other hand, mere quantity of grazing is not sufficient to ensure a healthy horse. Horses are pernickety feeders and will not thrive on poor scrubby pasture. The quality of grazing will depend on the location, the climate, the type of soil and the types of grass that will flourish in those conditions. With land being at such a premium horse-owners must often make do with second best, but there is no reason why they should not make improvements.

Drainage is an important factor in grassland management, particularly on clay soils. Sand-, chalk- or gravel-based pasture should not present too many problems, being naturally well drained. Nonetheless ditches must be kept clean so that they can do their job properly, and for safety's sake should be fenced off. On the other hand clay-based pasture, which will become waterlogged in wet weather, ideally needs pipe drainage, an expensive business initially, but one which will pay dividends in the long run.

To flourish, grass needs soil containing lime, phosphate, potash and nitrogen. When deficiencies of any or all of these occur, growth will suffer. By having a soil sample taken (through the Agricultural Development Advisory Service or by a good agricultural merchant) it is possible to determine what, if any, deficiencies there are and to decide on a suitable fertilizer. Ordinary farmyard manure, which will correct all deficiencies other than lime, can be applied in the autumn. Liming, when necessary, is best carried out in November. Nitrogen needs to be replaced annually, although an excess will produce growth more suited to hay crops than to grazing. Consequently, a light dressing only of nitrogen fertilizer may be applied in the early spring just as the grass is beginning to grow. Unless the paddock is very small and can be sprayed by hand, it will be necessary to enlist the help of a farmer or contractor. In all cases of fertilizer application, horses must be removed from the pasture for at least three to four weeks, until the rain has thoroughly washed the fertilizer into the soil. If there is no alternative pasture available for this purpose, the paddock must be divided into two or more sections, one portion of it being given over to the horses while the other(s) is being treated. Wire or electric fences can be used for this purpose and, indeed, can be used on a permanent basis to effect a system of rotational grazing. By employing this system portions of pasture can be rested alternately and overgrazing will be avoided.

Where really poor quality grazing is concerned it might be necessary

Be careful that no poisonous plants grow in the fields or hedgerows. These are some of the plants that are dangerous when eaten to excess.

1. *Laburnum*
2. *Ragwort*
3. *Bryony*
4. *Foxglove*
5. *Privet*
6. *Hemlock*
7. *Laurel*

to start afresh by ploughing and re-seeding the entire area. Again advice should be taken as to the most suitable seed mixture to use. It is possible, with correct seeding, harrowing and rolling, to convert really poor grazing into good pasture in about twelve months.

Between periods of grazing in spring, summer and autumn, when the land is not too wet, all grassland will benefit from harrowing (which aerates the soil and removes old, clogging growth) and rolling (which makes the topsoil firm for optimum growth).

Since horses will only graze the best grass, any areas of weeds, nettles, docks, etc., which may be present, will become increasingly well established. One answer is to adopt the mixed grazing method, whereby the horses are removed to another paddock for a few weeks and their grazing is given over to bullocks. The bullocks will graze much more evenly and will also help to reduce worm parasites to which they are immune. Weeds can also be treated with chemical sprays, which are not detrimental to the grass, but again the animals must be removed for at least three weeks or they could be poisoned.

When turning horses out to grass, great care must be taken to ensure that they do not have access to poisonous plants or trees. Horses are particularly vulnerable to yew, laurel, ivy, deadly nightshade and ragwort which can, if eaten in sufficient quantity, prove fatal. Privet, hemlock, rhododendron, laburnum and briony are also poisonous to horses. Poisonous trees must be fenced off so that there is no chance of the horse reaching them and poisonous shrubs and plants should be dug up and burnt outside the paddock.

The paddock must also be checked regularly for anything which could cause injury to the horse: bricks, tins, bottles, stakes, and so on.

Being nomads at heart horses will wander out of their paddocks if they are given half a chance. Safe fences or hedges are therefore essential. Post and rail fencing is ideal but expensive, and it has the one disadvantage of affording no shelter from prevailing winds. Hedged fields are fine, provided the hedges are stout and solid and do not contain poisonous growths. They must be regularly inspected for gaps and where these occur they must be blocked with strong post and rails or wire fencing. Paddocks can be entirely fenced with wire, provided the right type is used. Several strands of the plain heavy gauge variety strung tautly between solid wooden posts should cause no problems, provided the lowest strand is placed at least 1ft (0.3m) above ground level – thus ensuring that the horse cannot get a foot caught over it. Barbed wire should never be used. When building new paddock fences, it is advisable to round the corners, since right-angled corners can be dangerous to horses when galloping about.

Gates must be strong, wooden ones being safer than the metal variety; there is more chance of their breaking in the event of a horse getting his leg between the bars. Safety catches are essential as horses quickly learn how to open things, and if the gate opens on to a road a chain and padlock is a wise investment. The siting of the gate is also important. If possible, a well-drained area of the paddock should be chosen as this will help to prevent the area becoming badly poached in wet weather. Avoid siting gates in corners where horses will crowd round at feed time.

Shelters

Although many horses will ignore a field shelter and stay out in the vilest weather, the provision of some sort of shelter is important, particularly in exposed areas where there are no trees or hedges to act as a windbreak. The shelter will probably be appreciated a good deal in very hot weather when it will serve as a haven from the worst of the flies, and many horses will use one during periods of sleet, snow or driving rain. It should have an open front so that when it is being used by more than one horse there is no danger of one becoming cornered by a bossy companion. For horse-owners with no stabling facilities the shelter will be useful for tying up, grooming and tacking up the horse or pony.

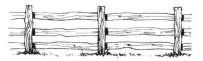
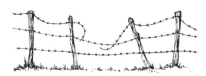

Fences should be made of strong wood. Post and rail (top) is best, though expensive. Loose barbed wire can be extremely dangerous.

A good type of gate-fastening. A chain and padlock will give still greater security in a field.

A shelter is a good idea, particularly in fields lacking trees and tall hedges. It should face away from the prevailing winds and be built on dry well-drained ground. In bad weather the horse can be fed inside so the food remains dry and palatable.

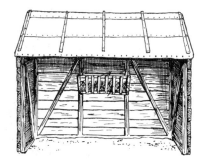

Feeding and Watering

by Elwyn Hartley Edwards

In the feral state the food on which horses and ponies can sustain life comfortably, is provided by various grasses and wild-growing herbs. Obviously, the grazing area has to be large enough to provide food in sufficient quantity, but so long as that is the case the horses can survive the year round. In some instances this is true of the domestic horse or pony, but more usually there is insufficient pasture area available to keep horses in good condition without their being supplied with supplementary rations in winter. Additionally, if the animals are to be used to some degree, a "natural" diet of grass will not provide sufficient energy for the purpose or maintain a satisfactory body condition.

The domestic horse is called upon to perform at speed, sometimes over obstacles and always while carrying weight. Fundamentally, this is an unnatural pursuit for the horse and one for which his natural food is in no way suitable. If, therefore, the horse is to work satisfactorily he must be fed a ration of energising, protein food in the correct quantity and balance and with due regard for a digestive apparatus designed to cope with a diet of soft grass.

Four requirements

Food is used to fulfil four requirements of life:

1. The maintenance of body temperature. 2. Replacement of tissue wastage. 3. The build-up and maintenance of body condition. 4. The supply of energy required for movement and for the internal processes of digestion, circulation, etc.

The first of these two requirements are paramount and, if there is insufficient food for their maintenance, death ensues. It follows that when food is scarce these two requirements will be met at the expense of the others.

In the feral state severe weather and shortage of food would result in the horses losing condition and energy. Conversely, the body condition and the provision of energy would improve with milder weather and a new growth of herbiage.

Exactly the same would apply to the domestic horse that was kept out without being given a supplementary ration during the winter months. Continuing in the rob-Peter-to-pay-Paul analogy, if a horse were to be put into hard work requiring a large energy output without any allowance being made in his diet for the extra expenditure the food available would be used first for the maintenance of body temperature and tissue replacement and then what was left would be used in the interests of energy. Since there would be none left for the body condition, the horse would lose flesh rapidly. Thereafter he would become increasingly weak and in the end, when the temperature fell and the tissue wastage was no longer replaced, the animal would die.

In brief, work which involves an expenditure of energy must be allowed for by an increase in food supplying energy. In other words, *the intake of energy foods must equal the output of energy*, and for perfection the former should be a shade above the latter.

Work, in fact, is at the root of the feeding problem. Horses, out in a field the year round, doing a minimum of work or none at all, present some management problems but their feeding often amounts to nothing much more than the provision of a substantial, but simple, supplementary ration during the winter.

A horse that hunts regularly or is involved in any of the competitive sports is something different. To condition him for the strenuous work expected of him, it is necessary, for ease of management as for much else, that he be stabled, clipped out in winter, fed a high protein diet, groomed, strapped and exercised each day.

The horse's natural diet, of grasses and herbs, play no part in the conditioning process beyond the turning out of the horse for an hour or so each day as a relaxation. In place of the grass a variety of concentrate foods are given, supported by hay (dried grass) which provides the necessary bulk and assists in the digestion of the rich concentrates.

The natural diet, however, achieved a balance between the various ingredients which must, of course, be repeated in the artificial diet fed to the stabled horse, and must be given to him in a manner as nearly related to the natural intake of food as possible.

The food fed to the stabled horse must contain the six prime constituents in proportions suitable to the demands made of the animal. These constituents are: *protein; fats, starches, and sugar; water; fibrous roughage; salts; vitamins.* All of these occur in varying proportions in all kinds of food, including, of course, the natural food, grass, which represents a *subsistence* diet for horses doing no work. In the case of the working horse, in whom the expenditure of energy increases the wastage of tissue, the balance of the diet and of the six constituents has to be altered.

The functions of the diet constituents are as follows:

PROTEIN replaces muscular wastage, forms body tissue, produces heat and energy. It is therefore an essential element in the diet without which life cannot be supported. Animals in work require a high-protein diet to repair the muscular wastage which occurs. Similarly, young horses require high-protein diets to promote muscular development. Too high a protein diet will only result in fat and, if continued without the requisite balance of equal work, will cause serious disorders of the digestion, swollen legs, liver troubles and so on.

FATS, STARCHES and SUGAR are, in simple terms, producers of fat, energy and heat. Fats produce up to two and a half times more heat and energy than the other two. None, however, is of any value unless protein is also present. No food consists entirely of protein or solely of fats, starches and sugar, but where there is too large a proportion of starch and sugar the digestibility of the protein content is reduced very considerably.

A bran mash. It acts as a laxative control. Add boiling water and a handful of salt, mix well and cover for 30 minutes to keep in the steam.

147

WATER is essential to life and the horse's body, like those of other animals, consists of 80 per cent water. Without a constant supply of water the body processes break down, all food being passed through the system in solution. Horses can live for only about a week without water, whereas without food they can survive for about 30 days.

The intake of water varies from one individual to another and also with temperature and circumstance. Horses may drink up to 10 gallons (about 45 litres) per day in very hot weather. Water should, therefore, always be available and it should be clean and fresh. In stables, the ideal is an automatic drinker which horses soon learn to operate. In a paddock the best method, other than clean, running water, is piped water to a trough. Stagnant pools and water left for days on end in slime-gathering, bath-like vessels cannot really be considered suitable.

FIBROUS ROUGHAGE provides the necessary bulk element in the diet. It is an essential in the feeding of herbivores. Its purpose is to assist in the digestion and absorption of concentrate foods, which cannot be fed without roughage being present. In themselves the fibrous elements are not easily digested. They occur, in varying proportions, in all vegetable foods; hay, a principal source, contains between 25 and 35 per cent woody fibre, while straw can contain as much as 40 per cent.

SALTS are essential to the organism as the means of controlling the continual body changes. They must, therefore, be replaced constantly. Salts are principally compounds of lime, soda and potash and are present to a high degree in hay and oat straw, but are not present in such high proportions in grain. Maize, for instance, is very low in salts and must always be fed in conjunction with an adequate and compensatory hay ration. If salts were not present in the food, death would result. Imbalances of salt, sometimes produced in modern, chemical farming, can cause disorders.

VITAMINS are present in very small quantities in all foods and their presence in the diet is of enormous and primary importance. They may be destroyed when foods are subjected to prolonged heating and in boiled foods.

Although improved farming methods may increase yields, they are not always advantageous in the feeding of horses. It is likely that the modern horse does not get the quality food of his predecessors and, in order to replace deficiencies, it is advisable for horse-owners to feed one or other of the proprietary vitamin-mineral supplements.

Foods, which supply the six constituents and when fed in proper proportions constitute a balanced diet for working horses, can be divided conveniently into bulk, energising foods and auxiliaries. (Proper proportions in this context refer to the *nitrogenous ratio*, the ratio of protein to fats, starches and sugar, which is 1:5 for horses in hard work and 1:10 for horses resting; and the *fatty* ration, i.e. fat to protein, which is estimated at $1:2\frac{1}{2}$).

Bulk foods consist in the main of hay, chaff (a mixture of chopped hay and oat straw) and also include bran, sugar beet pulp, carrots and other roots, although these latter are also considered as auxiliary feedstuffs. Grass, of course, is also a source of bulk.

A good sample of meadow hay will contain woody fibre in the percentage mentioned and can have a 13 per cent protein content with a protein/starch equivalent (*i.e.* the proportion of *digestible* protein to starch) of 48 per cent, a ratio of 1:4.

Lucerne hay, known as *alfalfa* in America where it is used extensively, is not much used in Europe, although it is the most valuable nutritionally. It has a 19 per cent protein content and a 37 per cent protein/starch equivalent. Oat straw contains a lower protein content and protein/starch equivalent and has a higher fibrous content. None the less good oat straw can be a better feed than the poorest meadow hays with less than 7 per cent protein content.

Energising foods contain high percentages of starches and fats and for practical purposes are exemplified by oats (which are the best), barley, maize, split beans and peas. The latter are excessively heating

A horse may drink up to six gallons (27 litres) of water a day in hot weather, so it is essential to have a constant supply. It is best supplied by pipe and the flow controlled by a ball-cock.

There should be enough room at the trough for at least two horses to drink at the same time.

and very indigestible. They can, therefore, be fed only in small quantities. Oats contain 11 per cent protein and have a 57 per cent starch equivalent. The heating and energising element is therefore high and the proportion of digestible protein is low in comparison with hay, which emphasises the need for feeding the latter.

Auxiliary foods is a term covering numerous feedstuffs outside the main categories. Nevertheless, they may be of considerable importance.

Bran can be placed under this heading. It is an excellent food, rich in salts. Bran is the ground husk of the wheat grain and where it is coarse ground (broad bran), it is a valuable adjunct to the diet. It is easily digestible and acts as a laxative control – *i.e.* bran, fed damp, acts as a laxative on the bowels; when fed dry it has an opposite effect.

Bran is mixed with other foods and forms the main constituent of the bran mash as well as figuring in the linseed mash.

It is normal for horses in work to receive a bran mash once a week and to be fed a mash after periods of exertion because of its easily digested properties.

A mash is made by adding boiling water to bran (3lb 1.5kg per horse), adding a handful of household salt (1oz 25grams) and stirring well. The bucket should then be covered, to keep the steam in, for about 30 minutes.

Linseed can also come under this heading. It is a noted fattening food with an oil or fat content of 37 per cent as well as a substantial protein content. Linseed is good feed for ailing or debilitated horses or for those in a state of exhaustion, because again it makes so little demand on the processes of digestion. Linseed cannot be fed raw. It has to be cooked and given as a mash or jelly. A linseed mash is made by soaking the linseed overnight (1–1½lb/450–670 grams per horse). On the day following, the seed is boiled for three hours over low heat. The mixture can then be added to bran (about 2lb/1kg per horse), stirred well and allowed to stand for 30 minutes or so before feeding.

Linseed jelly is made by adding the soaked seed to boiling water (1lb to 2 gallons/9 litres water), adding cold water and boiling for 20–30 minutes. The jelly can be mixed with either oats or bran but the ration given to the horse should not exceed ½–1lb (225 grams) per day.

Other useful auxiliaries are sugar-beet pulp, which has to be soaked overnight, the various roots which horses so much appreciate, and the very numerous range of mineral/vitamin additives.

Horse nuts constitute a system of feeding on their own. They can be fed with hay and will provide a balanced diet without further additions, or there are those which claim to be a complete feed and can be fed without the addition of any hay. It is, however, necessary to put an animal on to a "complete" feed very gradually. There are various types of nuts with differing protein contents. Some are intended for ponies in light work, others for nursing mares, and still more for racehorses and horses in hard and fast work. It is advisable to check the type of nut that is being purchased. By using nuts (12–16lb 5.50–7.25 kg per day for stabled horses and ponies in work) the hay ration can be reduced. But these convenience foods are without doubt one of the more expensive ways to feed.

Proportions and quantities

It is relatively easy to lay down the correct proportions in which food should be given. It is more difficult to give a clear indication of quantities, since the food intake varies from one horse to another. It is indeed quite possible for one horse to take a ration of 18lb (8kg) of oats per day for the work required of him, while another, doing the same work, might manage very well on half that amount of corn.

The following is a fairly accurate guide for the proportion of bulk to concentrate.

Horses in *moderate* work, *i.e.* hunted once a week and exercised each day, should receive approximately 50 per cent bulk food to 50 per cent concentrates. Horses in hard, fast work require extra concentrates, *but*

"A good horsemaster is one who can get the maximum amount of work out of his horse at the minimum cost without the animals losing condition."

the proportion of bulk to concentrate must never be below one-third of the total amount. Horses in light work, general hacking, weekend use and so on should do well on a ration of two-thirds bulk and one-third concentrates.

The table below is a reasonable guide to quantities, although it should be remembered that the necessary food intake varies according to the skin surface of the animal and not according to weight or height. A 15 hand cob for instance, will require more food than a lightly built Thoroughbred of the same height.

Horses and ponies at grass

Provided there is sufficient acreage, animals kept at grass without working will live well without an additional ration from the end of April until September. Thereafter grass has lost its nutrient value and horses should be fed hay, or a mixture of hay and oat straw, *ad lib* through the winter months.

If the animals are kept out but lightly worked (hacking and weekend work), a concentrate ration will also be required either in the form of oats and bran or as horse nuts.

As a guide, horses but not ponies, who are better-behaved on a ration of nuts, can be given 1lb (450 grams) of oats for every mile (1.6km) of exercise completed. This at least, is a good basis on which to start, but it may be found that the ration has to be cut back, if the horse is too fresh, until an acceptable level is found.

Food can be wasted if horses are not wormed regularly, since it will not be used to best effect. It will be wasted if teeth are not looked at regularly. Hay is wasted when fed from the ground instead of from haynets, since it becomes trodden underfoot. Poor quality food is wasteful and so is the practice of not weighing a ration so that the amount each horse receives is known exactly. Bruised oats are more nutritious and less wasteful than crushed oats from which much of the goodness has been lost.

Food is cheaper when bought in bulk, with the exception of bran which is best purchased in fairly small quantities because it absorbs moisture easily and can become sour. Hay is best stored in the dry on a base of boards or something similar which will allow some circulation of air. If stored outside, the same applies but a weighted tarpaulin is necessary to keep out rain. All other food should be stored in vermin-proof bins.

Between September and April, horses should be fed hay and other food to supplement grass which has then lost much of its nutrient value. The least wasteful method of feeding hay is from a net fastened sufficiently high so as to make the catching up of a pawing foot an impossibility.

Total Daily Food Intake		
Under 12h.h.	*12–13h.h.*	*13–14h.h.*
14–16lb	16–18lb	20–22lb
6.7–7.5kg	7.5–8.5kg	9–10kg
14–15h.h.	*15–16h.h.*	*over 16h.h.*
22–24lb	24–26lb	26–28lb
10–11kg	11–12kg	12–13kg

Grooming

by Robert Owen

The objects behind grooming are five-fold: to make a positive contribution towards the animal's health; to maintain overall condition; to keep the horse or pony clean; to prevent disease; to improve appearance. It is only by keeping to a regular routine that the above-mentioned objectives can be achieved.

There is a difference between the needs of a stable-kept horse and one which is permanently kept at grass. The former demands a daily and complete grooming; the latter requires daily attention but a modified routine, as will be discussed later.

The grooming kit, an essential part of every owner's equipment, will comprise: a *hoof pick* for cleaning out the feet; a *dandy brush* for

The hoof pick. Deposits of mud and stone can pierce the sole of the horse's foot. The hoof must be picked out regularly.

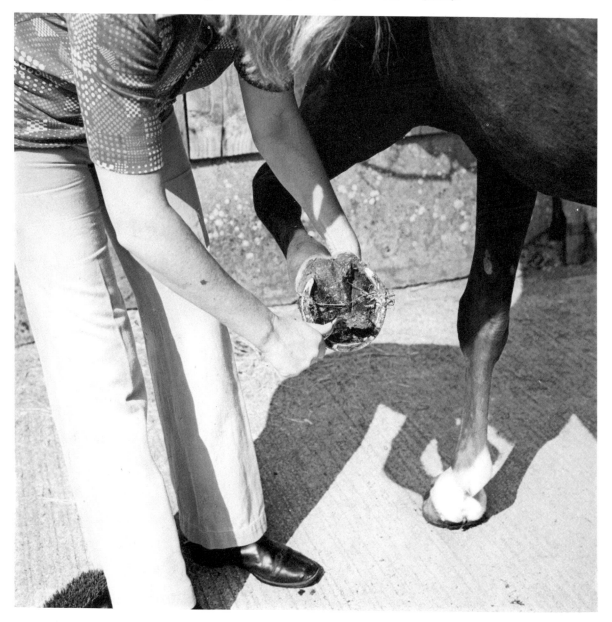

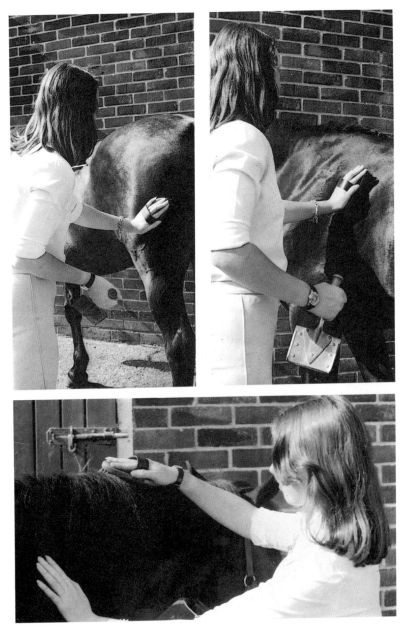

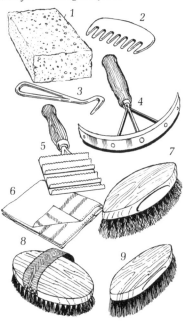

Far left: When using the body brush, use firm, short, circular strokes in the direction of the "lay" of the hair.

Below left: The body brush is used before the mane comb to separate the locks in the mane.

Left: Remove dust and scurf from the horse's coat by using a body brush. To remove hair from the body brush, draw it through the curry comb.

Bottom: The grooming kit.
1. Sponge. 2. Large mane comb.
3. Hoof pick. 4. Sweat scraper.
5. Curry comb. 6. Stable rubber –
gives final polish after grooming.
7. Dandy brush – removes caked mud and sweat. 8. Body brush. 9. Water brush – dampens mane and tail and is used for washing the feet.

removing dirt and caked mud; a *body brush* to remove dust and scurf from the horse's coat, mane and tail; a *curry comb* for cleaning the body brush (sometimes a rubber curry comb can be used with effect on the horse's coat, especially when the mud is caked deep); at least two *sponges*, one for use on the eyes, muzzle and nostrils, the other for the dock; a *water brush* used on the mane, tail and also to clean the feet; a *wisp* to encourage circulation and to give a form of massage; a *stable rubber* or duster to remove, as a final touch, any traces of dust.

Using grooming equipment will only prove effective when physical effort is applied. Too frequently, younger riders will attempt to get away with a "lick and a promise", a quick run over with a body brush and a liberal amount of water to "set" rather than "lay" the mane and tail! The importance of grooming to the well-being of the horse or pony is something which must be appreciated and understood by riders of all ages. In another section of this book the need for a regular check on the condition of the horse has been emphasised. A wise owner will use each grooming period to examine and then treat the

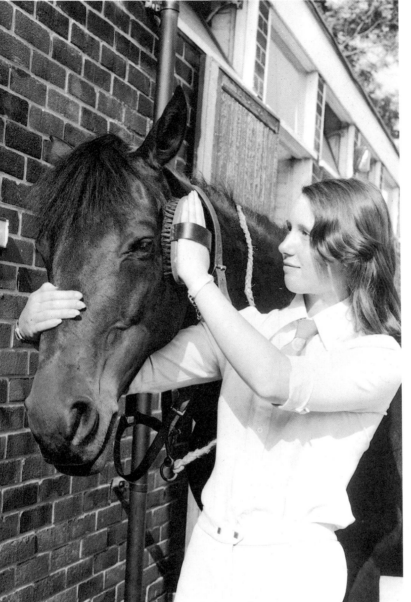

Because the body brush has such soft hairs, it can be used to clean the horse's head. Make sure the head collar has been removed first.

horse for cuts and bruises and signs of swelling or lameness.

Most horsemen agree grooming should start with the feet. The hoof pick removes stones, mud and dirt from the area between the shoe and the frog. Work from the heel towards the toe, and take care not to damage the softer parts of the frog. As each foot is cleaned a check should be made to see that the shoe is secure and not worn. Also feel round the hoof for any signs of risen clenches. Next, taking the dandy brush, remove all traces of caked mud, sweat marks and so on. Where the mud is deep seated a rubber curry comb can be used. With all stages of grooming it is best if work starts on the near-side before moving the off-side.

Once the dandy brush is put aside, the body brush, with its shorter hairs, is used to penetrate through the coat to the skin. And this part of grooming demands extra physical effort. First, brush the mane to the side away from its normal fall and thoroughly brush the crest. On completion the mane is brushed through and into its correct position, ensuring that it is free from tangles and knots. The attention to the

Use a body brush to groom the tail. Release a few locks at a time and brush them through. A dandy brush is unsuitable as it is too severe.

body is given in circular strokes and in the direction of the "lay" of the coat. Short strokes are best, and frequent cleaning of the brush is made by use of the curry comb. Do not stand too close to the horse, but close enough to apply sufficient pressure.

Some owners are never happy when using the body brush on the head of the horse, though most horses enjoy having their heads groomed. If the horse fights at this stage it is usually a sign of some mistreatment or having at one time been roughly handled. The head is one of the most delicate parts to be groomed, demanding quiet, careful attention.

Since before the grooming started the horse will have been tied to a ring or post, the headstall will need to be removed before grooming the head. Do not take this off and leave the horse free – even though he may always be patient and quiet. The headstall should be undone and dropped (see page 68). When the headstall has been replaced, and one is satisfied that both flanks of the horse are thoroughly groomed, attention is given to the tail. To groom the tail a few locks at a time are released (see illustration) and these are gently brushed through. Never use a dandy brush on the tail for this can be too severe and cause breaks in the hairs.

The wisp is used when slightly dampened; when applied with vigour to the muscular parts of the body it gives the horse a form of massage, at the same time it will improve the blood supply and stimulate the skin. Avoid the tender parts of the horse's body and especially take care not to wisp the bony areas.

Before using the sponges ensure there is a sufficient supply of clean water available. First squeeze one of the sponges and wipe the eyes, the inside and outside of the nostrils, and the muzzle. Then, taking a second sponge, thoroughly clean the dock and the entire area around the dock.

The water brush will "lay" the mane and can be used when washing the feet. It is also used on the tail. Finally, a stable rubber will remove any final traces of dust.

The grass-kept horse or pony will never be groomed to such a detailed routine. In autumn and winter months it is important not to remove any grease and dandruff since these contribute to body warmth and waterproofing. It is best if the daily routine is kept to the use of a dandy brush to remove mud. Attention must always be given to the spongeing of eyes, muzzle and dock. And, a daily cleaning of the feet will, as with a stable-kept horse, enable the owner to make a thorough check on the condition of the horse and to examine shoes and the overall appearance.

Use a damp sponge to clean the dirt from around the horse's eyes.

Taking a clean sponge, lift the tail and clean the dock area.

The damp stable rubber is used to give a final shine. Wipe the coat briskly in the direction of the "lay" of the hair.

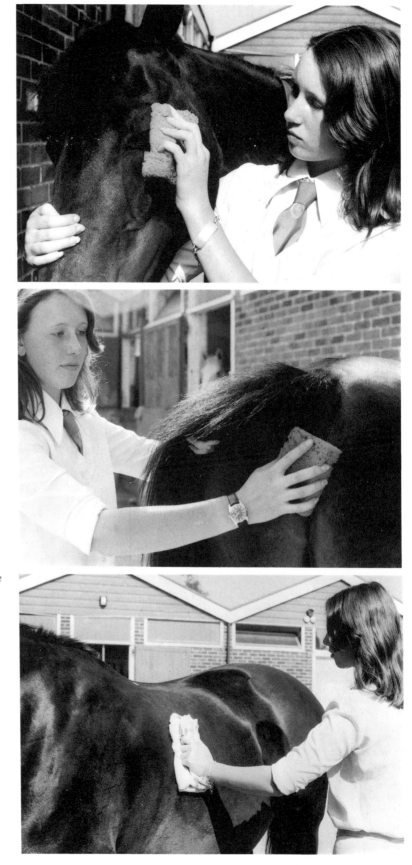

The Horse's Feet

by Gareth L. M. Hunter

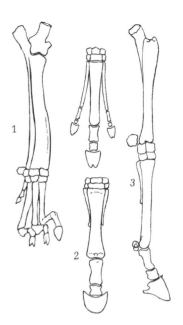

The foot of the horse developed from that of Eohippus (1), which had a dog-like foot. Gradually the lateral toes became less functional until the modern horse (2 and 3) is left with an enlarged central toe, the hoof. The lateral toes have become vestigial.

The horse's leg and foot have evolved over the past millions of years to enable it to move at high speed over a variety of terrains to escape danger. Fossil remains show that the foreleg and the hindleg are both evolved central digits. The bones of the knee are similar to those of our wrist, and those of the hock correspond to the human ankle. On each side of the cannon bone are the remains of two other digits, the splint bones. At the bottom of all this is the highly evolved foot.

The horn of the wall grows down from the coronary band. It consists of tubes of horn cemented together. The whole wall is covered with a varnish-like layer, the periople, which waterproofs the horn, and contains the moisture necessary to prevent it from becoming brittle. The sole is produced by a membrane lying above it, and is thinner than the wall. This, combined with its concave shape, allows the slight spring that is part of the complex concussion absorbing device. The frog, which extends up to the bulbs of the heel, is also composed of horn, but is rubbery. The cleft in its centre contains glands that secrete the fluid to keep it moist. The triangular shape assists in preventing the foot sliding forward, and the grooves to either side prevent side-slipping. Besides absorbing concussion the frog is part of the pumping device that drives blood back up the leg. To either side of the frog are the bars, the turned-back ends of the wall. These strengthen the foot.

As the wall grows down past the sole, the two cannot be solidly united. To allow a flexible union where the wall slides past the sole, a cheese-like substance exists, and when the shoe is removed this can be seen as the white line. In the unshod foot, small stones sometimes work their way up into this, causing a lameness known as gravel.

In the wild the downward growth of the wall compensates for the wear incurred, but domestication, especially with work on modern roads, results in excessive wear and the horse becomes footsore. To overcome this, shoes have been in use for centuries, and they have evolved into the modern fullered and concaved type in popular use today. The concaving on the inside continues the natural shape of the foot. While providing a narrower surface, that is less likely to be sucked off in heavy going, it also provides a sharper rim to the hoof, thereby increasing grip. The fullering is the groove that runs around the ground surface of the shoe. This rapidly becomes packed with mud and grit, providing grip on hard, smooth surfaces.

The heels of the foreshoes are usually pencilled, that is rasped to follow the slope of the heels. On the foreshoe this removes any projection at the back of the shoe that may get caught by the hind toe, which could rip it off as a result. Pencilled hind heels do at least reduce the damage done when a horse kicks. Studs are now used to replace the wedge and calkin of the more old-fashioned shoe. Many studs are available, and the blacksmith will fit a threaded hole in the outside branch of the hind shoes for a small charge.

Wear of the shoe is one of the obvious reasons for replacement, but unless most of the work done is on a hard surface, other reasons are likely to necessitate a visit to the farrier before the shoe is worn out. With the wall protected from wear, the foot will become overlong. Taking the shoes off, cutting back the foot and replacing the same shoes is a process known as having removes. It is usually necessary to visit the farrier about every five or six weeks, regardless of wear to the shoe, but this will depend on the growth rate of the wall.

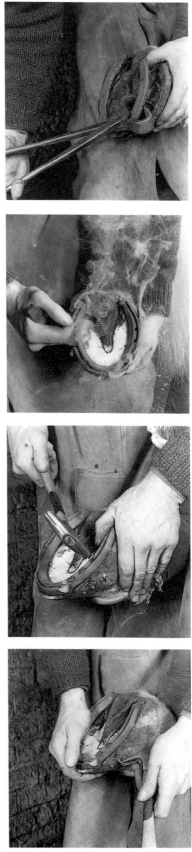

Above: Shoeing a horse. First the farrier knocks up the old clenches with a hammer and the end of his buffer. Right from the top: 1. Starting at the heel, the old shoe is gently prised off with the pincers, taking great care not to damage the wall of the foot. 2. The foot is cleaned and rasped to ensure an equal distribution of weight on all parts of the foot. Taking the shoe from the fire by means of a pritchel, it is placed on the foot. If the shoe fits properly, the burn mark on the wall of the hoof will be even. 3. The new shoe is nailed on with the driving hammer, starting at the toe. The outside nails are driven in last. The nails should pierce the wall of the foot without penetrating the sole. 4. The farrier is pulling the nails tight with the claw of the hammer, before turning over the clenches and tapping them into the wall of the foot.

The farrier removes the shoe by cutting the clenches with a buffer, and then levering the shoe off with the pincers, starting at the heels and finishing across the toes so that none of the horn is split away. The wall is then cut back with hoof cutters and levelled with the rasp. It is the rasp that is used to obtain a flat surface and therefore an accurate fit between the wall and shoe. It is at this stage that the advantages of hot shoeing becomes apparent.

Cold shoes can be fitted fairly well, but the finished result can only be judged by the farrier's eye. In hot shoeing the hot shoe is held in place on the foot for a few seconds. The burn marks on the foot show how level the wall is, as proud areas will be burnt a darker brown. These can be removed with the rasp and the shoe retried, ensuring a very accurate fit.

The shoe is then nailed on. The first nail is driven through near the toe and the heel alignment checked again before the second is put in. The normal number of nails used is four on the outside and three on the inside. This is because the outside of the foot is longer than the inside. It also cuts the risk of brushing injuries.

The nails are bevelled on one side at the point, to curve them away from the inner foot. The points of each nail are twisted off with the claw of the hammer as they come out of the wall, leaving a small stump, and this, when hammered down, will form the clench which holds the shoe on.

The rasp is then run around the edge of the shoe to remove any overlapping wall. If this is not done, it will split up. Excessive rasping, especially at the toe, known as dumping, is a serious fault. Besides changing the shape of the foot, this removes the protective periople, allowing the foot to dry out and become brittle.

Clipping and Trimming

by Gareth L. M. Hunter

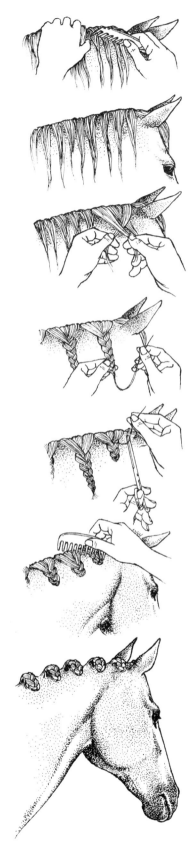

At the end of the autumn the horse's thick winter coat grows, and although this is necessary to keep the horse warm in the natural environment, it prevents him working properly in a domestic one. If worked hard he will sweat, become exhausted quickly, and eventually lose condition. To overcome this the hair is removed with clippers. With a short coat he will also dry more quickly when wet, avoiding the risk of chills, and will be easier to keep clean.

The disadvantages are that clothing will be necessary, and the horse will normally have to be stabled, unless a very small amount of hair only has been removed. The considerations of management and work being done will therefore determine the type of clip, of which there are a variety.

With a full clip all the hair is removed, except for the mane and tail, which are never taken off as the normal part of the clipping process. The disadvantage of this clip is that the short hair under the saddle is more prone to rubbing, and the legs have no protection against mud and thorns. To overcome this a hunter clip is more usually employed, leaving the hair on the saddle patch and legs as high up as the elbow and stifle. If the line here is sloped down the back of the leg, it will make the leg look longer.

A blanket clip leaves on the legs, and an area corresponding to a blanket, thereby covering the loins. For ponies and animals not working too hard, or being turned out for part of the day in milder weather, a trace clip only removes the hair as high up as a harness trace, and leaves the legs on. The chest and gullet are also normally removed.

For the private horse-owner it is probably best to have the horse professionally clipped, unless the owner himself is experienced and already owns his own clippers. The process is not particularly complicated.

The most common type of clipper is the electrically powered type, with the motor in the handle. On all clippers the bottom blade is stationary, and the upper blade slices from side to side, cutting the hair. It is the thickness of the bottom blade that determines the length of the cut. The tension of the blades is adjusted by a nut. If they are too loose they will not cut, and if too tight they will heat up rapidly. In either case they become blunt quickly. Manufacturers' instructions should be followed as to how to tension.

The horse to be clipped should be as clean as possible, and a tail bandage will help to prevent tail hairs getting caught. The operation should be carried out in a safe area, such as a stall or box, although daylight is better than artificial. A haynet will help keep the horse quiet, although an assistant may be needed if the horse is difficult. The person clipping should wear an overall to save clothing, and strong shoes, preferably with rubber soles as an extra protection against electrocution. Some form of mask should be worn if a lot of clipping is to be done.

The clippers must be used against the lay of the coat, and they should be allowed to do the work, lying flat against the coat, otherwise lines will show. Long, overlapping strokes will also help to avoid these.

Left: Plaiting the mane. The mane is first dampened with a water brush. The end of the plait is secured with thread. This is folded underneath and stitched again.

Right: The final stage. Rolling up the loop into a knob, by stitching it tight to the poll.

Below: Hunter clip. Hair is left on the saddle area for comfort and on the legs, up to the elbow, to protect them against mud and thorns. The trim slopes down the back of the legs so that they appear longer.

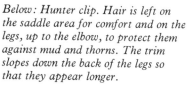

A blanket clip. This leaves the legs and an area corresponding to a blanket untrimmed. It is used on horses that do not sweat excessively.

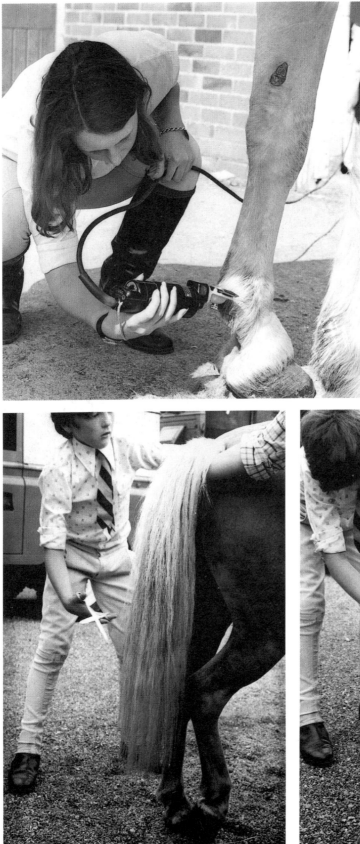

Left: An electric clipper being used to trim a fetlock. The clippers should be used against the "lay" of the hair.

Below: Trimming the tail. Because a horse only carries its tail when moving, an arm must be put under the dock to cut the tail to the right length.

Right: Tail plaiting. First dampen the hair. Then starting at the top of the tail, plait the side hairs. Two thirds of the way down change to plaiting the middle hairs. Stitch the end of the plait, fold it under and tie it to the point where the plaiting of the side hair ends.

Bottom right: A variation is to tie the plaited loop to the top of the tail.

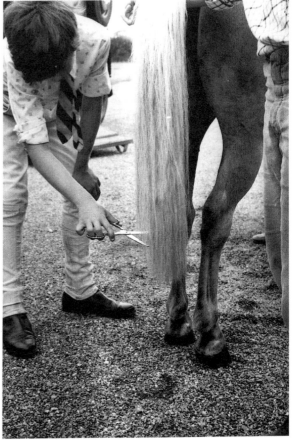

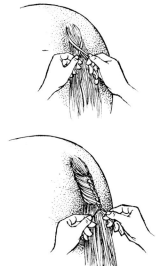

Unless the operator has a very experienced eye, lines should be marked in chalk. Fine baby oil or saddle soap may be used to mark a grey.

The blades must be cleaned and retensioned regularly during the process. Lubricating with a light mineral oil will help prevent the blades heating excessively, but dipping them in paraffin is discouraged by modern manufacturers, as it tends to blunt them. Finally a rug must be handy to cover areas as they are clipped.

The first clip is normally done at the beginning of October, and to keep the horse really smart, repeated every three weeks until the latter part of January, when the last clip is usually done.

Unlike clipping, trimming is done almost purely for the sake of appearance. The clippers may be used for this, but a neater result will be achieved with scissors, and a mane comb. Usually only the mane, when totally removed, known as hogging, is done with the clippers.

The degree of trimming will depend again on management. Leg hair protects against the elements in winter, and flies in summer. The muzzle hairs are of great use to the horse living out in foraging for food, but expendable if the horse lives in. But the hairs round the eyes should not be removed, as they prevent the horse bumping into anything in the dark, and damaging himself.

Legs are trimmed by lifting the hair with the comb and cutting it, thereby ensuring a smooth, even finish. The jaw can be treated in the same way. The coronary band hair should not be trimmed too short, as the top of the hoof tends to be rather pale. The ears can be trimmed by pushing the edges together and trimming the hair that sticks out. The hair inside the ears must not be trimmed. A piece of mane can be cut out behind the ears to allow the bridle to sit.

Mane and tail hairs are removed by pulling. Taking a few hairs, the rest are pushed up with the comb. The held hairs are then removed with a sharp downward tug of the comb. Opinions vary as to the length to pull to, but four inches (10cm) will be short enough to be neat, but have enough weight to make it lie. The bottom of the tail may be banged (cut off) about four inches (10cm) below the point of the hock. As the horse carries his tail when moving but not when standing, an arm should be placed under the dock before the hair is cut. If the tail is to be pulled, only the hairs at the side of the dock should be removed, and a tail bandage then employed daily for a few hours. Hair is far easier to remove if the horse is warm.

Rugs, Bandages and Clothing

by Gareth L. M. Hunter

Rugs may be divided into a number of basic types. The most common are jute, lined with wool, and usually fairly hard wearing, although this will depend on their price. Cheap rugs of any type tend to be cut short in the chest, the size stated being the length of the back line. If stains are scrubbed out daily and the leather soaped, these rugs should only need cleaning at the end of the winter, before storing.

Days rugs are woollen, usually bound with another colour, and with the owner's initials, and a matching roller. They are smart and warm, but difficult to clean, and are therefore only worn during the day, being replaced with a jute rug at night. They usually have a fillet string at the back, which passes under the tail above the hocks, preventing the rug from blowing up.

Cotton summer sheets are useful for keeping flies and dust off. Being very light, they must have a fillet string. They are useful in the summer for keeping the horse clean in the stable, and as they are easy to wash, they can be used in winter under rugs and blankets to save them from becoming soiled. They can also be worn over anti-sweat rugs. Anti-sweat rugs are made of open cotton mesh, and under a summer sheet they allow a limited amount of air circulation. This lets a wet horse dry without chilling, and helps to prevent excited horses from breaking into a sweat. Debatably they may be used on their own. In winter they provide extra warmth under rugs and blankets.

Quilted rugs are very light and warm, but those with attached surcingles can put pressure on the withers and are inclined to slip.

Blankets are used under rugs for extra warmth. A number of layers, especially wool, provides greater warmth than one heavy rug and blanket. The yellow blankets with stripes at each end are London or Kersey blankets. All blankets should be put on lengthways, along the length of the horse.

Rugs and blankets are held in place by either rollers, which are padded over the withers, or surcingles, which, being a plain length of webbing, need to be used with a wither pad. Anti-cast rollers have a raised steel arch over the withers, to prevent the horse from rolling right over, but due to the risks involved in not being able to turn the horse over if he does get stuck, they should have buckles on the right-hand side as well as the left. A breastplate may be used to prevent the roller from sliding back.

Breastplates and the front of rugs, must be fitted loosely enough to allow the horse's head to be lowered, and not to pull on the chest and withers. Rubbing sometimes occurs on the shoulders and withers, even when the rug fits well, so pieces of sheepskin can be sewn on the inside. Rollers must be firm enough to keep everything in place, but not be as tight as a girth. Blankets may have the front corners folded back over the withers, leaving a central point, which is then folded back over the rug, under the roller. If not long enough to do this, the front edge should be folded back as a cuff. For safety reasons the front of the rug should never be done up unless the roller is on, otherwise the rug may slip and get trapped around the front legs.

New Zealand rugs are designed to protect the horse from wind and rain. Made of waterproof material, and semi-lined with blanketing, they have an attached surcingle, and leg straps at the back. The leg straps should be looped through each other between the hind legs to

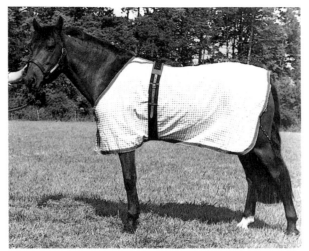

Above: A cotton summer sheet keeps the horse clean.
This one is kept in place by a roller.

Below: Quilted rugs combine lightness with warmth
This one has a fitted surcingle and has a tendency to slip.

New Zealand rugs are semi-lined and waterproof. They should be used on stable-kept horses put out to grass for protection against wind and rain.

The anti-sweat rug is like a string vest and is used in hot weather instead of a blanket. It can also be worn under a summer sheet so that the air can circulate a little.

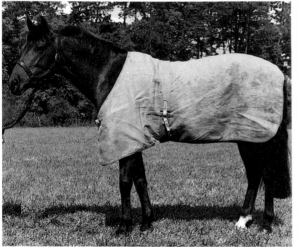

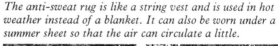

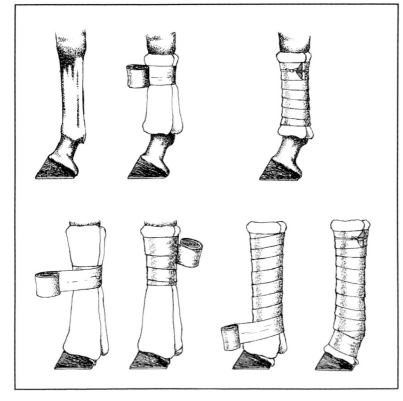

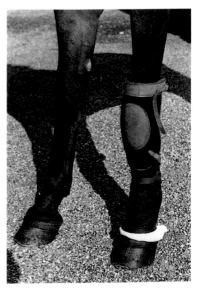

Bandages protect the legs and keep them warm. The upper sequence shows how to bandage the legs for exercise, the lower for travelling. Notice the greater protection given for the travelling horse. In both cases, the bandages should be applied over gamgee as shown.

Below: Knee caps are used for protection while travelling or riding on a hard road.

prevent rubbing when the horse moves. Being waterproof they should not be used in the stable as they can cause sweating.

Small exercise rugs that attach under the saddle, with a fillet string at the back, cover the loins and are useful for slow, fittening exercises. They are often seen on racehorses. Waterproof ones are also available.

Not so commonly seen in Britain are hoods. These cover the head and neck, with tie strings underneath, but are usually only necessary for sick horses and very severe climates.

Bandages and boots

The extremities of the horse are very prone to heat loss, and, when travelling, to possible injury. Woollen stable bandages, about five inches (12.5cm) wide, over gamgee, are very useful, especially when warmth is required, but they may be rather hot for summer travel. Woollen or stockinette stable bandages, besides providing warmth and protection, also support tired or injured legs. Applied more loosely than usual, possibly with some hay underneath, they help dry off wet or muddy legs.

Tail bandages and exercise bandages are usually crepe and about three inches (7.5cm) wide. Although stockinette can be used for the former, it does not have enough elastication to support tendons.

Exercise bandages are always applied over gamgee or some other form of padding. This evens out the pressure ridges that may otherwise damage the tendons and cannon bone. To avoid these dangers, the tapes of any bandage must be tied in the groove between the cannon bone and the tendons, and for exercise bandages on the outside of the leg rather than the inside, in a reef knot. Although this will make them very secure, it is still advisable to sew them in place for cross-country work.

Travelling boots are a more convenient method of protecting the legs than bandages, being quick and easy to put on and remove. Home-made ones are usually perfectly adequate, and the velcro strip tapes are good fasteners for these, although their tendency to come undone makes them dangerous for work boots.

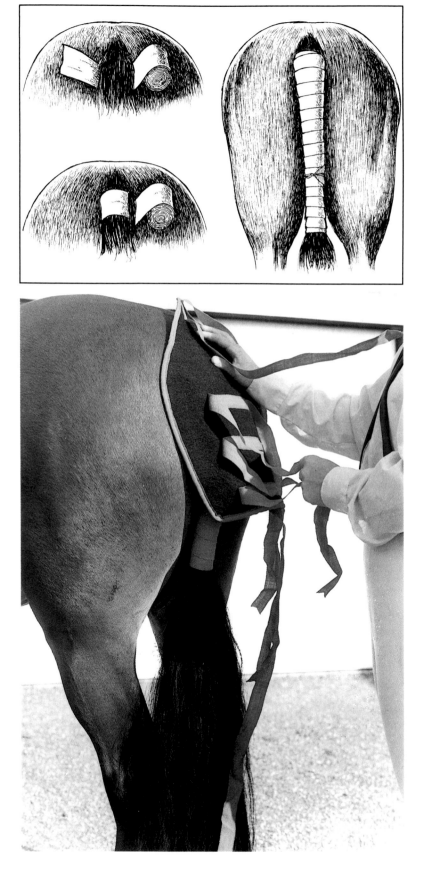

The tail bandage is used both for protection and for flattening the tail hairs. The tail should be damp when applying the bandage.

A tail guard is used only when travelling. It prevents the top of the tail being rubbed. The tail should be bandaged before the guard is applied.

Travelling

by Gareth L. M. Hunter

The most normal method of transporting horses today is by road, in a horse box or trailer. The former is preferable, providing a safer and more comfortable ride. It is impractical, however, for the average owner, and this is where the trailer comes into its own. The trailer, having a relatively narrow and low entrance, can present problems with horses that are not used to loading. But this can be overcome with a bit of forethought.

Vehicles must be checked before a journey to ensure that tow links, lights, and flooring are in good order, and that tyre pressures are correct. Safety chains are now required as an extra link between towing vehicle and trailer, but these must be heavy duty and correctly attached, if they are to be of any use.

The trailer should have a layer of bedding. Straw is best as this is easy to clean out and does not retain moisture, which will rot the boards. It should be packed down so that the horse stands on it, rather than in it. As an added precaution the horse should be tied to a loop of stout string attached to the ring. If he then falls, it will break rather than suspend him, and the partition will keep him in place until he is re-tied. A haynet can be tied to the ring itself, as high up as possible.

Unless the horse is used to travelling, it should be loaded a few times prior to the actual journey, and taken for a short ride. If this is possible, it allows problems to be ironed out before the last minute. Hurried, bad loading experiences may result in future refusals to load, as well as bad driving.

When deciding on the clothing and equipment necessary for travelling, the factors to consider are protection from injury, and comfort, especially warmth. A strong, well-fitting headcollar will allow the attachment of a poll guard. There are a variety on the market, but a foam sponge sleeve, slipped over the headpiece, can be easily made and is quite sufficient. They are more important in trailers than in boxes. A tail bandage will prevent the tail from rubbing, and a tail guard can be put on top, although these should not be used without a bandage under, as they tend to twist the hairs.

Legs should be protected from the knee and hock to just below the coronary band. Horses that tread on themselves badly can also wear over-reach boots, if low set gamgee is not sufficient. In summer, stockinette bandages over cotton pads will prevent the horse from becoming too hot. Knee caps are a wise precaution, as are hock boots, although some horses resent the latter, and they may cause them to kick. With both, the top strap should be firm to hold them in place, while the bottom one, which merely prevents them from flapping up, should be as loose as possible to allow the joint to flex.

Rugs are necessary during most of the year, especially as the animal can not move around to warm up. A jute rug is quite sufficient, although a day rug looks smarter. In warm weather the shoulders can be folded back under the roller. A sweat rug is a useful item to take, and in wet weather a New Zealand rug can be thrown over the horse while waiting to compete. Blankets will be necessary during the winter, but the best guide is to dress according to the weather, and take a few extras as precaution.

Checking equipment

Boxes or trailer and towing vehicles, and tack should be checked a few days before the journey in case any attention is required. The rest of the equipment should be assembled the day before. A list is vital, and it can be built up and used for future journeys. It will ensure that

This horse is perfectly clad for travelling. His tail and legs are properly bandaged. The knee guards fit. He is wearing a strong, well-fitting head collar and the day rug is secured with a padded surcingle. A poll guard and hock boots are sometimes worn.

This side-loading box has been prepared to receive the horse at the end of the competition.

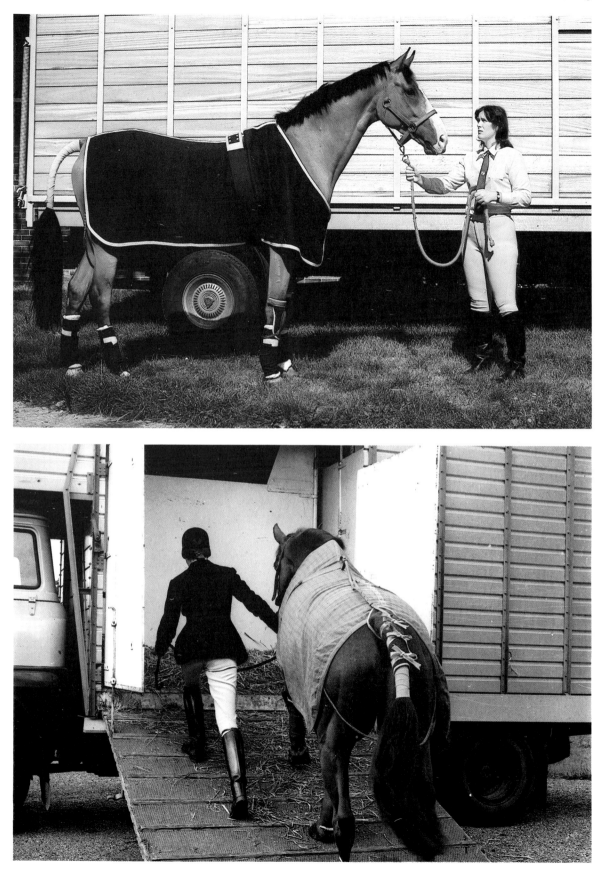

After a hard day's work the horse should be walked for a few minutes before putting him in the trailer and driving him home.

nothing is forgotten, as each item can be checked as it is loaded. A separate list of the rider's clothing etc, is also useful.

About half an hour after starting the journey the horse should be checked to ensure that he is not too hot or too cold. Provided the horse is not going to be doing fast work after arrival, a haynet should be provided for the journey, and on a long journey water should be offered.

On arrival it will be realised how useful an assistant is. The horse should be unloaded and walked around to allow him to stretch his legs and settle down before he is tacked up and worked in. If hunting, it is a good idea to do this about a mile from the meet and ride him the rest of the way. He will be quieter to prepare, and will have loosened up by the time he arrives. A good assistant will roll bandages and fold rugs, saving time later.

If the journey home is a long one, the horse should be walked for a few minutes before he is put in his box. After a long day, remove plaits and do everything else necessary quickly, so that the horse can be left to relax with a haynet without further disturbances. If he has been deprived of water for any length of time, or is still warm, offer him only half a bucket of water with the chill taken off, and increase the amount offered only as he stops showing a great interest in it. Meanwhile, the gear should be unloaded and sorted out. Finally it is important that the box or trailer is mucked out. Droppings and wet straw rot the flooring if not removed.

Foreign travel can be complicated and entry permits often require veterinary tests. This combined with the special requirements of air and sea travel mean that enquiries must be made well in advance, if delays are to be avoided.

Part Five: Competitive Sports

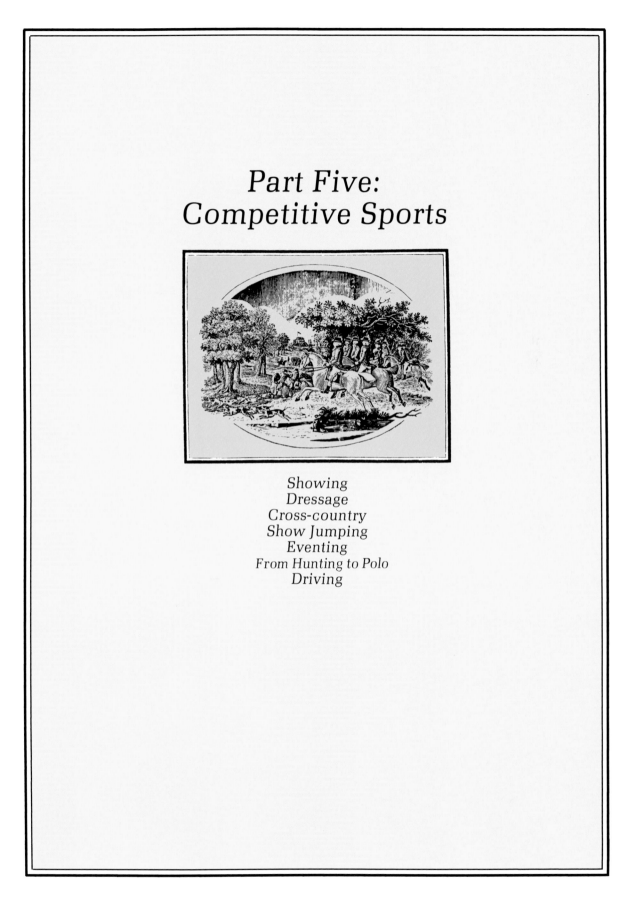

Showing
Dressage
Cross-country
Show Jumping
Eventing
From Hunting to Polo
Driving

Above: Harry Boldt (West Germany) on Woyceck performing an extended trot in the dressage competition at Goodwood in 1978.

Below: A young rider about to compete in the leading rein class at a horse show.

Above: The sport of combined driving was established in 1969. Here is a competitor, beautifully turned out, at Cirencester in 1975.

Bottom: B. Bentejac of France jumping an obstacle in the cross-country phase of the three-day event at the 1974 Burghley World Championships.

Showing

by Jane Holderness-Roddam

For a long time showing has been a most popular and enjoyable pastime and today there are classes for virtually every size, make and shape of horse or pony both under saddle and in hand. Anyone can take a horse to a show and have a lot of fun; but to produce one to win in the ring is an art only acquired through hard work, knowledge and experience.

Having decided to show your animal, it is important to consider exactly what class he is suitable for and then to ensure that he is correctly produced. If you are new to the game, it is well worth going along and seeing for yourself what is required before having a go. It is also essential to know the rules governing the judging of your class and to be sure you have registered yourself and/or your horse with the necessary society at the beginning of the season. In some classes height certificates are required and it is advisable to get these as early as possible to avoid disappointment if the certificates fail to arrive before your first show.

Presentation is probably the most important part and every aspect should be carefully considered. It is a good idea to study your horse with a critical eye and decide which are his good and bad points and how you can produce him looking his best. A lot can be done through careful plaiting, building up a poor neck or fining down a thick one, but to be able to do this a well pulled mane of the same length and thickness all the way down is necessary. The tail should be well pulled and the bottom not brushed out. This is done so often by over-enthusiastic grooms that before you start, your animal's tail has been ruined. So beware of this danger and be sure never to use more than a body brush on a tail. In youngstock and breeding classes a neat plaited tail is usual.

Trimming is essential and ears, jaw and heels should be neatly and carefully done, and the tail "banged" to the right length, remembering, of course, that in pure-bred Mountain and Moorland classes manes and tails are usually left.

Shoeing is vitally important. For the ridden show horse or pony, light steel or aluminium plates in front will help him to move well. A good farrier can do a lot to help the doubtful mover by careful shoeing. In-hand show horses should also have well-trimmed neat feet, and all horses should be produced in the ring with well-oiled or smartly polished hooves.

Show tack

Show tack should be spotlessly clean with polished bits. A coloured browband is quite correct for hacks, children's ponies and most youngstock in-hand classes, part-bred classes, and so on. But it is quite incorrect for all hunter classes, cobs, and doubtfully correct in working pony classes. There is often a lot of talk about what bit is best for ridden show classes. The correct bit is always the double bridle. However, there are occasions when for some reason a horse or pony hates two bits in its mouth. In such cases a pelham bit is the most suitable. In ridden novice pony classes, only a snaffle bridle may ever be used.

Ponies and hacks should be shown in neat, narrow, elegant bridles; hunters, cobs and working hunters and ponies should use more workman-like bridles. Saddles can improve or ruin the look of your horse and a straight cut show saddle is best as this shows off the horse's shoulder and front. If the judge is to ride, do ensure the saddle is a comfortable one and has the correct size of irons and leathers. A large gentleman judge will not appreciate short ladies' leathers with narrow irons that he cannot get his feet into, so a medium-sized pair should suit most judges! Hacks and ponies are often shown in white girths, but leather is correct for anything and are always used on cobs and hunters.

In-hand tack should be neat, spotlessly clean and suitable for the type of horse or pony classes in which it is being used. A bit should always be used when showing stallions, with a coupling attachment from which the lead rein is attached. Foals and yearlings are usually shown in neat head stalls with coupling and lead rein. If a bit is to be used, do remember that your animal's mouth could be ruined at this stage by rough handling and so, if possible, a very mild show bit or rubber in-hand bit should be used. A bit in youngstock should only be used when absolutely necessary or where the rules demand it, but always sympathetic handling is essential. Brood mares should be shown in a double bridle.

Picture of health
The condition of your show animal is most important. He should look superb in his coat. This can only be arrived at through a combination of good feeding and daily grooming. It is elementary to say that regular worming and yearly check-ups on your horse's teeth play a vital role as, if either of these two factors are wrong, your horse will be unable to get the full benefit from the food he is being given. The show horse should look round and well covered and a picture of health. Good quality food is well worth the extra cost. Flaked maize, mollasses, boiled barley and linseed make useful additions to the normal diet, as does milk powder which is a good fattener for youngstock, but do be careful not to over-do them.

Show animals undoubtedly benefit from some time out at grass two or three times a week, if not daily for a few hours. This not only relaxes them but also saves riding time. It is not usually necessary to ride a show horse every day as this tends to get them fitter – not always wanted if you have a rather excitable show horse! Children's ponies should be turned out regularly, if they are to remain suitable rides.

Manners
Manners in the show ring are extremely important. All too often one sees badly behaved animals in the ring. This does not reflect well on the horse's training, although we all know how difficult it sometimes is to produce a spirited four-year-old behaving as it should! However, if you do have a problem, do ask yourself if your horse is being given too much protein, too little work for the amount of food, or generally is one of those that needs hours of work before a class. There are show animals that have been known to need riding literally all through the night before they were sensible enough to go into the class. If you want to win, you have to be prepared to work for it – although luckily it is unusual to have to go without a whole night's sleep on too many occasions!

Training and schooling shows up in all ridden horses and ponies, and it is the ones that go well in the ring that are going to win the prizes in the end. Your horse should go confidently round the ring without spooking at everything. It should walk, trot and canter quietly and gallop well in the classes that require it without bucking, and yet remain under control at all times. If required to do a show, this should be an immaculate performance showing all paces and a change of rein, possibly a rein back, and a halt in front of the judge when the horse should remain stationary for some seconds before returning to the line. Most judges are pushed for time, so as quick a performance showing off the horse at his best will be far more appreciated than endless turns and circles and fancy circus tricks.

David Tatlow's Bunowen, the Champion Hunter at the Royal Horse Show in 1976, looking a superb picture of health.

If the judge is to ride, he will expect a quiet, safe ride that goes in any direction when asked, obeys the aids and is generally a pleasure to ride. If you have a young show horse, it is a good idea to get other people to ride it about at home so that the horse is used to having strange jockeys.

Leading your horse up in front of the judge is an art in itself, and it is the way this is done that can again win or lose a class. Practise this at home to make sure your horse stands correctly, showing himself off to his best advantage. Square on all four legs, head up, ears pricked and really looking a picture. He should then lead up willingly and trot back straight at the judges. Nothing is more annoying for the judge than to have horses weaving past them or going off at an angle.

Ring craft is another vital factor. Having gone to all the effort of producing your animal, it is now ready to be seen by the judge, which is not easy if there is a huge entry. Learn how to keep out of a bunch by riding a wider corner or doing a circle out of sight of the judge so that you can then go past in a nice space to yourself; keep your eye on what is happening and be in the right place at the right time without looking as if you have your eyes "glued" to the judges; concentrate on what you are doing and avoid making signs to your friends. Do not be unsporting and cover up rivals or do any other such tricks, you can be sure they will do far worse to you if they get the chance! When waiting to be called in, walk your horse on the bit and ensure you look the part yourself, making it all appear easy even if it has not been. Keep your horse standing up properly in line and do not allow it to rest a leg (the judge may glance at the line at any time). Above all watch the experts and study their techniques.

Showing in-hand

Showing in-hand is as much of an art as showing under saddle. The actual training is very important. It is essential that the horse leads well, moving freely and quietly with the handler walking by the shoulder and not having to pull it along or haul it back. Early lessons with a helper behind the horse will soon teach it the correct way to lead; or you can carry a long whip in your left hand to touch the pony behind your back if on your own. Of course everything should be done quietly and calmly so as not to upset or frighten the animal. If you have a rather bumptious youngster, make sure he is well disciplined before bringing him to a show. Firm handling is all that is required to make the horse respect you; this is necessary for all animals, some to a greater degree than others.

For small local shows, youngstock can usually be shown from the field, if they look well enough. They should be brought in, trimmed and their manes and tails washed the day before. However, it is not really possible to expect grass-kept mares and youngstock to travel all over the country and look their best; nor is it very good for them.

For serious in-hand showing the animals must be stabled for a while, although still turned out during the day, or if a stallion, exercised or lunged. Old coats must be removed by regular strapping, and rugging will be necessary to keep the coat looking good. Feeding linseed is very good for coats. Be very careful not to over-feed youngsters; this coarsens them, spoils their action, and in ponies, in particular, could lead to laminitis. Ponies were never designed to be pig fat and the happy medium should be your aim.

Stallions

Stallions and colts are more intelligent than geldings and can easily get out of hand if mismanaged and be a real danger. However, you should have no problems, provided you are quick-witted and remember to treat them with firmness when neccessary. A stick should always be carried with colts or stallions and a quick smart smack given if and only when necessary.

Tack is useful for schooling stallions in-hand, it balances and controls them, and some Mountain and Moorland stallions are shown

Holly of Spring winning first prize in a show.

The rider wearing traditional dress for side-saddle riding, holding her mount, while the judges assess the condition of the horse.

in tack. Thoroughbreds, Arabs and cross-bred stock are shown in a bridle and lead rein. Consequently so many people are under the impression that stallions are dangerous, which is simply not true, if they are properly handled and treated like other horses. But it is a wonder that there have not been terrible accidents when one sees the amazingly stupid things people do with them sometimes. Do not expect stallions to behave when a mare is right next to them, or when they are in a crowd with everyone far too close, or if they are always being fed tit-bits. Just use common sense and treat them accordingly.

When going to your show, do make sure that your helper or groom is neatly and tidily dressed. Nothing looks worse than a lot of scruffy humans crowding into the ring to "do" the horse with buckets, coloured rags and so on. A rug, body brush, sponge and clean stable cloth is all that is necessary to take into the ring. Neat and tidy hacking jackets, trousers or jodhpurs and riding hat or scarf are appropriate and several shows will no longer allow helpers into the ring unless dressed accordingly. Grooms should strip off saddles and sponge down saddle patches as quickly and quietly as possible, doing the essential but not unnecessarily fussing the animal in the process. A rug should be put over the animal if the weather is cold; a cotton sheet in hot weather will prevent the coat from becoming "stary". As soon as the rider is mounted again, grooms should leave the ring, ensuring that they do not at anytime interfere with the judging of the class while doing so.

Sidesaddle

Sidesaddle riding has again become increasingly popular in the last few years. There are large entries in ladies hacks, hunters and children's pony classes, the latter being by far the most popular. It is not difficult to ride sidesaddle, but it is important to do it well, as nothing looks worse than someone riding sidesaddle badly and not sitting correctly or straight. Most horses or ponies will carry a

An Irish Draught stallion winning its class at the Royal Horse Show in 1977.

sidesaddle but, before showing in one, do make sure that it improves your horse, this is because the saddle does cover up the horse a little, so he needs a good front and one with a poor wither will have the saddle tending to slide forward. Also, not every animal is a comfortable sidesaddle ride – however lovely he may be to sit on astride. Horses tend to miss the outside leg so a long stick will help solve this problem until the horse gets used to it. Ladies riding sidesaddle should always wear a veil with a bowler hat and tie or with a top hat and stock during an afternoon or evening performance at a "Royal" show. Children can wear hunting caps without veils and all should wear neat sidesaddle habits with the elastic loop underneath holding the skirt correctly over the right foot. Hair should be in a bun and kept off the collar.

Clothes

All riders in show classes should be correctly and neatly turned out. Bright, gay colours are inappropriate. Neat tweed coats should be used on hunters and at small shows; blue or black coats at larger shows with jodhpurs and jodhpur boots for children, breeches and boots for adults. Dark leather or string gloves should be worn. Hunting caps, bowlers or top hats are all used for different classes, but they must all be correctly put on with the brim horizontal to the ground. Nothing looks worse than a hat stuck on the back of the head. Hair should be neatly tied back or worn in a hair net. Correctly tied stocks should be used always with a top hat. A tie is appropriate with a bowler. Sometimes correct dress is not easy to establish as occasionally one sees an amazing array of different dress. It is best to ask a professional, if in doubt. A neat show cane or leather show stick should be carried in all classes, although a hunting crop may be carried in hunter classes with hunting dress. A lot of make-up is not appropriate when riding.

Some popular shows

The next few paragraphs consists of a run-down of some of the most popular show classes and some points relative to them:

All *hunters* have to be registered with the National Hunter and Light Horse Breeding Society. There are several breeding and youngstock in-hand classes. The ridden classes comprise Small, Novice, Lightweight, Middleweight, Heavyweight and Ladies' classes and Working Hunters, often divided into a Lightweight and Heavyweight section. The only height restriction is in the Small Hunter class when 15.2 hands is the limit. Hunters are expected to gallop and are ridden by the judge.

Hacks have two height classes, under 15 hands and not exceeding 15.3 hands. There are sometimes Novice and Ladies' Hack classes. The British Show Hack and Cob Society is the governing body. Hacks are judged on ride, performance, manners and conformation. Hacks are not expected to gallop and are ridden by the judge. Height certificates are required.

Cobs are governed by the British Show Hack and Cob Society and are ridden by the judge. They are expected to gallop.

Children's pony classes are governed by the British Show Pony Society. There are several different types. The show pony classes of 12.2 hands, 13.2 hands, and 14.2 hands, Leading Rein, Sidesaddle, First Pony classes. The Working Pony classes of 13.00 hands, 14.00 hands, and 15.00 hands, also Nursery Stakes. Children and ponies have to register with the B.S.P.S. Children need to send their birth certificates. Show ponies are not required to jump, but Working Ponies are. Height certificates are required. Ponies are not ridden by the judge.

Riding horses may be required to gallop and jump. Riding horses are ridden by the judge. In most cases you may not enter a riding horse class if you have entered for a hack or hunter class at the same show.

Arabs are governed by the Arab Horse Society. Ridden classes for Pure Bred Stallions, Mares and Geldings and also Part Breds and Anglo-Arabs are ridden by the judge. In-hand classes for all types.

There are several different classes of riding ponies in-hand for different ages, sex and heights. Ponies at shows are plaited, and youngstock in height classes may not exceed 12.2 hands, 13.2 hands, or 14.2 hands, at maturity.

The National Pony Society champions the cause of all the Native breeds. Each breed has its own society. All pure Native breeds are shown unplaited except for New Forest mares. (It is optional with Connemaras.) Welsh Mountain mares have one plait not turned up behind the ears. Welsh Section B are sometimes plaited but schedules usually state the requirements. There are several ridden pure-bred classes and mixed Mountain and Moorland classes and in-hand classes. Most Societies have their own breed shows.

Palominos are governed by the British Palomino Society, and all horses and ponies have to be registered. All horses and ponies are judged on their colour and conformation. Palominos are shown unplaited and will not be accepted for judging if produced plaited. There are some ridden Palomino classes and Palomino shows.

To conclude, showing should be fun and whether you win or lose there is usually another day with another judge with whom to fare better or worse. Every show attended will gain you valuable knowledge and experience, but however good you are yourself you are never so good that you could not be better, so there is still plenty to be absorbed by us all in the years to come.

Mrs Georgina Andrews, correctly dressed for side-saddle riding, on DAKS Blizzard, winning the Ladies' Hunter Class at The Royal Bath & West Show in 1978.

Left: A member of the Spanish Riding School performs one of the "Airs above the Ground".

Right: This is the larger of the two dressage test arenas. It is used for International Competitions.

Below: Jennie Loriston Clarke, bronze medallist in the 1978 World Championships, performs at Goodwood.

Dressage

by Jane Kidd

All over the world riders are taking up competitive dressage. They are discovering the fascination of trying to master the techniques that enable riders to control, train and be in harmony with their horses. How successful a rider is in this purpose is decided, in competitions, by judges who give marks according to how well they believe a competitor performed a movement.

Dressage, however, is an art, and the mark must be based on human judgement. Dressage competitors find that one day a judge may be a little hard with his marks, and another can be equally lenient; but they usually end up all square at the end of the season. After all, show jumpers have to face an element of unfairness too, for a pole might fall when only lightly brushed while another will stay when hit very hard. Every sportsman needs his luck.

The dressage competitor is tested in an arena, the perimeter of which is marked with white boards. At specified intervals around the outside of the arena there are markers with letters which are used to indicate where movements should begin and end. Cutting the arena in half longitudinally is the centre line, which is either a mown strip, a painted line or sawdust.

Two arenas are used for dressage tests, the smaller one measuring 44 yards × 22 yards (40 metres × 20 metres), and the larger arena measuring 166yd × 22yd (60m × 20m) has four extra markers, and is used for all the more advanced tests.

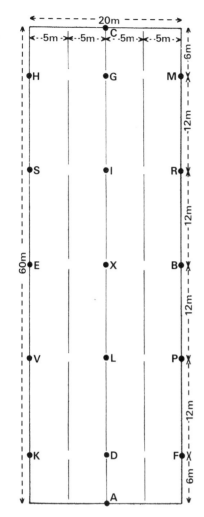

Dressage tests are made up of movements performed at the walk in which the four hoof-beats should be distinctive and regular; at the trot which should show elasticity, rhythm, impulsion and cadence (springiness of step); and at the canter which should be united, light, regular and cadenced.

Variations are asked of these paces, the most difficult being the Collected paces when high and short steps are taken. The Extended paces have longer, flatter steps, but not quicker ones, and Medium paces have steps that are rounder than the Extended, but longer than the Collected.

At the canter, even in the easier tests, the horse is asked to *counter canter* when the outside instead of the inside leg is the leading leg on a curve or circle. Legs can be changed in the canter through a *simple change* when the horse is brought back to the walk, and after one or two steps moves off into the canter on the other leg; and for the more advanced horses with a *flying change*. In this the change is made at the canter with the fore and hind lead changing simultaneously with straightness, impulsion and rhythm. Flying changes can be single ones, or in series at every fourth, third, second and eventually, single stride.

The *rein-back* is used from medium standard tests upwards when the feet are raised and moved backwards in diagonal pairs, almost simultaneously.

The *pirouette* is a small circle performed on two tracks with a radius of the length of the horse, the forehand moving around the hindquarters. At the walk it is part of medium tests, but at the canter only advanced horses are expected to perform it.

Lateral movements, which entail the horse stepping sideways as well as forward, are introduced at the medium level. The *leg yield* is the simplest with the animal moving sideways, straight except for a slight bend at the poll away from the direction of the movement. The *shoulder-in* requires some collection and is therefore more difficult. The forehand of the horse is brought in to move on a different track from the hindlegs, which continue on the original track.

The shoulder-in is only performed at the trot, but the *half-pass* can also be done at the canter with the horse moving on two tracks across a diagonal and remaining as close as possible parallel to the longside of the arena.

The most advanced movements asked for in dressage tests are the *piaffe*, a very cadenced, elevated and collected trot on the spot, and the *passage*, a very collected, very elevated and cadenced trot, in which the moment of suspension is longer than for any other form of trot.

The figures asked for in dressage tests include the *volte*, which is a circle of 6m (20ft) in diameter, and a *serpentine*, which is a series of loops which may be to either side of the arena or a specified distance on either side of the centre line.

There are dressage tests for a wide range of standards. It is normal for a national dressage federation to have a set of progressively more difficult tests and to grade their horses so that the easiest tests are only open to horses that have not won x number of points or y amount of prize money. In the United Kingdom the easiest tests are the Preliminaries in which the horse is merely asked to show his basic paces. Then there are the Novice, followed by the Elementary and Medium sets of tests. The most difficult nationally devised tests are Advanced in which canter pirouettes, and series of flying changes have to be performed.

The most advanced tests of all are the international tests. These are devised by the FEI to be used at all international shows and championships, but they are also used at national shows a good deal. The easiest is the Prix St George (equivalent to Britain's most advanced national test), then the Intermediaire I, Intermediaire II, Grand Prix and Grand Prix Special are progressively more difficult.

Every test is divided into sections containing movements and transitions, and for each section a judge awards a maximum of 10

Left: Harry Boldt on Woyceck, runners-up for the 1976 Olympic title, the 1977 European Championship and third in the 1978 World Championships.

Right: Movements.
1. Work on two tracks. The diagram shows the position of the horse when traversing. 2. Serpentine. 3. Change through the circle. 4. Figure of eight. 5. Half volte.

Below: Going down the centre line in the Dressage at Wolfsburg in West Germany.

marks. The scale of marks is as follows: 10 excellent, 9 very good, 8 good, 7 fairly good, 6 satisfactory, 5 sufficient, 4 insufficient, 3 fairly bad, 2 bad, 1 very bad, 0 not executed. At the end of the test marks are given for general impression and the usual sections are: 1 Impulsion. 2 Paces. 3 Submission. 4 Seat and correct application of aids by the rider.

The Judge who determines the marks usually has to pass tests himself. The national federation grades judges so that the inexperienced are limited to judging novice tests, and only the experienced and perceptive, can judge the international tests.

The judge has a writer who takes down both the mark and the judges comments about the performance of the rider in each section. Competitors can collect their own test sheet at the end of a competition and can learn a great deal by studying the comments.

The important factor for a competitor is to find out just what is required of him. Consequently, it is well worth careful study of the definitions of paces and movements as laid down by the FEI. After all, a test sheet merely asks for a halt but what the FEI asks the judge to look for is a halt in which the horse stands attentive, motionless and straight with the weight evenly distributed over all four legs and with the feet positioned in pairs the feet forming a rectangle. The neck should be raised with the head slightly in front of the vertical (not overbent or above the bit). The horse can champ at the bit but should at all times maintain a light contact with the rider's hand.

At home prior to the competition it is advisable to read the rule book and check that all the proposed tack is allowed by the national federation. Many bits are prohibited, and such things as spurs need not be worn at novice levels but have to be worn for medium and levels above.

It is also important that careful attention is given to the turnout. A pleasing smart overall effect can help to put the judge into a more generous frame of mind – after all dressage is supposed to be an elegant activity. Consequently, horses' tails need pulling, coats need grooming, manes need plaiting, tack needs polishing and hooves need blacking. The rider, too, must see to his dress; almost anything that is

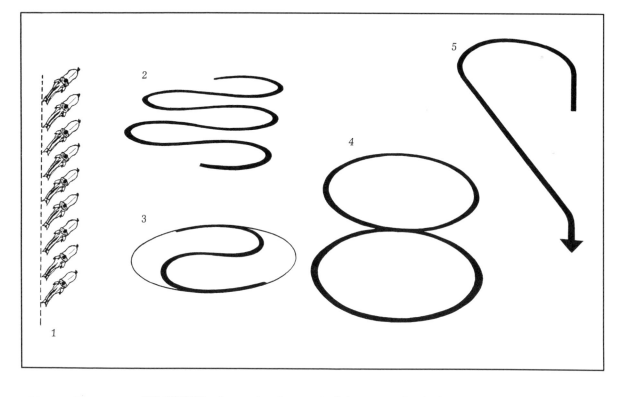

becoming is permissible, except in the international tests when a top hat and a tail coat are required.

The horse's training, it is to be hoped, will have taken him to, or above the standard of the test. It is, however, important to get arena practice. An arena of the appropriate size can be laid at home, with boards or poles on the ground and buckets for the markers. Although the test can be run through once or twice in its entirety, there is danger in doing it too often as the horse starts to anticipate. It is wisest just to run through sections or parts of sections and mix them in with other movements. It is a help to have someone watching to make remarks on the rider's position and to see if the horse is straight and going correctly.

The competitor should direct his training towards the achievement of the FEI's explicit definitions. But the rider must not forget that last mark on the test sheet – position and seat of rider and correct application of aids. Although this only provides a small percentage of the marks, unless the rider is capable of getting a good mark in this section, then he is going to find it very difficult to train his horse. It is well worth spending time on the lunge and getting the best possible position, for a bouncing, crooked rider who gives cumbersome aids will find it extremely difficult to achieve that highly prized harmony with the horse.

The aspiring dressage competitor needs to study the dressage tests and decide which his horse is capable of performing reasonably smoothly and effortlessly. It does not pay to be over ambitious, for if the horse has to be hauled in the mouth and kicked in the ribs to perform a movement then he not surprisingly objects, and develops resistances which will be difficult to cure. It is also best for the debutant to find a local dressage show run by a Riding Club where it will be easier for the rider not to develop those handicapping nerves.

Another important preparation that can be done at home is to find out how long it takes to "ride in" the horse – the length of time it takes to get him going in his best possible way. This will vary according to the temperament and stiffness of the horse. Excitable horses may be best off with a good deal of work the day before and then a lunge and a short "ride in" prior to the test. It is up to the rider to experiment – a successful dressage rider needs to understand his horse's mind.

On the day of the show, arrive in plenty of time – time for what should, by now, be a determined "riding in" period. But the rider needs some suppling up too. Even those who are not nervous tend to get keyed up and tense and this can ruin the seat. Most top riders can be seen riding in without stirrups as this helps to get them deeper into their saddles.

As the time for the test approaches, it is important to get totally absorbed in what lies ahead. Relaxed concentration is vital and it can help to run through the test "imagining" how to ride each movement.

Check must be taken, too, of the type of horse being ridden. If he is highly strung, then the aim must be calmness, sympathy and not asking too much of him. If he is lazy and hefty, then he has to be alerted and worked on to give his best. If the test is difficult for him, then do not ask too much; aim for a satisfactory but calm performance. If the test is well within his (and your) capability, then dare much more. Ask for as much extension as possible, and ask for precise and definite transitions.

When the prior competitor finishes there will be a few minutes for working around the arena while the judge makes the summary and gives the last general marks. This time can be used to get the horse used to the arena, to ensure that he is supple and relaxed when working there, but make it look good, for the judge may glance up and get the first overall picture.

A dressage test

When the bell or horn sounds try not to leap out of the saddle with nerves, but forget everything other than getting the best out of the horse in the test ahead.

Enter on the rein which the horse is straightest, for the judge will mark severely horses that are bent or have their quarters to one side when approaching down the centre line. A straight course is essential and, like riding a bicycle, the best way of achieving this is not to look down, but for the rider to hold his head high and look well ahead.

Come gently to a halt at X. It is far better, in the novice tests, to take a few steps at the walk rather than to haul on the reins and make the horse resist. Then it is time to show some respect to the judge or judges. A proud dignified salute – the men doffing their hats and the ladies putting their right hand to their side – sets the tone and helps to make the judge think the rider must be good.

In the move off it is important to keep steering that straight course, so keep looking up, sit straight and keep the legs around the horse.

From now on tests differ in their demands, but we can run through a typical novice one, the British Horse Society's Dressage Test number 12 (see illustration). Keep the horse well together on the move off, for tracking right at C entails a sharp turn. Try not to cut the corner, but do not lose the balance. Keep up the rhythm, keep the horse going forward well on to the bit all along the long side.

The three-looped serpentine from C has to be manoeuvred thoughtfully to get three equal loops; there must be definite changes in the horse's bend from one direction into the next and the correct rhythm is vital.

Now it is into the canter. Prepare for that transition, build up the impulsion and do not give one hefty kick which will catch the horse unawares. Try to keep the forehand in, to prevent the quarters coming in, and again think of the all-important rhythm and keeping the horse on the bit.

Make sure that 20-metre circle is a circle and not a square or an oblong. Use the inside leg to keep up the impulsion and help maintain an inside bend around it.

Now comes that tricky half circle. That is easier to do if the turn is not started until just before H, and come up to the top end of the arena. Think of the rhythm, the balance, and the bend. Take care the horse is

THE BRITISH HORSE SOCIETY'S

DRESSAGE TEST

NUMBER 12

(Novice standard) 1974

		Test	Max. Marks
1.	A X 	Enter at working trot (sitting) Halt. Salute. Proceed at working trot (rising)	10
2.	C	Track right	10
3.	A	Working trot (sitting) serpentine 3 loops, each loop to go to the side of the arena finishing at C	10
4.	M B BAE	Working canter right Circle right 20m diameter Working canter	10
5.	Between E&H K	Half circle right 15m diameter returning to the track between E&K Working trot (sitting)	10
6.	A C	Working trot (rising) serpentine 3 loops each loop to go to the side of the arena finishing at C Working trot (sitting)	10
7.	H E EAB	Working canter left Circle left 20m diameter Working canter	10
8.	Between B&M F	Half circle left 15m diameter returning to the track between B&F Working trot (sitting)	10
9.	A KXM	Working trot (rising) Change rein and show a few lengthened strides	10
10.	C HXF	Medium walk Change rein at a free walk on a long rein	10
11.	F A G	Working trot (sitting) Down centre line Halt. Salute. Leave arena at walk on a long rein at A	10
12.		General impression, obedience and calmness	10
13.		Paces and impulsion	10
14.		Position and seat of the rider and correct application of the aids	10
		TOTAL	140

A score sheet for a novice dressage test. The letters in the second column refer to where in the arena each part of the test should be performed.

Right: A reprise at the Spanish Riding School in Vienna.

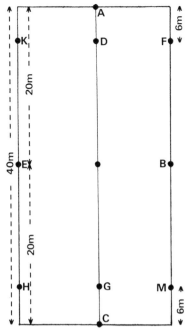

Above: The smaller Dressage arena measuring 44 yards by 22 yards (40 m × 20 m). This is used for less advanced tests.

straight and not on two tracks when returning towards the long side, so bring the forehand well around. Keep the legs around him for that short piece of counter canter and push into that transition, so he does not fall into the trot.

Aim for the same points on the other rein, in the serpentine, the canter left and the like, but when coming back to the trot at F there is a tricky bit ahead. Those lengthened strides across the arena are very difficult to get if the horse is on his forehand, not on the bit, and not going forward; so try to get all this organised between F and K. When setting off across the diagonal, take it easy at first – after all it is only a *few* lengthened strides. Get the horse balanced, get the hindquarters engaged and then ask him, but keep the rhythm. Steady him before M by using the seat and legs to a resistant, not pulling hand.

In the walk the important point is to get him to walk out in four time, not to run, and in the free walk to give him plenty of rein so that he can stretch his head downwards. Trot at F with a smooth transition and turn down the centre line aiming for straightness etc., as in the beginning.

When it is all over, remember a test is never perfect. The important point is to realise what went wrong and aim to correct it, but at the same time not to forget to enjoy those bits that went well.

Cross-country

by Michael Clayton

The cross-country phase of a Three Day Event is the focus of most public attention. Inevitably, it produces the thrills which entertain the crowd, and it does this most effectively. There are more spectators on the Duke of Beaufort's delectable estate, Badminton, on the cross-country day of the famous Three Day Event than are present at the FA cup final.

How much fun is it for the competitor? This question is at the heart of sport. Of course, a skilful rider and a good horse should enjoy the cross-country phase, but some clearly relish it more than others.

Enjoyment and the reservoirs of courage and dash available to horse and rider, are closely related. The truly successful combinations are those which enjoy the challenge of cross-country riding to the utmost, and which can genuinely be said to follow the age-old advice to the novice rider over fences: "Throw your heart over first".

The elements which bring success in the other two phases of an event – dressage and show jumping – are of course a great help in succeeding in the speed and endurance phase: discipline, accuracy and balance.

Courage – key to success

Yet these assets will not be enough in crossing country effectively, if there is lack of zest and courage.

The FEI regulations giving the object of the endurance competition do not include the word "courage", but it is the key to success. The rule simply says that the object of the competition is "to prove the speed, endurance and jumping ability of the true cross-country horse when he is well trained and brought to the peak of condition. At the same time it demonstrates the competitor's knowledge of pace and the use of his horse across country".

Combined training, or eventing, evolved as a specific competition from the variety of long-distance rides and other contests held by European cavalry regiments up to the start of the First World War. Their aim was mainly to test the chargers ridden by the officers and men, and therefore endurance was always an important element in these competitions.

Early this century the French devised championships with four phases, for dressage, a steeplechase, a long-distance roads and tracks phase, and a final show jumping competition.

In 1912 Sweden held the Olympic Games in Stockholm, and included a "military" equestrian competition which was the forerunner of the modern Three Day Event. Combined training is merely the English term for what the French have always known as *concours complet*, the complete test.

The FEI now rules that the endurance competition in an international Three Day Event is divided into four phases: A, roads and tracks normally carried out at the trot or slow canter; B, steeplechase with obstacles, at the gallop; C, roads and tracks, at a trot or slow canter; D cross country, with obstacles, at the gallop.

In an international Three Day Event under FEI rules (known as a CCI) phases A and C (roads and tracks) a total of 10 to 16km (6 to 10 miles) has to be carried out at a speed of 240 metres per minute (260 yards per minute). In phase B (steeplechase) a distance of between 3,150yds and 3,775yds (2,880m and 3,450m) has to be carried out at a speed of between 700 and 750 yards (640 and 690 metres) per minute. In phase D (cross country) the distance is from 5,685yds to 8,100yds

Richard Meade on Wayfarer at full-stretch at Badminton.

(5,200m to 7,410m), and the required speed from 570 to 625yds (520 to 570 metres) per minute.

At the highest category, the official International Three Day Event (known as CCIO – Concours Complet International Officiel) the distances and speeds are: phases A and C 10 to 12½ miles (16 to 20 km) at a speed of 262 yards (240 metres) per minute; phase B, 3,735, 4,150 or 4,525 yards (3,450, 3,795 or 4,140m) at a speed of 755 yards (690 metres) per minute; phase D 8,100, 8,415 or 8,725 yards (7,410, 7,695 or 7,980m) at a speed of 625 yards (570 metres) per minute.

The Badminton Three Day Event was started in Britain in 1949. It soon became apparent that a shorter, less daunting competition was also needed as a practice and trial event. So in 1950, at Ewelme in Oxfordshire, there was held the first One Day Event. It was an immediate success.

In the cross-country phase of a Three Day Event there will be between 30 and 35 fixed obstacles on the course. A One Day Event has a course varying between 2.8 and 4km (1¾ and 2½ miles), with 20 to 25 obstacles in Advanced and Intermediate classes, and 16 to 20 obstacles in Novice classes.

Altogether there are 73 One Day Events, held all over Britain, and offering a remarkable range of Novice, Intermediate and Open Intermediate classes. Yet with more than 3,500 horses competing, events in Britain are frequently oversubscribed; the sport continues to boom.

Above: Old Fort combination jump at Lexington.

From the start, the British welcomed the challenge of the cross-country phase of eventing because so much of the tradition of riding throughout the United Kingdom and Ireland was based on riding to hounds in the hunting field.

No other country in the world offers more variety of fences and different terrains than are available in the British Isles. The great galloping grasslands of Leicestershire, intersected with neat brush fences and post and rails, offered the cream of the riding country for the foxhunter, and despite the increase of modern ploughing, the Quorn, Belvoir and Cottesmore hunting countries still attract among the largest mounted fields. Elsewhere in Britain there are stone walls, and an amazing variety of ditches, hedges and timber to be encountered in the hunting field.

British successes at Olympic and international championship level undoubtedly owe much to this background of natural cross-country riding. North American, European, and Australian teams have also excelled at the top level of the sport and continue to make great progress, but the British are still able to draw upon a great reservoir of talent in young riders.

Above: Giant's Table jump at Lexington.

Unfortunately, it is not so easy nowadays to find suitable horses for young riders to graduate to the highest realms of international eventing. The growth of the sport has produced an increasing demand, and consequently much higher prices, for the best horses. The sport requires complete soundness as well as considerable aptitude in young horses.

What type of horse?

What type of horse is needed for the challenge of cross-country riding in the modern event? Nothing less than a three-quarters bred horse is likely to fill the bill. Seven-eighths Thoroughbred will do, but there is an increasing trend towards the completely clean-bred horse.

A half-bred horse can jump the obstacles if he is well trained, but time is the vital factor in eventing. In the steeplechase course the competitor receives 0.8 of a penalty point in excess of the optimum time; in the cross-country course the figure is 0.4. Thus it is essential to ride a horse which can really gallop as well as jump, and the Thoroughbred has been evolved to do this more effectively than any other equine.

The Thoroughbred's long stride, his elasticity of tendons and suppleness of joints, are ideally suited to the shocks and strains of

Below: Typical rustic cross-country jump.

quick turns on an event course, and the need for a ground devouring gallop in getting from one obstacle to the next.

The problem with the Thoroughbred is his temperament; he may take far more skilful training and handling to settle quietly enough to get good marks in the initial dressage phase, and to be calm enough to clear in a show ring atmosphere on the final day's jumping phase.

The American team, on Thoroughbreds, showed how successfully they can be used in top level eventing when they won the team and individual Olympic medals in 1976. The cross-country course fences at Bromont, in Canada, appeared comparatively easy by Olympic standards, but the course's major changes in gradients and its stretches of dead going provided a severe test of a horse's physique and stamina. On the whole, the Thoroughbreds, especially the younger horses, stood up to the test the best. The American team said afterwards that they had chosen to ride their younger horses after inspecting the terrain.

Mike Plumb, competing in his fifth Olympic Games, explained why he chose to ride his seven-year old Better and Better, rather than his superb 14-year old Good Mixture: "I did not think it was going to be an easy course. The fences were not really a problem, but the uphill nature of the terrain, the uneveness of the going, and the sand track on the steeplechase course meant that a horse could never get settled down in a gallop, and never knew where its feet could be placed safely."

Where are suitable horses to be found nowadays? Britain and Ireland still remain excellent sources of the Thoroughbred and near Thoroughbred horse. International buyers may be seen for example, at the great annual Dublin Horse Show, looking out for animals which have quality and scope. Prices have soared in recent years, and the Irish Horse Board, and the Hunters' Improvement Society in the United Kingdom, both play a vital role in helping to stimulate the breeding of suitable horses for eventing. These bodies can give potential buyers invaluable advice and information about special sales of potential event horses held annually in Ireland and the United Kingdom.

Training for the cross country

The training of a horse for the cross-country element in eventing is inevitably linked with the schooling on the flat needed for the dressage phase. Balance, suppleness and response to the aids are the requirements. Working in an enclosed area, or an indoor school, is usually a great help in the early stages, the horse making transitions from walk to trot, and trot to walk in a circle with a light contact on the mouth.

Most event riders seriously engaged in making progress with a good horse nowadays undertake a great deal of their ground work under the guidance of an instructor or trainer.

It is vital not to persevere in ground work in one direction at a time. Frequent changes of direction are important, not only aiding suppleness and responsiveness, but in keeping the horse's interest and attention throughout the schooling period. Training on the flat continues regularly throughout the horse's career.

Jumping training for the eventer starts with trotting over poles on the ground, and progresses to jumping individual obstacles, before going on to lines of cavelleti (low single rails) at 5ft (1.5 to 2m) intervals. This is often used to graduate from two or three cavelleti to a longer distance, perhaps up to 12 feet (3.5 metres), before jumping a small fence.

The eventer must gain early experience in jumping ditches, water and drop fences. It is as much a question of familiarisation as actual jumping skill. How often does one see a novice horse poke his nose uncertainly at a black looking ditch because he has lost impulsion.

It is essential that the young horse is trained to jump *into* water fearlessly, as well as over it. Spreads and drop fences are vital in the training programme for the novice. It is obvious that some experience in the hunting field is an invaluable asset to the young horse in gaining confidence.

The essential of the cross-country course is that the obstacles are fixed, and should be as imposing as possible. Colonel Frank Weldon, the course builder and director of Badminton Three Day Event, has often explained that his object is to build obstacles which can "frighten the rider" but are always fair and never trappy, thus reducing the risk of injuring the horse to the minimum.

The Coffin obstacle is still a regular "stopper" in event courses. It comprises a combination of a rail, a drop down to a black looking ditch, then another rail to be jumped on the far side. All too often, horses will not jump the first rail because they are intimidated by the sight of the ditch beyond.

Novice riders frequently make the mistake of riding the timber too fast. Most horses tend to flatten when galloped at an obstacle; it is better to jump timber with the horse well balanced and his hocks well under him.

The need for balance and plenty of impulsion is emphasised by some of the modern combinations of timber fences being used by course builders. The quickest route through an apparent maze of timber may be a "bounce" stride between two post and rails. This calls for accuracy and balance, and saves a great deal of time; the course builder carefully ensures that the alternative easier route takes much longer to complete.

The FEI rules stipulate that the fixed and solid part of all cross-country obstacles in Three Day Events will not exceed a height of 3ft 11in. (1.20m). In a CCI (Concours Complet International), obstacles with a spread must not exceed 9ft 11in. (3.50m); a water jump with a spread must have a maximum spread of 13ft 1in. (4m) inclusive of any guard rail. The fixed and solid part of the steeplechase obstacles must not exceed 3ft 3in. (1m), with the brush not exceeding an overall height of 4ft 7in. (1.40m).

For a bold, fit horse the steeplechase element in the speed and endurance section of a Three Day Event should present no problems, but all too frequently upsets occur through error on the rider's part.

The problem is one of pace; obviously it is vital to finish within the optimum time, avoiding time penalties. But it is a great mistake to "bash on" too fast round the steeplechase course. The usual brush fences encountered on this course in themselves should offer no difficulties and a good steady gallop at a pace to finish well within the time should be accurately worked out at practice sessions with the aid of stop watches, and a rider has the benefit of consulting a watch during the event.

Too much speed may, at the very least, impair the horse's stamina unnecessarily; a considerable handicap, since the cross-country course is still to be faced. And all too often "invincible" combinations of horse and rider incur slip-ups and falls on steeplechase courses through indulging in unnecessarily reckless galloping and careless jumping.

The time element is equally important in the cross-country ride, and although changes of pace are inevitable here, the horse which can be settled into a good strong consistent pace between the fences will be far more likely to arrive at each obstacle effectively balanced and stands much more chance of finishing within the time limit. Each three seconds over the limit costs one penalty point.

Falls and refusals only count if they occur in the penalty zones marked round the obstacle, but leaving the penalty zone without having jumped the obstacle to be negotiated costs 20 penalties. On the steeplechase course or the cross-country course a first refusal incurs 20 penalties, the second 40, and the third causes elimination. A fall of horse and/or rider costs 60 penalties on the steeplechase course, and elimination for the second fall. On the cross country the first two falls cost 60 penalties each. If the horse falls a third time, then he is eliminated and must retire.

The 1976 Olympic course

The cross country built by Barbara Kemp for the 1976 Olympic Games at Bromont gives a good idea of the immense variety of obstacles which the modern event horse has to face at top level. He may encounter modified examples of such fences at lower levels of this exciting sport.

The first fence was an inviting stone wall, then came a "stopper" for some horses in the form of a steep bank to descend, with a post and rails one stride from the foot of it. This rode much better than it looked, but it caused three falls.

Parallel rails and a substantial post and rail into a woodland track led to a double zig-zag of timber, followed by large crossed tree trunks. This called for accuracy, and three horses fell here.

A table fence was encountered on the woodland track, and then came a pile of birch logs. Then came the Bromont Slalom, one of the most difficult of fences: three timber jumps at different angles downhill.

A staircase jump across the angle of the hill, some spruce parallels, a timber pen, and some rails uphill were encountered next. Fence number 15 caused six falls, more than any other obstacle. It comprised post and rails on a downhill slope, involving horses in a difficult landing on a gradient, with only a couple of strides following, to jump a rustic table. Some horses were put at the rails too fast and over jumped, thus being unable to check sufficiently to jump the next obstacle. Other horses were put at the post and rails too slowly, got "under" it on take-off, and then tipped up on landing.

Four more upright timber fences and a stone wall followed, then came a curious combination at a lake. Horses had to jump two boats lying on their sides, into the lake, then in and out of water over a brush fence "growing" in the middle of the lake. Finally there was another timber fence out of the lake. Horses who took the first fence too fast tended to crumple and fall on landing in the water.

After this three more timber fences, including a bounce in-and-out of a corral, led to a stone wall. There followed a small bank and a "ski jump" – a jump down off a ramp, which caused no trouble; then came a bullfinch of corn stooks, an open ditch and timber, a simple open water, and then three large terraced banks, with a steep descent on the far side to a log pile. Straw bales in a manger comprised the final fence.

Compared with some Badminton and Burghley courses in Britain, this Olympic course did not contain many fences where horses could gallop on boldly at imposing obstacles. There appeared to be a great deal of "hooking up" to be done in tackling many of the fences; nevertheless, it undoubtedly called for considerable riding skill and great ability on the part of the horse to remain balanced on a variety of gradients. Altogether there were 36 obstacles in a distance of 8,410 yards (7,695 metres) to be completed in an optimum time of 13 minutes 30 seconds.

It can be seen that the demands of cross-country riding are immense at top level; it is undoubtedly one of the toughest risk sports in the Olympic Games, and no woman took part in an Olympic Three Day Event until 1964 when the honour fell to an American, Helen du Pont. Since then, women riders – including Princess Anne at Bromont – have represented Britain and other countries with considerable distinction.

Standards of training and expertise have improved enormously in the postwar years, but it must always be remembered that owners, riders and organisers have a prime responsibility in ensuring that modern event horses are genuinely capable of tackling courses which are a fair test of their ability without undue risk of serious injury. In the main this precept is well observed, and cross-country riding has a great future as a challenge to new generations of young riders, and as a thrilling spectacle.

HRH Princess Anne on Goodwill riding down a slope towards an obstacle

The water jump always attracts a large crowd at any Horse Trials. Illustrated right is the jump as seen at a recent Badminton three-day event.

Show Jumping

by Jane Kidd

A perfect example of how to jump an oxer by Eddie Macken on Boomerang at the Horse of the Year Show. Notice how he has kept his balance and let the horse have his head.

For a competitor to see his country's flag being raised, to hear his national anthem being played in honour of his horse's victory, is the most glorious feeling. It makes the inevitable heartaches, setbacks, and injuries involved in becoming good enough to win International competitions all worthwhile. It is the *raison d'être* of any ambitious rider.

Yet international competitions have more to offer than these glorious moments. Just to participate provides that exciting challenge of testing ability against "the" or at least "some of the" best in the world. Because, too, international shows take pride in being good hosts, there are usually exceptional opportunities to meet leading people in the land and to view the country. The horse, too, seems to provide a rather more endearing common denominator than a swimming pool or an athletics track and communication between everybody from Russian communists to South American revolutionaries and American capitalists is a feature of international shows. To be an international competitor provides an exceptional passport to see and learn about other nations.

In the equestrian field there are four types of international sports. Show jumping is the most lucrative, the most publicised and the most frequently performed, with the season running all year round.

Eventing is the most dashing and sporting form of international equestrianism, but because of the strains put on the horses and the need for outdoor venues events are only held from May to October and on limited occasions.

Dressage is the equestrian sport with the closest connections to art. Yet competitors need self-discipline as much as talent, and spectators need knowledge really to enjoy it. At the international competitions these demanding requirements make the atmosphere more dignified and erudite than in other equestrian sports.

Combined Driving is the newcomer to the international equestrian circuit. The rules were only drawn up in 1969 when an event on wheels was devised for teams (4 horses) and carriages. They have to complete 3 tests – dressage and presentation, the marathon and obstacle driving. It has proved a huge success – spectators love to watch the old means of transport hurry across country and through dressage tests; competitors enjoy the thrill of getting their horses to pull carriages through these demanding tests.

These international sports are controlled by the Fédération Equestre Internationale (FEI) which co-ordinates, standardises and publishes rules and supervises the organisation of international competitions. The foundations for this organisation were laid in 1921 when eight countries (France, Sweden, Belgium, Denmark, Italy, Japan, Norway and the USA) got together to control international show-jumping events. Until that time, although competitions were held, the rules varied from country to country and from show to show. Sometimes marks were given for style and practically all the time penalty marks were varied.

Standardisation of rules was a start, but after the Second World War the FEI extended its scope to run international championships. The first was held in Ostend in 1952 for Juniors. Although support for this initial venture was poor – only two teams – much grander, and more successful championships have been held ever since.

The format of these championships have been changed over the last 20 years, but they have now settled into a generally acceptable form. In dressage, jumping and eventing (not driving) there are Junior European Championships every year. For the adults in dressage, jumping and eventing there are the Olympic Games – the ultimate test – every four years. And every four years (two away from the Olympics) there are World Championships, but driving has an extra World Championship in Olympic Year to compensate this new sport for not yet gaining a place at the Games. All four sports then stage a European Championship every two years.

These yearly championships are the feature of the equestrian's year. The gold medals (Olympic, and FEI versions for Continental Championships) are given to winning members of teams, and victorious individuals; they are the most prized possessions of any international rider.

The venues of these championships change, and except for the Olympics are usually staged by the defenders of the title. One of the attractions of international competitions, however, are the events held every year at the same venue. Competitions at each of these develop a certain flavour and become famed for particular jumps or aspects of the competitions. The atmosphere at each of these events will depend much on its host country and although each country can only hold one official show with a team championship, they can stage any number of ordinary international shows as long as they are well enough run to be approved by the FEI.

It is show jumping that has both the largest number of Official Internationals (CSIOs Concours de Saut International Officiel) and ordinary Internationals (CSIs). There are enough to run an annual Team Championship based on cumulative successes. Points are given at each CSIOs team competition – the Nations cups or Prix des Nations. The country accummulating the most points in these Nations Cups wins the trophy – the Presidents Cup – and since its inauguration in 1965 the United Kingdom has been the most frequent winner.

A CSIO is held by all foremost jumping nations – except Australia where quarantine regulations and geographical situation make international jumping impossible. Probably the most famous CSIO is Aachen in Germany – the leading nation of show jumpers. Aachen is the biggest test for a competitor outside the Olympic Games, for it is renowned for its imposing huge courses, formidable natural obstacles and the largest number of participants. Rome another of the best known CSIOs has tricky courses but the obstacles tend to fall more easily. A careful horse is best in Rome and a bold one in Aachen. At Madrid, where the arena is in the picturesque grounds of Club de Campo, the fences are just as big as Aachen but they are not so solid. Holland holds one of the most popular shows at Rotterdam where a permanent arena is filled with imaginatively built fences that are inviting and not trappy to jump. Ireland has one of the most famous shows and not just for horses, as Dublin Hunt Balls make it a favourite show for the party-loving competitors. But Dublin, too, has some of the biggest prize money in the world, so the commercial competitors also queue up for a place on a team.

Indoor jumping

A feature of modern jumping has been the development of indoor jumping. The North Americans were the first to use such enclosed arenas for major shows running the Fall circuit which featured Madison Square Garden in New York (CSIO) and the Toronto Royal Winter Fair in Canada (CSIO). The victories at these are prestigious, and the hospitality of the host countries generous, so it has become a coveted trip for international show jumpers.

The United Kingdom compromises by running the individual competitions indoors at Wembley and the team competition outdoors at Hickstead. Few horses manage to do well at both, for the small space

Right: David Broome clearing a very high wall on Philco.

Below: A good picture showing the rider in the right position and the horse basculing well. Notice the use of the running martingale.

at Wembley demands quick, springy, bouncy horses and the large arena and the imposing huge fences at Hickstead demands bold horses with great scope.

Hickstead, though, is probably more famous for the British Jumping Derby than as the venue of the British Nations Cup. A Jumping Derby is one of the most exciting forms of international competitions with the course demanding endurance and courage in addition to normal jumping skills. There are more jumps, the distance is longer and most of the obstacles are natural types rather than fly fences – Hickstead has its famous 10ft 6in. (3.20m) bank to slide down. Derby courses remain unaltered from year to year and it is some indication of comparative standards that clear rounds are still rare.

Jumping Derbys are held in such countries as South Africa, France and Australia, but the only one to rival the prestige of Hickstead is the originator – the Hamburg Derby which was first held in 1929. It took 15 years before a competitor jumped clear over this hazardous course.

The international circuit for eventers has developed a great deal over the past decade. Originally, the only major international Trials apart from the Olympic Games or Continental Championships were Badminton. These British Horse Trials were started by the Duke of Beaufort after the 1948 Olympic Games and still remain the major event of the spring season, attracting participants from all over the world. In the autumn the United Kingdom now has another important event at Burghley where the lovely parklands have been the venue of World and European Championships.

Then Holland has Boekelo; Germany Luhmuhlen, France Haras du Pin, the United States Ledyard Farm, and Belgium Heide-Kalmthout.

There are thus a growing number of opportunities for an eventer to compete in foreign countries, but, unlike a show jumper he will need more than one horse if he is to compete frequently. The Three Day Event tests endurance and no horse can stand up to many Trials in a year. As the international event circuit expands, many of the leading riders are extending their horse power in order to make the most of the opportunities to compete abroad.

Aachen – mecca for dressage

For dressage riders the mecca is, as for show jumpers, Aachen. Germany is the only country where riders are brought up to dressage, so that much of the population understands, this rather complicated sport and enjoys watching it. The result is grandstands packed with knowledgeable spectators, a vibrant atmosphere and domination by the German riders in international classes. The young Christine Stückelberger from Switzerland and the occasional Russian have been the only serious challengers to the Germans in this sport which they love so much. Although Aachen is the pinnacle of the international dressage rider's year, Rotterdam holds popular championships in conjunction with the show jumping at the end of August. France stages some very remunerative events alternating between Fontainebleau and Nice; and the United Kingdom holds probably the most picturesque at Goodwood in Sussex.

The international dressage rider, however, does not lead the circus-like life of show-jumping riders. For the jumper competitive experience is vital and the rider earns more by frequent appearance in the ring. For the dressage rider it is work at home rather than experience in the arena that is so vital. Continuous travelling, and competitive appearance could jeopardise this and also make it difficult to train the replacement horses. Top dressage combinations therefore only appear half a dozen times a year. Most of the time is spent training at home.

Driving is the "baby" of international equestrian sports, but it is also one of the fastest growing. Once again it is Aachen that is the mecca of the sport, and also the originator, for they ran international competitions for teams (4 horses) and pairs in the 1960s before the FEI had drawn up rules for the sport. It was also in Germany, at Munich, that the first ever World Driving Championships was held in 1972; but it was Britain that staged the first international driving competitions under the FEI rules. These took place at Royal Windsor Horse Show in 1970 and since then these British driving Trials have been annual features in international driving competitions.

For riders at international competitions the opportunities to compete all over the world have expanded enormously over the last 20 years. So, too, have the international competitions for the younger, the less talented and inexperienced competitors. Today there are international competitions for school children, pony clubs, university undergraduates, riding clubs and even farmers. More and more equestrian sportsmen are enjoying the benefits of international competitions.

Right: Christine Stückelberger of Switzerland, one of the best dressage riders in the world, riding Granat at the World Championships in 1978.

Right below: Marc Roguet easily clearing a water jump.

Below: A team of four greys in the dressage and presentation section of combined driving.

Eventing

by Jane Kidd

The original competitors in Eventing (also known as Horse Trials, The Military and Combined Training) were soldiers. It was thought an excellent test of the stamina and versatility of military chargers to make them do dressage tests, go across country and tackle some show jumping; and for the first part of this century the sport was almost confined to the military. It was only after the last war that civilians started to participate in any great numbers and they turned it into a booming sport.

Since the 1950s the format of eventing has been streamlined to cope with an enormous increase in numbers of competitors and a wide range of standards. Although there are always the three tests – dressage, cross country and show jumping – they can now take place in a One Day Event, a Two Day Event and for the major trials only, the original Three Day Event.

In a One Day Horse Trial with all three tests taking place on one day the cross-country test is quite short and endurance is not on trial. In a Two Day Horse Trial the cross-country test is extended to include a modified steeplechase and a roads and tracks phase so that endurance does become more important. In the Three Day Event endurance becomes vital, for the cross-country then includes two separate phases of roads and tracks, a steeplechase and a cross-country section. This format for the cross-country test in a Three Day Event is known as the Speed and Endurance test.

All variations of Horse Trials are judged on a system of penalty points which are cumulative over the three tests. Penalty points awarded for the dressage are added to those gained by refusing, falling or being over the time in the cross-country test, or by knocking fences down in the show jumping. The winner has the least number of penalty points.

Most national federations grade their horses and then stage Horse Trials of varying standards. In the United Kingdom there are three grades – 1, 2 and 3; and there are Novice, Intermediate, Open Intermediate and Advanced Horse Trials. Novice Horse Trials are restricted to Grade 3 horse, Intermediate to Grade 2 or in some cases 2 and 3, with the result that horses can make their debut over the relatively easy courses of Novice Trials, and if successful progress to the more difficult. It shows some progress from the days when Sheila Willcox, the triple winner of Badminton, made her debut; her first ever event was one of the most difficult – the European Championships at Windsor in 1955!

The relative influence of the first test – the dressage – on an event is supposed to be slightly more than that exerted by the jumping but much less than the cross-country. Consequently, when a competitor is judged (in the same way as for pure dressage) his total marks (averaged if there is more than one judge) are subtracted from the maximum marks obtainable in the test, i.e. converted into penalty points, and then a multiplying factor applied according to the test being used. In the case of the FEI test it is 2/5.

The dressage tests used in Horse Trials vary from the very easiest for Novice Trials to those of a medium standard for Three Day Events, in which the horse is asked to perform lateral work, medium and extended paces and counter canter. Event horses are not asked for any collection as for them dressage is a means of improving the jumping and not as an end in itself.

The cross-country phase is run over solid, fixed and imposing fences. For novices these can not exceed 3ft 6in. (1.07m) in height, but for international events they can be 4ft (1.22m). The length of the course varies from a minimum of one mile (1.6km) with 16 to 20 obstacles for novices in a One Day Event, to five miles (8km) with 30 to 40 obstacles for the ultimate test at the Olympic Games.

These obstacles have to be tackled at speed, and time penalties are easily incurred. In Novice events the optimum time is 525 metres (574 yards) per minute and for every three seconds over this a penalty point is given. A competitor can be eliminated if he exceeds the time limit which is twice the optimum time.

In international events competitors are expected to go at an even faster rate, for they have to complete the cross-country section at a speed of 570 metres (623 yards) per minute.

A fine demonstration of the extended trot in the dressage phase.

Penalties are also incurred when tackling an obstacle. In national events it is the jump judge who decides if the errors were made when negotiating or attempting to negotiate an obstacle. In international events, however, there is a marked penalty zone, and outside it competitors can fall, turn circles with the only penalty being a loss of time. The penalties when tackling an obstacle are 20 for the first refusal, 40 for the second and elimination for the third at the same obstacle. A fall of horse or rider results in 60 penalties.

The cross-country (known as Phase D) is part of all Horse Trials, but in Two and Three Day events other phases are added. The roads and tracks help to test the endurance of the horse as he has to go at a fast trot (240 metres – 262 yards – per minute) for up to ten miles (16km). The chosen total distance is, however, completed in two halves, for there is a Phase A, and Phase C to the roads and tracks. In the Two Day Event, though, Phase A is not obligatory and therefore is usually omitted.

Separating the two phases of the roads and tracks is the section that tests the speed of the horse. This is the steeplechase (Phase B) which can vary from one to two and half miles (1.6 to 4km) in length and is over brush or hurdle fences. Horses have to complete this at a speed of 690 metres (755 yards) per minute which for all but the best of the Thoroughbreds means going flat out. Penalties are as for the cross-country, one point for every three seconds over the optimum time. It is a phase which can exhaust many horses, but they do have Phase C (roads and tracks) followed by a compulsory ten-minute halt to recover themselves before the most demanding section – the cross-country.

The jumping test is traditionally the final test and is rarely very demanding in itself for the object is that, after testing endurance across country, the horse is still supple, energetic and obedient enough to negotiate with precision obstacles that can be knocked down. In a Three Day Event every horse is inspected by a vet to ensure soundness before being allowed to jump. In Three Day Events too (except in team events) the competitors jump in reversed order of merit with the leader after two of the tests going last. They have to jump a course of not more than 3ft 11in. (1.19m) in height or 5ft 11in. (1.8m) in spread. The possible penalties are 10 for a fallen obstacle or first refusal and 15 for a fall. In national competitions the penalties are usually less – just 5 for a knock down.

Dressage with Jumping

In a One Day Event, where endurance is not being tested, the jumping phase is often prior to the cross country. The size of the fences for the novices is also less, 3ft 9in. (1.14m) being the maximum height and 5ft (1.52m) the spread.

Eventing is one type of Combined Training, and a rather less demanding form of this sport is Dressage with Jumping. It is popular with event riders as a means of giving their horses experience without the rigours of going across country, and for the fun of competing at the larger Horse Shows. Without the cross-country test this competition can be staged at Horse Shows, and organisers like using this opportunity to get event riders to participate.

It is not a competition which has international championships and countries make up their own rules. In Britain the dressage is marked as in pure Dressage with good points and this is followed by the jumping phase which is marked as in Show Jumping. Hence a competitor knocking a fence incurs four faults which is deducted from his dressage score. The winner has the highest number of points i.e. the points are good ones not penalty ones as in eventing.

The first essential requirement for those setting out to do some eventing is a horse, and the ideal mount will depend a good deal upon the rider and his ambitions. For the inexperienced rider tackling novice events a horse with a little "common" blood may be best. This less distinguished type usually has a more sensible temperament.

Those aiming at Three Day Events need more of a "blue blooded" Thoroughbred in order to get the speed and the stamina; but they will also need more skill to train these sensitive temperamental creatures.

Whatever the type decided upon there are certain common requirements. Firstly soundness. Eventing tests fitness and toughness, so the horse needs to have good conformation and no weaknesses. He is also more likely to stay sound if he is well up to his rider's weight. An underhorsed jockey is the first to break his mount down when going across country.

The horse must also be bold. It takes great bravery to tackle unknown cross-country fences. The best indications of this are a horse with a good eye, his previous competitive record (if any), and when trying the horse, judge his reactions to any spooky obstacles.

The event horse must have the ability as well as the courage to jump. He need not be so powerful or careful as a show jumper, but he must be clever and have the scope to get himself out of tricky situations. Important too, he must also have the temperament to be obedient during the dressage test.

Bruce Davidson (USA) won the World three-day event Championship in 1974 and 1978, seen here with his horse Might Tango.

Training for Eventing

Only freak horses can be talented in all the fields required of an eventer, but careful training can help in the spheres that do not come naturally. The work at home is vital for an eventer, not just to improve his skills but also to make him fit. Thoughtful, clever preparation for eventing is as important as being an able competitor on the day. To do it well it needs skilful adaptable riding, knowledgable conscientious stable management, careful planning and a good deal of hard work.

The dressage training can be approached in a similar fashion to that for pure dressage although the emphasis is on calmness and getting the horse relaxed. An event horse is a very fit animal, and usually has a good deal of spirited Thoroughbred blood, so one of the biggest dangers is explosive reactions in the dressage arena. It is usually best for dressage to become part of the everyday activities and most riders find it beneficial to practise it for 20 minutes or so each day.

For the jumping test the goal is to make the horse careful. He does not have to be made to jump high and wide like a show jumper. Horses find it easiest to be careful if taught to approach fences calmly with balance and impulsion, and to jump the fence with a bascule (rounding the neck and back). This style is best achieved by schooling the young horse over grids (see page 117).

To go across country, boldness needs to be added to jumping ability. This is best achieved by building up confidence to jump every sort of obstacle. Initially, before the horse becomes too valuable, hunting can be a wonderful aid. Following hounds is an enjoyable and efficient way of teaching a young horse to be bold, clever and go forward.

The events have become so sophisticated, however, that many of the fences are not found in the hunting field. Ditches, drops, coffins (post and rails with a non-jumping stride before a ditch, and another non-jumping stride to a second post and rails), waters that are jumped over and into, have to be tackled. Some can be constructed at home especially as the training fences are best kept very small; there also are equestrian centres where riders may, as members or by payment, practise over various obstacles.

Most riders find the events themselves excellent practice. In the initial competitions the pace can be kept slow and only increased to the speed needed for victory when the horse is sufficiently experienced.

Getting a horse fit is a vital part of events, for endurance, especially in Three Day Events, is tested as much as ability. Even for the novices who have to complete a comparatively short course it is still easier for them to tackle the obstacles if they have plenty of energy.

To get a horse fit for a Three Day Event takes about four months; for a One Day Event about three months. The important aspect is that the work is progressive so that the horse is never put under undue strain.

Remember that a large number of horses go wrong at home and not in the competition.

It is best to prepare a programme which is varied according to the horse and his projects. Some horses are stuffy and hard to get fit, so that they need longer and faster work; others may be quick to muscle up and clear their wind but are temperamental and need a great deal of practice at jumping and dressage to get them to settle.

Importance of fitness

Although schooling for jumping and dressage is important, much of the time has to be spent hacking, preferably in hilly country. When hacking though, schooling can still be continued. Grassy tracks are ideal for teaching the horse to go straight, on the bit, and to learn to lengthen or shorten his strides at the trot and canter.

As the horse gets fitter, he has to be treated more and more like a racehorse. Long steady canters are needed with the stuffy horses probably benefitting from occasional sharp bursts to clear the lungs. Great care must be taken about the state of the ground. Stony hard ground can so easily jar the joints or strain the tendons and end hopes of competing.

It is not just riding that is important in eventing, for success can be limited by poor stable management. Feeding is a vital factor. With novices, where fitness is not at a premium, oats (energy food) can be limited to keep the horse sensible enough to concentrate on his work. Advanced horses, however, need to assimilate as much energy food as possible (without creating protein poisoning) and this usually entails four feeds a day and a variety of feedstuffs to make them eat up.

The other vital aspect of stable management is perceptiveness. It is important to know a horse's weaknesses, to recognise symptoms such as going off food, warm tendons, and to be able to take the appropriate action before serious damage is done.

The ambitious competitor has to remember, too, that it is not just the horse's fitness that is important. The rider will only be able to give maximum assistance if he is feeling strong and fit. Jogging or skipping are pretty good occupations for any eventer who does not ride large numbers of horses.

At the event the most important preparation prior to the riding is to walk the cross-country course. Many riders will do so twice. The first time will allow them to see it as the horse does – whether, for example, a fence looks formidable far away or a frightening ditch only reveals itself at the last moment. All these reactions will help the rider to be ready for the moment when a horse needs to be given that extra bit of confidence with the voice, leg or sometimes whip.

The second time around the course the details of angles of approach, exactly which track to take and the speed to approach each fence can be decided. The risks to be taken must depend on the experience and ability of the horse and rider, the state of the going, the gradients, and the problems raised by each individual fence. There is a great deal to be thought out, and although the dashing rider who heads at all fences flat out might have some successes, it is rarely for long; a crashing fall is usually the result of this dare-devil policy.

Nor must the show-jumping course be forgotten. It might not be so formidable, but by a careful walking of the course the rider can analyse turns, approaches, length of stride in doubles and trebles which can make those tiresome and sometimes vital penalties avoidable.

For the dressage the most important points are, to remember the test and to have worked out the best possible "riding in" routine for the horse. The chapter on Dressage competitions gives some idea how the test should be ridden (see page 180).

In One Day Events jumping follows the dressage and if the horse has been put back in the box before it, he will need about 15 minutes warming up.

When the show jumping follows the cross country then this warming up is much more vital. The horse is usually a little stiff, he has also got used to jumping fast, rather flat and not bothering about brushing fences. All this has to be changed before entering the jumping arena. He has to be made supple, careful and more steady.

In riding the course, styles and methods vary for each horse and rider, but the common requirements are relaxation and determination to clear every single obstacle.

The cross country is the thrilling stage and it is best to be ready at the start – dressed in a sweater and crash helmet – about 10 minutes before take off. About five minutes before setting off a short gallop is needed to clear the horse's wind. The starter will count down from five seconds and then it is away as fast as the horse can keep his rhythm and tackle the fences.

If all goes according to plan, very little else can match the exhilaration of going fast over fixed obstacles, a pleasure that is enhanced by most horses loving it too.

Whatever the outcome of the gallop across country, the horse usually needs some appreciation for his efforts, and always some attention. He has to be washed down, dried off, inspected for damage, his legs bandaged with cooling lotion, rugged up, put away with a haynet and taken home as soon as possible. Any animal that can give a rider as much excitement and pleasure as an eventer does across country, deserves very special care.

Wolfgang Jurgens (West Germany) jumping a drop fence.

*Dramatic action in front of the goal,
with a player riding off an opponent
attempting a forehander.*

From Hunting to Polo

by Dorian Williams, O.B.E., M.F.H.

It would seem absurd to brandish riding as a danger sport. It is true, nevertheless, that down the ages people have increasingly associated riding with adventure and risk. It is not surprising that even in the less competitive sports there is frequently an element of excitement.

Perhaps the most exciting is hunting, although hunting first became an absorbing interest to man through the art of venery, pursuing a quarry with a pack of hounds. In the Middle Ages, though the hunting rights in Britain were vested in the Crown, most great landlords kept their own packs of hounds, some of the better known being the Dukes of Beaufort, Grafton, Rutland, Richmond and Gordon, Northumberland, the Earls of Berkeley, Fitzwilliam and Halifax. The sport in those days was entirely private, the great landlord, who was not then known as Master, inviting a few of his friends and neighbours to join him for a day's hunting. Vast areas of country were hunted, the land hunted coinciding with the territory owned by the landlord. The Duke of Beaufort, for instance, hunted from Bath to Oxford, the Earl of Berkeley from Bristol to the western outskirts of London, which in those days was Marble Arch. The Duke of Grafton hunted his estates in Surrey, Northamptonshire and Suffolk, his hounds being moved round from kennel to kennel. He was, in fact, instrumental in having a bridge built at Westminster to make the transportation of his hounds that much easier.

The change for a private, leisurely, but intensely interesting occupation into the crowded exciting sport depicted in sporting prints was due to two things. First was the division of the land into enclosures or fields which meant that the boundary fences had to be negotiated if one was to keep with hounds. Jumping was thus introduced and very quickly horsemen found that it was an exhilarating experience to leave the ground. Moreover, especially in the late 18th and early 19th centuries, the element of risk was very much to their liking: as Robert Smith Surtees said through his famous character John Jorrocks, the grocer-Master of Handley Cross, hunting is the image of war without the danger.

The second cause of the change in the character of hunting was financial. Even in those days, between 150 and 200 years ago, the great landlords found the expense of maintaining a private pack of hounds in the lavish style which was then expected, too much for their spacious pockets. They, therefore, invited subscriptions. Coincidentally the industrial revolution of the late 18th and early 19th centuries had created a new wealthy class. Finding themselves with vast fortunes the new rich built themselves great country houses and, naturally, wished to join in the country sports. They were happy enough to pay for them, but being hard men of business they did not always take kindly to putting up the money and then being entirely under the control of gentlemen whose wealth was entirely inherited.

The gradual result of this was the disappearance of many of the great feudal, privately owned packs which were replaced by subscription packs, with an elected committee which appointed a Master.

This revolution was as significant as the industrial revolution itself, being a revolution in the whole way of life in the countryside which for so many centuries had been considered virtually the private property of the great landlords. Declining fortunes now forced them to sell parts of their estates which were taken over by the new barons of industry. Not surprisingly it took several decades for everything to sort itself out. Meanwhile hunting flourished as never before, with more and more people wanting to take up hunting. In the more fashionable countries, particularly in the shires, adjacent to the great industrial towns and cities, yet almost wholly grass with few big woodlands, fields of 600 or 700 were not unusual.

The onus on the Master and his huntsman to provide sport for this great horde was enormous and led no doubt to the discreditable practice of hunting foxes provided unnaturally, rather than hunting the fox in its natural state. The situation was aggravated by the value of the fox's pelt, which led to a great deal of poaching. Shortage of foxes could only be counteracted by importing them: a sizeable trade

Hunting in Germany, where it is only permitted to have a drag hunt.

in foxes being brought down to London from Scotland and sold at Leadenhall market. They became known as Leadenhallers or, of course, bagmen. It was all very unethical and while many of those following hounds, perhaps most, cared little about what they were hunting as long as they could gallop and jump, there were others who were far from happy about the situation. Not only was the bagged fox put down out of his own territory, but frequently he was "touched up", that is to say made to smell stronger with a touch of aniseed or even urine. In strange country, their scent enhanced, they had little option to run straight, chased at a tremendous speed by hounds. With few roads, no railways or barbed wire the hunt became a straight steeplechase. The young bloods and madcaps, often with more money than brains, enjoyed it enormously, even to trying to bring about their rivals downfall by tricking them into jumping an unjumpable fence; or pounding them by jumping something such as canal lock-gates or iron park railings which they knew others would not be able to jump; or, if they could, would break their necks doing so. To those more genuinely interested in the art of venery it was anathema. One of the greatest critics was the Duke of Rutland over whose beautiful Belvoir vale some of the worst distortions of hunting were perpetuated.

Fortunately there were enough of such people in influential positions gradually to get the sport back into proper control. They formed, at the end of the 19th century, the Master of Foxhounds Association with a very strict set of rules, the first of which was to the effect that the fox could only be hunted in its natural state, at no time being handled in any way. The penalties were extreme, involving the immediate resignation from the Association if any malpractice was reported, or proved. This virtually meant the closing down of the Hunt of which he was Master, only Hunts whose Masters were members of the Association being allowed to hunt.

While there is no doubt that the tightening up of the controls at the end of the 19th century resulted in a return to hunting proper, nevertheless it cannot be denied that the legacy of the days when hunting was a mad gallop across country still lingers. And perhaps it is no bad thing: for while the priority in hunting must always be the venery, the working of hounds in all conditions, pitting their wits and those of their huntsman against those of the quarry, yet inevitably for those, the majority, not close enough to be able to observe the working of hounds, something rather more exciting is wanted: something that can, too, be a challenge.

It is claimed, with justification, that hunting has frequently moulded the character of a soldier. In the hunting field he has learned initiative, he has experienced frustration, even disaster. He has had to exercise control, patience, courage. Many foreigners still assert that part of the English character, the ability to survive, the spirit of adventure, the acceptance of leadership, has been acquired in the hunting field. Between the wars army officers from other countries were frequently sent to England to enable them to have the experience of the hunting field, something denied them in their own countries.

The proper enjoyment of hunting, it would seem, is an acceptance of priorities. Hunting is concerned with hounds, hunting a wild animal, following hounds, keeping up with them on a good scenting day, then there is the need for courage and skilled horsemanship: for most, obviously, it is the latter that provides the real enjoyment of hunting: hence, despite the very big costs, the enormous fields that most Hunts have today.

This chapter is supposed to be on the non-competitive equestrian sports, yet it cannot be denied that there is frequently a good deal of competition to be experienced in hunting. Regrettably, one finds oneself all too often hoping that, while one has been lucky enough to take the right turn, someone else has taken the wrong turn and so misses the hunt: one finds oneself hoping that whereas one has oneself survived some particularly fearsome obstacle, someone else has been less lucky and refused it, or even had a fall. Yet all this is taken in good part: though by the very nature of human reactions one likes winning, scoring off someone else, yet it would be stupid to pretend that hunting is a cut throat sport such as racing, or a sport in which there is a definite winner such as in show jumping or eventing.

Polo

Nor is there an individual winner in polo, which is essentially a team sport, coming therefore, somewhere between hunting and its mass excitement and the individual sports such as jumping or eventing. In the opinion of many it is the most exciting game in the world and, with the possible exception of ice hockey, the fastest. It has been played in various forms for many centuries, and still is in different parts of the world. Originating, it is generally agreed, in Persia it was developed in its modern form in India where it was played by the Indian Princes during the 19th century, the word polo coming from Pulu, the Tibetan for a ball. The British Cavalry started playing the game as a form of recreation in India in the second half of the 19th century, the heyday of the British Empire. Only towards the end of the century was it introduced to the west, largely through the father of English polo, John Watson. America adopted the game a few years later, instituting the famous Westchester Cup, the annual match between England and America.

Because of the speed of the game, each chukka, another legacy from India, is only seven and a half minutes in length, ponies being changed for each chukka. Such was the popularity of polo that it was included in the Olympic Games of 1908, 1920, 1924 and 1936. In 1908 and 1920 Britain won gold medals. As there were seldom more than three or four teams competing, when the Olympics were revived in London in 1948 polo was excluded and has never since been part of the Olympics. As one who believes that there should be no team events in the Olympic Games the decision seems a right one.

Between the wars polo was very much part of the British Cavalry scene, there being few civilian teams. Since the Second World War, however, with little polo played in the Army, since the Cavalry became mechanised, there has, largely due to the enthusiasm of Prince Philip, been an upsurgence in the interest of polo all over the country, with centres firmly established at Windsor, Cowdray, Cirencester, Oulton Park (Cheshire), Woolmers Park (Herts), and Ham (Surrey). Particularly encouraging is the number of young players taking up the game. Good for the sport, too, the number of top class Argentinians who come over to play. Compared with the 700 or 800 who play polo in Britain, in Argentina no less than 4,000 people play at different levels. In fact polo is to the Argentinians what hunting is to Britain.

Long Distance Riding

It has sometimes been said that the newly popular equestrian sport – newly popular in Britain that is – of Long Distance Riding is like hunting without jumping fences. Although an over simplification, it is true that it demands many of the qualities of a good man across country. It needs judge of pace, the ability to nurse one's horse, patience, control and a head for direction. Long distance rides can be anything from 40 to 100 miles (65 to 160 kilometres), necessitating stamina both on the part of the horse and the rider. Long distance riding has in Britain introduced a new kind of rider into a form of equestrian sport which, while competitive, could never be described as cut-throat. Those who take part are frequently people who have neither the desire nor means to show jump, event, show or even hunt. Long distance riding provides them with something both worthwhile and rewarding. In America and Australia long distance riding is a long established equestrian activity as might be expected in those countries with wide open spaces. In Britain it has been practised for less than a decade, but it is increasing in popularity every year, not surprisingly.

There are two other forms of cross-country riding which have also become very popular, though they could hardly be more different: one

is trekking, the other is the new sport of cross-country riding itself. The latter is based, initially, on the old point-to-point with riders crossing natural country from one point to another. With the risk of infringing the Jockey Club rules, which could make such races "flappers", a team element was soon introduced, particularly success-fully by Douglas Bunn at Hickstead. Teams consist of four or five riders, the time of the third of the four, or the fourth of the five to pass the winning post being the time of the team. As far as possible the fences are natural, but not too big. Recently the idea of having one or two fences which have to be jumped by the whole team together has been introduced. This has prevented teams adopting a follow-my-leader technique, making the performance much more interesting to the spectator. Obviously, it is essential that this new sport should be controlled to the extent that it is not dangerous, nor infringes Jockey Club requirements, but essentially, like long distance riding, it is the ordinary horseman's rather than the specialist's sport. This is as it should be.

Trekking is even more for the less experienced rider, trekking holidays which can be most attractive, being provided for riders, many of whom have hardly ever ridden before, in many of the most beautiful parts of the country. The number of trekking centres increases each holiday season which can only testify to the ever increasing popularity of this very pleasant way of having a holiday and seeing the loveliest of the countryside.

There is, in Britain, for the rider who does not wish to indulge in competitive equestrianism, an enormous range of equestrian acti-vities, from the leisurely pastime of trekking to the thrill and excitement of the hunting field. It is probably true to say that there is no country in the world that can offer a wider variety of riding than Britain. Every taste is catered for.

Team jumping is a race over fences, in which a whole team is timed over a course of obstacles. The time for the team is measured from the start to when the last rider in the team crosses the finishing line.

Driving

by Sallie Walrond

A hackney, wearing a light set of harness with breast collar and tilbury tugs, to a show wagon.

The sport of driving has grown beyond all expectations since 1957, the year in which the British Driving Society was started – with such tremendous foresight – by Mr Sanders Watney, Mr Reg. Brown, Captain Frank Gilbey and Colonel A. Main. At the time it was thought that maybe a hundred or so enthusiasts might enrol, to perpetuate the fast fading skills of handling the reins and whip. Certainly no one could have predicted that in less than a quarter of a century membership would have risen to around 3,000 with new additions daily, nor that teams would be sent abroad to compete for honours in European and World Championships.

The decline in driving meant that the skills of harness making, carriage building and coach painting were becoming dying crafts. The current upsurge in the sport has encouraged young people to learn these trades in order to supply the numerous demands. It is now possible to get both harness and carriages made to suit exact requirements.

The increasing number of Whips (drivers) has inevitably led to the need for competitions.

For those who want to specialise in pure showing, there are the private driving classes which are held at numerous shows throughout the country. If the fixture is affiliated to the BDS, then the classification is standardised and a judge is chosen from their panel. The class is normally open to singles, pairs and tandems. Horses and ponies have

HRH The Duke of Edinburgh driving Her Majesty the Queen's Cleveland Bay team at a Combined Driving Trial.

to be four years old or more. Sometimes the class is split into Hackney type and non-Hackney type. Frequently it is divided into pairs, or tandems, and singles. If there is a large entry in the single, non-Hackney type section, then this may be sub-divided into two heights. Turnouts are required to trot round the ring while the judge assesses the entries. He observes the suitability of the animal for the vehicle. A light Arab looks as out of place in a substantial Country Cart as does a tough Welsh Cob put to a spindly Phaeton. Action and way of going are taken into consideration. The turnouts are then lined up in the centre of the ring so that the judge can inspect each exhibit for correctness of the harness and vehicle. Both must fit and be in clean, sound condition. The driver's and passengers' dress are considered, as are the appointments. The horse is viewed for lumps, which are likely to cause unsoundness, and blemishes, which are unsightly. Each turnout will then be asked to give an individual show. This usually entails walking out of line, trotting away from the judge and turning and trotting towards the judge before halting and reining back. Any tendency to dish or plait will be noted, as will reluctance to go forward from the line or resistance in the rein back. Some judges drive the exhibits.

A number of shows include a five- to ten-mile drive which, perhaps a little confusingly, is called a marathon. This drive is not a speed competition. The schedule usually states that excessive speed is not required and that the suitability of turnouts for private driving purposes will be specially considered. Competitors are sent on a selected route (often preceded by a police escort). The judge is taken round in a car and stops at strategic points, such as the top of a hill, in order to watch the performance of the turnouts. Animals which pull hard, or are bad in traffic, will be placed accordingly. The final judging is usually held in the main ring on returning from the marathon.

Some shows put on a class known as Concours d'Elegance. This is frequently judged by an artist and the winner is the turnout which he would most like to paint. Fancy dress and period costume are not permitted.

The ride and drive classes are popular for those who keep just one horse – perhaps to hunt in the winter and drive in the summer. These events are held in two sections; the entries are judged as riding horses under saddle and as harness horses between the shafts. The aggregate score of placing is taken to decide the winner. In the event of a tie, whichever was placed the higher in harness takes the overall award.

Mr David Morgan-Davies with his delightful Shetland pony team at a Combined Driving event. The dressage arena can be seen in the background.

Combined driving

The sport of Combined Driving began in Great Britain in the early 1970s. The Combined Driving Group is now a discipline of the British Horse Society and has about 500 members. A combined driving event, which has classes for singles, pairs, tandems and teams, usually consists of three phases. Competition A is divided into two sections. The first is known as "Presentation" and is always judged at the halt. It is equivalent to pure showing and marks are given entirely for cleanliness and correctness of turnout. Section two is the "Dressage Test" which is driven in an arena 110 yards by 44 yards (100 metres by 40 metres) and is similar to a ridden test. The paces which are required are walk, collected, working and extended trots, halt and rein back. Various movements such as circles, loops and serpentines have to be executed. Unlike ridden dressage, the use of the voice and whip are permitted.

Competition B is the "Marathon" which, at a full event, can be a rugged drive taking about two hours. It is wise to have a substantial vehicle for this, as hills, rough terrain and water crossings have to be negotiated. The horse needs to be extremely fit, in order to complete the distance within the time allowed under such demanding conditions. Competition C is the "Obstacle Test" which is usually held in the arena. Competitors endeavour to drive a clear round between pairs of yellow cones, and sometimes through obstacles, in order not to add any further penalties to their existing scores.

For drivers who enjoy speed events there is scurry driving in which pairs of horses or ponies are tooled, against the clock, between cones.

Obstacle driving against the clock has become a very popular sport. Here the carriage passes between the cones with little room to spare.

Where to begin

The newcomer to the sport of driving frequently wonders just where to begin. Many say that they only want to jog along the lanes on a sunny day behind a quiet horse. Most people start with a single horse or outgrown pony which they break to harness.

There are no mysteries in training a horse to harness. As long as common sense is applied and the animal is not a confirmed kicker or bad in traffic, there is no reason why he should not be persuaded to go quietly.

A set of harness and a vehicle must be purchased. It is probably best to go to an expert for help before spending a lot of money on equipment which may turn out to be unsuitable. The local BDS Area Commissioner will probably be willing to give advice on the subject.

Many beginners start by purchasing a Governess Cart; they are relatively cheap and reasonably plentiful. Although these tub-shaped vehicles are ideal for taking small children for drives, they leave a lot to be desired, and it is not long before the Whip is looking for a replacement, having discovered that he does not like sitting sideways and facing forwards. A gig is the most popular vehicle for exhibiting a single horse. The two, facing-forward seats set on springs between the shafts and two wheels, form an elegant outline to show a horse to advantage.

If showing a single turnout is to be taken seriously, it will be found necessary to have a set of black show harness which is trimmed with patent leather. The bridle will probably have a rolled throat latch and matching winker stays attaching the patent covered winkers to the head piece. A patent covered, neatly shaped, full collar which fits correctly is preferable to a breast collar (though the latter is always

A team being driven through the water during the marathon section of a Combined Driving Event.

better than an ill-fitting full collar). The saddle will be patent covered and should have lined (two layers of leather which are stitched together) girth straps, back band and belly band. The crupper, breeching and tugs will all be designed to match the rest of the harness. The shape of the buckles and the type of keepers must be similar throughout the set. Brown reins are always used, because black reins would leave dye on the Whip's clothes.

Lady drivers will find that a trouser suit or matching jacket and skirt is practical. Flat, comfortable shoes and leather gloves one size too large are best. The hat should be neat and secure. Large brims are disastrous on a windy day with a pulling horse.

Gentleman Whips can wear a suit and a bowler hat.

Social passengers should dress as neatly and unobtrusively as possible. Girl grooms look very smart in a hacking jacket, well cut trousers and a small hat.

Aprons which buckle round the waist and reach well down the legs look efficient and keep the horse's hairs and grease from the reins off the clothes.

Appointments such as the lamps are important. The metal should match that of the harness buckles and vehicle fittings. The whip needs to have a holly or similar stick; the thong should be well oiled and never whitened.

A spares kit of some kind should be carried in case of an emergency. Combined Driving rules specify such spares as hame straps, traces and reins as essentials and those judges must not ask for anything else. However, judges in private driving classes are inclined to inquire if more than these are carried; so it is quite a good idea to add a knife, a

Mrs Colville's highly successful Welsh section C gelding, Synod Cerdin, showing in the Private Driving section of the Royal Show in 1978.

leather boot lace and a box of matches to those mentioned above. A neatly set out spares kit can be an impressive detail.

During the early stages of driving the single horse, it is essential to master the art of handling the whip and reins correctly, as this forms the foundation for all future driving – whether it be pair, tandem, unicorn or team.

The reins should be held firmly in the left hand with the nearside rein over the index finger and the offside rein between the middle and third fingers. The wrist should be kept rounded and supple as the reins are secured firmly against the palm by the lowest three fingers.

The whip is held between the index finger and thumb of the right hand lying across the palm at the point of balance at an angle of "ten to twelve" in relation to the reins. The right hand is placed in front of the left hand on the reins to assist in turns, steadying the horse and shortening the reins. The left rein lies between the index and middle finger; the right rein goes under the third finger. The reins are shortened by sliding the right hand forward and taking the contact on the horse's mouth, while the left hand is pushed up to lie behind the right hand again. A pulling horse can be steadied by both hands working together. On no account must the hands be separated with two loops of rein hanging between the hands, as this would mean that the right hand was taking all the contact and the left hand rendered redundant. Nor must the reins be separated into two hands. The habit will be hard to break and when the time comes to hold four reins for tandem, unicorn or team there will be difficulties which may lead to disaster.

Turns to the right can be made by placing the right hand (still holding the whip) over the offside rein, and to the left by placing the right hand on to the nearside rein to bring the horse round in that direction. Turns to the left and right can, with a light-mouthed and obedient horse, be made with just the left hand by turning the wrist. A turn to the left is made as the knuckles of the hand face upwards thus tightening the nearside rein. A single-handed right incline can be made by turning the left hand so that the palm faces uppermost and so putting pressure onto the right rein and releasing the left. The hands should, at all times be kept in the centre of the body with the elbows to the sides. Any tendency to carry the hands to the side of the body will tighten the opposite rein and, although this is an effective method of making an intentional incline, it causes erratic steering if practised inadvertently. It is a common fault among beginners to driving, who have ridden for years, to swing their hands to the side in an effort to turn the horse. The more the hands are brought to the left, the tighter the right rein becomes and vice versa. It is important to see that a comfortable sitting position is adopted with the legs together and sloping downwards from the box seat to the floor or foot rest. A seat which is too low, causing the Whip to sit with his knees folded like a garden gnome, will be very uncomfortable and will not be of much help if the horse catches hold. Equally, inability to reach the floor and inadequate purchase for the feet can be disastrous. It will be found that pulling horses can be controlled far more easily if the feet, legs and back can be used to assist the arms and hands.

Driving a pair

Once the Whip has got his single equipage going to his satisfaction, he may start thinking about finding a pair for his horse. However, it is often easier to find a matching pair than another horse to go with an existing one. A visit to a stud which specialises in one of our native breeds will probably result in the purchase of a couple of foals or yearlings of similar blood lines which are likely to grow to match. In many ways, type and action is more important than colour. It is preferable to bring on youngsters, though this is a slow process. The result is well trained, confident animals. It also allows time for the harness and vehicle to be found.

Pair harness differs in many ways from single harness. Fortunately the bridles remain the same, so the bridle which was originally used for the single turnout can be employed for one of the pair. If full colllars are used, these, too, are the same. The hames are different, those used for pair work have a kidney link and kidney link ring at the bottom to take the pole strap from the pole head. The hame tug is longer and the buckle differs in having a dee at the top. A strap and buckle is sewn to the dee and this is fastened to the point strap which comes down from the pad. There is also a dee on the lower side of the tug buckle to which a point strap is sewn. This is fastened to the belly band. The traces have either quick release, square dees and tags, or loops at their ends, instead of crew holes. The cruppers are similar to those used for single harness. Trace bearers and breechings are employed by some people.

There are only two reins to the hands with a pair. They are known as the draught reins and go down to the outer sides of each horse's mouth. Buckled to one of about 15 holes on the centre of the draught reins are the coupling reins, which cross after they have passed through the hame terrets to the inner sides of each horse's mouth. The adjustment of the coupling reins is of great importance in order to get the pair working evenly and going straight. When the right rein is pulled, contact is taken on the right side of the offside horse's mouth and the right side of the nearside horse's mouth, and vice versa. The handling of the reins is identical to that of a single, though a wider, heavier, contact is felt in the fingers because the reins spread down sideways to each horse.

A pair is most usually driven to a four-wheeled vehicle. Dog Carts, so named because shooting dogs were carried under the four back to back seats, and Waggonettes, which have two forward seats at the

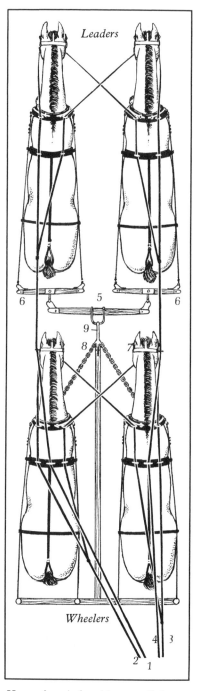

How a four-in hand is controlled.

1. *Near lead rein*
2. *Near wheel rein*
3. *Off lead rein*
4. *Off wheel rein*
5. *Main bar*
6. *Lead bars or single bars*
7. *Leading eye rosette*
8. *Pole chain*
9. *Crab*

front and inner-facing seats at the rear, are popular. Many people drive their pairs to one of the numerous members of the Phaeton tribe.

Once the horses are going quietly side by side, some Whips become ambitious and start thinking of the complications of four reins and the uneconomical and dangerous pastime of tandem driving in which two horses are harnessed one before the other.

With two horses and the Gig, which was used for single driving, there is only the harness to be considered. The single set can be used for the shaft horse with just a few adaptations. If a snaffle is not used, then a bar bit is essential, to prevent the leader's reins from getting caught in the cheeks of the Liverpool bit. The bridle also needs leading eye terrets to carry the reins from the leader on the way to the saddle terrets which have to be replaced by those with a dividing roller bar. An auxiliary throat latch is best added as a safety precaution, to prevent the shaft horse's bridle from being pulled off, if the leader should come round. One way of fitting this is to have an extra loop put onto the browband through which a long strap, with a buckle at one end and point with holes at the other end, passes. The strap is connected to the back of the noseband by a double loop of leather to keep it in place. Then, any pressure exerted onto the bridle from the front is taken on the jaw bones, which is preferable to trying to drive with an overtight throat latch. The only other modification to the shaft horse's harness is an adapter, in order to fix the leader's trace to the wheeler's hame tug buckles. This can be made from a metal fitting with a small hole which passes over the tongue of the tug buckle to hold it in place and a larger hole through which the leader's trace spring cock eye is hooked.

The leader can quite easily be driven in one side of a set of pair harness, with longer traces, until such time as a lead pair can be obtained. A martingale crupper is best, otherwise the lead rein may get caught in the back strap point.

The handling of four reins is based on that of single and pair. The reins are initially anchored in the left hand which is assisted by the right hand placed on the reins in front of the left. The near lead rein lies over the index finger; the off lead goes under the index finger and on top of the near wheel rein. The off wheel rein lies on top of the third finger. The middle and third fingers of the right hand are placed

A team of Haflingers, wearing traditional harness, to a landau in West Germany.

between the left and right reins. Simple turns, where there is plenty of space can be made by putting pressure onto whichever side is needed, treating the two reins as one. It will be found, with tight turns, that as much, if not more, attention has to be paid to opposing the shaft horse as in bringing the leader round if hubs are to be kept clear of gate posts. The wheeler nearly always falls in on turns once the leader comes round. Care must be taken to keep the leader out of draught, unless it is being called upon to assist the shaft horse through deep going.

Once four reins have been mastered, it is inevitable that Whips should start considering unicorns (two horses abreast and one in front) and four horse teams. Another visit to the stud will probably follow.

The existing pair harness can be used for either one leader (in unicorn) or for two leaders (in a four horse team). Matching collars, hames and bridles will be needed for the wheelers. For a unicorn, the tandem lead reins will be all right. A team will need new reins for the leaders. They are of the same principle as a pair with longer draught reins to pass through the wheelers' leading eye rosettes (those from the tandem wheeler will do) and through the centre terrets of the wheelers' pads which will have to be acquired.

The four reins, whether for unicorn or team are handled in the same way as for tandem driving. The extra weight and wider pull of the team reins makes the reins heavier in the hand so looping is often necessary in executing turns. A tight turn to the right could well be made by first looping the near wheel rein to hold the wheelers firmly to the left in opposition on approaching the corner. A loop of rein is picked up with the right hand and placed under the left thumb where it is secured; this enables the right hand to exert pressure on the off lead rein, to bring the leaders to the right. Once the leaders have come round, then the loop can be dropped allowing the wheelers to follow.

Many vehicles which are used for pair driving can also be used with a team, though it is necessary to have a pole head with a hook to take the main bar. The lead bars, on to which the leader's traces are hooked, are attached to hooks at each end of the main bar.

The once "newcomer to driving" may eventually find himself with a stable full of horses, a garage full of carriages and secret hopes of a gold medal in the World Championships.

Sallie Walrond (UK) driving her tandem, to a skeleton Gig, to win their class at a country show.

Glossary

Aged a horse of seven years or more

Aids the signals used by a rider to convey instructions to the horse. The *natural* aids are those produced by use of the body, legs, hands and voice; the *artificial* aids include the use of spurs, whips, martingales etc.

Amble a slow leisurely walking pace, commonly used in the United States of America

Anti-sweat rug a sheet of cotton mesh used to assist horses to cool off after exercise or work. The anti-sweat rug prevents a too rapid reduction in the body temperature

Backing mounting a young horse at the time of breaking it in

Balance a horse without a rider has no problem with its balance, but this is immediately upset once the horse is mounted. The rider's skill and experience in sitting correctly and making necessary adjustments will assist the horse to be better balanced

Bedding can be made of straw, sawdust, wood shavings, dried bracken or peat

Bed down to make a bed for a horse

Behind the bit when a horse refuses to take hold of the bit, invariably accompanied by a shaking of the head

Bit the metal, vulcanite or rubber device which is attached to the bridle and placed in the horse's mouth in order to give the rider control over the pace and direction. The bit is also used to control and regulate the position of the horse's head

Bitless bridle any of the bridles used without bits. Pressure from these bits is applied on the nose and the curb groove. The most common in use today is the Hackamore

Blacksmith see Farrier

Blaze a white marking which extends the length of the face

Blood horse an English Thoroughbred

Bloom the shine on a horse's coat

Braiding see Plaiting

Bridle the part of the saddlery that is placed over the horse's head, to which are attached the bitting device and reins. There are several different types of bridle; all have a headpiece, throat lash, browband, noseband and cheekpiece. Among the better-known bridles are the Double bridle, Pelham bridle, Kimblewick and Snaffle bridle

Breaking out is an unnatural sweating despite the horse having been previously dried. This is usually caused through strenuous exercise or over-excitement

Brood mare a female horse used for breeding

Brushing caused when the shoe or plate catches the opposite leg. Brushing boots are fitted as protection

Canter one of the paces or gaits of the horse

Cantle the upward and curved part of the saddle

Cast a word with two meanings, when a shoe has been lost it is said to have been 'cast'. A horse is 'cast' when it is down, usually in its box, and is unable to rise by its own efforts

Cavaletti a word meaning a number of small wooden jumps which can be used for a variety of purposes. They help always in the basic training of a horse, teaching it collection and balance. When used correctly they also assist in the strengthening of muscles and will help a rider to attain confidence and a better seat and balance

Chef d'Equipe the manager of an equestrian team

Clench the pointed end of a nail which protrudes through the hoof after a shoe has been fitted. This is hammered flat and downwards against the hoof. Risen clenches, that is when the nail head comes away from the hoof, are dangerous in that these can cause severe cutting

Cold shoeing a method of shoeing using shoes which are not heated and shaped to the horse's foot

Colt an ungelded male horse which has not reached the age of four years

Conformation the build of a horse. This word describes the way a horse has been 'put together'

Cow hocks these are weak hocks which turn inwards

Crupper a leather strap which passes under the horse's tail and is attached to the back of the saddle to ensure this is kept in place

Dam the female parent of a foal

D-cheek snaffle a bit similar to the eggbutt snaffle, but having D-shaped rings as opposed to the oval of the eggbutt

Double bridle a form of bridle which has two bits, a snaffle and a curb bit. These are separately attached by means of cheekpieces and through which the reins can be individually operated

Draught horse a horse that is used to draw a vehicle of any size, though normally this expression is used for horses which come under the heading of heavy horses, including the Shires, the Suffolk Punch, Clydesdale, Breton, Percheron, Ardennes etc.

Eggbutt snaffle a snaffle bit with a jointed mouthpiece and egg-shaped rings

Ewe neck a neck which is concave between the poll and the withers

Extended paces the extended walk, trot and canter is a lengthening of the stride and is extremely important in all aspects of riding. The walk is comparatively fast and the horse is asked to cover as much ground as possible. With a trot it is a controlled trot but extended in length and at the same time it must have a smooth rhythm. The word extension is also used when lengthening the stride perhaps in approaching certain fences and obstacles

Farrier the craftsman who makes and fits horse shoes, the process is described on pages 156–157

Fédération Equestre Internationale the governing body of international equestrian sport founded in 1921 with its headquarters in Brussels. The FEI makes the rules and regulations for the conduct of all equestrian sport including the equestrian part of the Olympic Games. All national federations have to comply with these rules and many competitions are run under the FEI rule book, which in many cases only differs slightly from the various national rule books

Filly female foal

Flash broad white stripe running down a horse's face

Flexion action of a horse when it relaxes its jaw to the pressure being applied to the bit

Foal the young horse up to the age of twelve months referred to either as a colt foal or a filly foal, depending on its sex

Forearm the part of the horse's foreleg between the elbow and the knee

Forehand the part of a horse which is in front of the rider, i.e. the head, neck, shoulders, withers and forelegs

Gait the movement or pace of a horse or pony. The four basic gaits or paces are the walk, trot, canter and gallop (q.v.)

Gall a skin sore which usually occurs under the saddle region or girth and is normally caused by dirty, damaged or badly fitted saddlery

Gallop one of the paces or gaits of a horse

Gaskin the part of the horse's hind leg between the stifle and the hock

Gelding a male horse which has been castrated

Girth the circumference of the horse measured behind the withers around the deepest part of the body, or the band usually made of leather, webbing or nylon fixed to the saddle which passes under the belly of the horse to keep the saddle in position

Goose rump is when the hind-quarters fall away sharply from the highest part of the quarters down between the tail

Grade horse a term used in America to indicate a horse bred from a pure-bred on the one hand and a mix-bred on the other

Hackamore the oldest and best known form of the bitless bridle which is operated by a single rein. This is a very severe bridle to use, since the pressure is applied on the nose of the animal, and it is one not recommended for an inexperienced or younger rider

Halter a rope headpiece which usually has a lead rope attached

Hand the measurement equalling four inches (10 cm) used when giving the height of a horse. In Europe the hand, though still used, is now being replaced by a metric measure

Hogging a term used for removing the mane

Impulsion denotes the impetus to move forward that is built up in a horse by the correct use of the seat, body, weight and legs of the rider. The rider's hands control impulsion through the reins and the bit

In foal a pregnant mare

Irish rings one of the artificial aids and a type of martingale

Irons a word sometimes used for stirrups

Jog a term used in Western riding which indicates the natural gait of the stock horse

Joint Pelham a Pelham bit which has a jointed mouthpiece similar to that of the jointed snaffle

Keeping on a tight rein restrains the horse by exerting greater pressure on the bit

Kimblewick a combination of snaffle and curb bit

Laminitis an inflammation or fever of the feet, invariably caused by fast work on hard going or too much body-heating feed without sufficient exercise

Left behind is an expression when the rider is found back in the saddle when the horse is jumping

Livery stable at which privately owned horses are kept, groomed, exercised and are looked after for agreed charges

Lope in Western riding this is the natural fast gait or pace of the stock horse

Mare a female horse

Market Harborough this may only be used when jumping under the BSJA rules with a snaffle. It is a device rather like a martingale fixed to regulate and control the position of the horse's head

Native breeds are those which are native to a particular country or region, for example there are nine known British native pony breeds: the Connemara, Dales, Dartmoor and Exmoor, Fell, Highland, New Forest, Shetland and the Welsh

Near-fore the left front leg of a horse

Near-hind the left hind leg of a horse

Near-side the left-hand side of a horse

Neck rein used to steer the horse by applying pressure against the neck rather than the mouth

Numnah a pad placed under the saddle, made from sheepskin, felt or a manmade fibre

Off-fore the right foreleg of a horse

Off-hind the right hind leg of a horse

Off-side the right-hand side of a horse

On the bit is when the rider feels through the reins that the horse is actually on the bit

Over-reaching is when the hind shoe comes up to strike the foot in front. This can be dangerous and upsetting especially when jumping. Over-reach boots are frequently used for protection

Pastern the part of the horse's limb between the fetlock joint and the hoof

Pastern joint the joint between the short pastern bone and the long pastern bone

Pelham bit is a bit designed to reproduce the action of a double bridle with only one mouthpiece. This gives the combined effect of a snaffle and curb bit. The basic shape is similar to that of the Weymouth bit

Pelham bridle is a type of bridle used with the Pelham bit. Pressure is applied to the corners of the mouth when the snaffle rein is used and on the poll and curb groove when the curb rein is brought into play. Again this is not a bit encouraged for the inexperienced or younger riders but is one now very commonly used throughout the world

Pommel the front and highest part of the saddle

Posting a term used in America for what is sometimes called a 'rising' gait or pace. This is the action obtained by alternately rising from the saddle and then sitting back in it in rhythm with the horse's movement

Pulse the pulse of a horse normally beats between 38 and 43 times per minute

Quarters the area of the horse's body which extends from the rear of the flank to the root of the tail and downwards on either side to the top of the gaskin

Resistance the act of refusing to go forward or stopping, moving backwards or rearing. This in show jumping or under the rules normally laid down in horse trials is a penalty and is classed as a disobedience

Rig a male horse which has been unsuccessfully and incompletely castrated

Roller is a form of girth made from leather, webbing or nylon which goes round a horse's body, used frequently for keeping rugs in place. See also Surcingle

Roughing-off a procedure followed before turning a stabled horse out to grass. In roughing-off one omits giving heating food – stuffs such as oats, and apart from the grooming needed for an animal kept at grass, the daily grooming procedures for the stable-kept horse are omitted

Rowel the small wheel forming the extremity of certain types of spurs

Running martingale consists of a strap which is attached to the girth by a loop and divides at the chest into two arms each terminating in a ring, through which each rein is passed

Slow gait is one of the gaits of the five-gaited American saddle horse. It is a prancing action and is something not frequently seen in horses in the United Kingdom or Europe

Snaffle bit the oldest and simplest form of bit which consists of a single bar with a ring at each end to which one pair of reins is attached. This is the most gentle of all bitting devices and the one recommended for novice and younger riders

Sock a white marking extending from the coronet as far as the fetlock joint

Stallion an ungelded male horse aged four years or over

Star a white mark of any shape or size on the forehead of a horse

Stock a word used in America for a stock horse, so called because they were originally used for working with cattle or stock

Stud the place or establishment at which horses are bred

Surcingle a webbing belt usually three or four inches wide which passes over a saddle and girth and is used to hold the saddle in position. Alternatively this may be used in place of a roller to secure a day or night rug

Tack saddlery

Tail guard a rectangular piece of soft leather or canvas fastened around the dock by means of tapes or buckles over a tail bandage. This is used specifically in order to protect the tail when a horse is travelling

Temperature the normal temperature of a horse is 35°C (100.5°F)

Throat lash or latch a strap incorporated into the headpiece of a bridle which fastens under the horse's throat in order to prevent the bridle slipping over the head. When properly fastened the throat lash should allow for the insertion of two or three fingers between the strap and the throat

Track is the prescribed path which riders are expected to follow in jumping events. The track is the line on which the course has been measured and is one which allows the smoothest possible turns

Trot one of the paces or gaits of a horse

Turned out is an expression used when a horse has been turned out to grass as opposed to being stable-kept

Walk one of the paces or gaits of a horse

Yearling a horse which is more than one year old and which has not reached two years

Index

Italic numerals indicate an illustration

Photographic acknowledgements

All Sport pages: 193 (top); 198 (bottom). Bruce Colman pages: 35; 41. Jesse Davis pages: 180; 214 (bottom). Eaglemont pages: 55; 71; 126. E. Hartley Edwards pages: 87 (bottom); 102. Equestrian (Photographic Services) Ltd Front cover (top; bottom left); pages: 2; 5; 21; 30; 59; 61; 67; 68; 69; 78; 79; 80; 82; 88; 89; 90; 94; 95; 96; 97; 98; 101; 113; 114; 117; 118; 120; 122; 131; 135; 136; 137; 138; 139; 145; 147; 148; 149; 151; 152; 153; 154; 157; 159; 160; 161; 163; 164; 165; 167; 168; 170 (bottom); 188 (top); back cover. Mary Evans Picture Library pages: 8; 87 (top). David Guiver page 220. Horse & Hound page 179. Kit Houghton pages: 2; 74; 75; 84; 125; 128; 170 (top); 173; 176 (top); 177; 181; 182; 188 (top & middle); 191 (top); 194; 198 (top); 199; 203; 212; 216; 217. Keystone Press Agency pages: 106 (top); 107 (top); 108. E. D. Lacey page 205. Novosti page 9. Tom Parker page 31. Riding magazine page 14. Saphier pages: 27; 28; 29. Selwyn Photos page 211. Robin Serfass pages: 50 (top); 52 (top); 72; 73; 76. Shalia page 85. Sally Anne Thompson pages: 4; 33 (top); 36 (bottom); 37; 38; 39; 40; 43; 47; 48; 50 (bottom); 52; 58; 105; 121; 141; 150; 171; 176 (bottom); 187; 191 (bottom); 193 (bottom); 197; 213; 214 (top); 219. ZEFA Front cover (Bottom right); pages: 6; 16; 33; 107 (bottom); 115; 174; 183; 185; 196; 201; 206; 208.